Banking has always played a central role in the nation's economy and Citibank has played a leading role in banking and American business for more than 180 years. Established in June 1812, Citibank's history began at the same time that a young Buffalo was emerging as a center of trade and transportation.

Former Citicorp Chairman Walter B. Wriston wrote of Citibank, "History is the story of people, the organizations they create and how those institutions cope with the constantly changing challenges of society. Citibank is one of the few private institutions that have survived since 1812, through wars and panics, through good times and bad, while steadily building and maintaining a position of leadership at home and abroad. Like all institutions that flourish over time, the bank was and is driven by its customers' needs. These requirements are never static."

Since 1972, Citibank has worked in partnership with communities in Western New York. Our goal has always been to provide quality banking with personal, professional service and innovative products—banking that builds community growth and success. Together we have achieved that success and together we face the responsibilities of the present and challenges of the future. It is in that spirit that we continue our third decade of business and community partnership in Western New York.

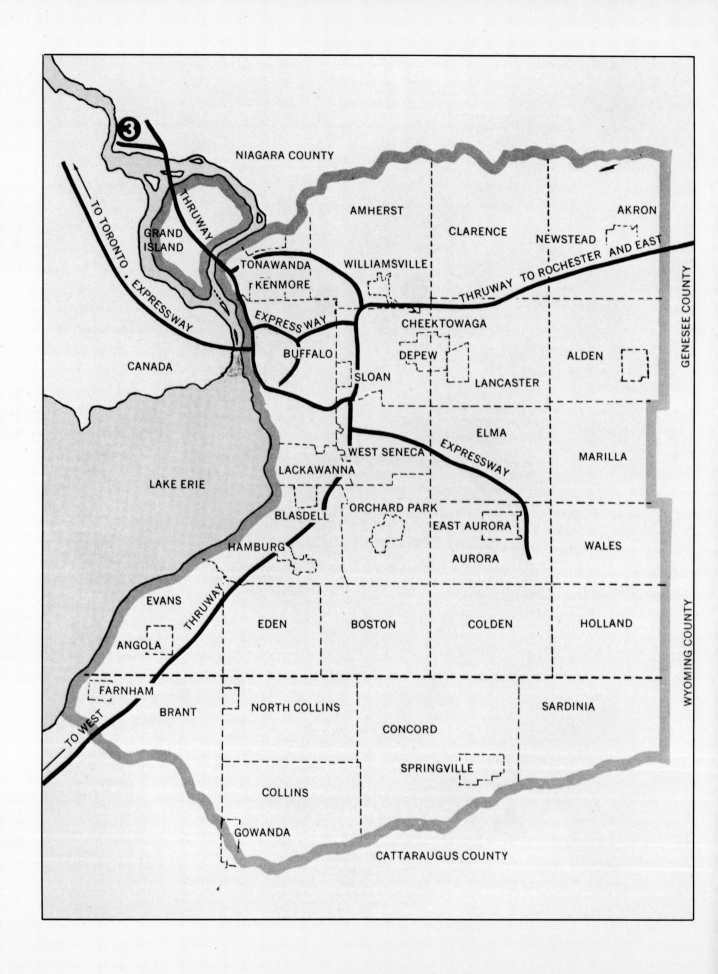

A
Pictorial History

SECOND LOOKS

*of Buffalo
and Erie County*

by Scott Eberle and Joseph A. Grande

design by
Patrick S. Smith

THE
DONNING COMPANY
PUBLISHERS
NORFOLK/VIRGINIA BEACH

Edited by Nancy O. Phillips and Richard A. Horwege
Debra Y. Quesnel, Reprint Project Director
Tracey Emmons-Schneider, Reprint Research Coordinator

Library of Congress Cataloging-in-Publication Data

Eberle, Scott G., 1952–
    Second looks: a pictorial history of Buffalo and Erie County
        by Scott Eberle and Joseph A. Grande.
    p.   cm.
    Bibliography: p.
    Includes index
    1. Buffalo (N.Y.)—Description—Views. 2. Erie County
(N.Y.)—Description and travel—Views. 3. Buffalo (N.Y.)—
History—Pictorial works. 4. Erie County (N.Y.)—History—
Pictorial works.
I. Grande, Joseph A. II. Title.
F129.F843E24   1987   974.7'96—dc 19   87-27402
ISBN 0-89865-609-5 (lim. ed.)

Printed in the United States of America

Contents

Acknowledgments 6

Chapter One
Foundations: Land, Lake, River
by Scott Eberle 9

Chapter Two
Frontier Days
by Joseph A. Grande 13

Chapter Three
Settlement and Boom
by Joseph A. Grande 25

Chapter Four
In Pursuit of Greatness
by Joseph A. Grande 47

Chapter Five
Neighbors: The People of Erie County
by Scott Eberle 73

Chapter Six
The Caring Impulse
by Scott Eberle 103

Chapter Seven
Growing Up and Out
by Scott Eberle and Joseph Grande 129

Chapter Eight
War, Boom and Depression
by Joseph A. Grande 173

Chapter Nine
The Creation of Greater Buffalo
by Scott Eberle 201

Bibliography 235

Index 237

About the Authors 240

Acknowledgments

I am grateful to Dr. William Siener, executive director of the Buffalo and Erie County Historical Society, and David Rumsey, its president, for making time for me to write this book in the thick of a busy exhibit schedule. My colleagues at the museum, especially Mary Bell, Yvonne Foote, and Molly Howard, smoothed the task of charting local history through photographs. The work and assistance of historians Monroe Fordham, David Gerber, Mark Goldman, Julia Boyer Reinstein, Brenda Shelton, and others has been invaluable. Shonnie Finnegan, archivist at the State University of Buffalo, lent her eye for the quirky and interesting in suggesting photographs for inclusion. Despite a demanding schedule of her own, Sister Martin Joseph patiently guided me through the *Courier-Express* Collection housed at Buffalo State College. Donning Publishers editors Nancy Phillips and Richard Horwege helped restore ailing sentences. Christine Narum-Eberle cheerfully endured the missed dinners and lost weekends of a brief (but absorbing) period of composition. Finally, I owe thanks to the Canisius College Dana Grant Program for funding the work of research assistant Maria Schmit. Her energy, good humor and stamina were crucial to sailing this project home on schedule.

SCOTT EBERLE
AUGUST 1987

Invaluable assistance for this project was provided by Mary Bell, head librarian, and the staff of the Buffalo and Erie County Historical Society Library. Thanks also go to Ellen Smith, head librarian, and the staff of the D'Youville College Library for the many kindnesses shown me. A special debt of gratitude is extended to the authors of senior local history theses done at D'Youville College over the last quarter century. Similarly thanks go to the authors of the town history series done to observe Erie County's Sesquicentennial in 1971.

Very special acknowledgments must be extended to the many historical societies and town or village historians who provided pictures and information for this project. And last but not least, I extend to my wife, Marguerite Edwards Grande, my sincerest appreciation for her patience and forbearance, for her editorial assistance, and for her many hours at the word processor laboring to give my scribblings readable form.

JOSEPH A. GRANDE
AUGUST 1987

From a Drawing by W.R. Callington Engineer, Boston, from an Actual Survey made in 1837.

A Birds eye View of the river Niagara from Lake Erie to Lake Ontario shewing the situation and extent of NAVY ISLAND, and the Towns and Villages on the banks of the river in Canada and the United States.

UNITED STATES.		CANADA.	
1 Town of Buffalo	6 Hotel at the falls	A Lake Erie	F Rapids
2 Black Rock	7 Lewiston	B Fort Erie	G Cataracts of Niagara
3 Grand Island	8 Fort Niagara	C Waterloo	H Queens Town
4 Tonewanta Creek	9 Lake Ontario	D Navy Island	I Fort George
5 Grand Canal		E Chippewa	J Welland Canal

Published by J. Robins, Bride Court, Fleet Street.

Behind those uncultivated and uninhabitable mountains [the Niagara Gorge] you enjoy the sight of a rich country, magnificent forests, beautiful fruitful hills....Situated between the two lakes...you breathe the purest air under the mildest and most temperate climate imaginable.... —Fr. F. X. Charlevoix, March 1721. *From the Collections, Courtesy Buffalo and Erie County Historical Society*

Chapter One

Foundations: Land, Lake, River

by Scott Eberle

Seventeen thousand years ago it was springtime on the planet. The glaciers began to recede for the last time. Meltwater from these giant frozen reservoirs gouged and recarved the land. It now seems possible that human eyes witnessed the process in North America, people having crossed over a land bridge from Asia thousands of years before when the ice was still accumulating. These changes in the landscape were exquisitely slow. Whether or not people saw the change, the span of a lifetime would not have been long enough to recognize a *process* at all.

Over many generations the primordial Lake Iroquois receded leaving behind the body of water we call Lake Ontario. Just to the south, and stretching west for some three hundred miles, another Great Lake formed. Large enough to be called inland seas, Lakes Erie and Ontario are connected by a "strait," so pretty, fast-flowing, and blue, that wordsmiths concocted a fanciful origin of the name for the principal city of the region out of the French words "beau fleuve." Freed from the weight of two miles of ice, the land gradually uplifted. In the geologists' joke the region "re-bounded," and it continues to creak and groan. Twelve thousand years ago the Niagara River ran its northerly course uninterrupted into Lake Ontario. At the rate of a few inches or as fast as several feet per year the river has cut a gorge backward into the rock. Fourteen miles upstream of its mouth the Niagara now empties into thin air, and falls 167 feet at the "colossal cataract."

Though remote from human history these events of climate and geology nevertheless have an important bearing on the lives that people have lived in this region. The Great Lakes are giant engines that pump heat and moisture into the atmosphere. The November snow squalls and April ice storms which result have gained Western New York a reputation for ferocious and unforgiving weather. But more important to the inhabitants of this area over the last thousands of years, the lakes have a moderating and evening effect on the climate, tempering the summer, lengthening the fall. Erie County enjoys a growing season a full sixty days longer than parts of Cattaraugus, only two counties away, where the killing frosts come just 110 days apart. Surprisingly, wild fruits common in more southerly climates thrive here.

The ups and downs of a varied postglacial landscape provided niches for many different kinds of plants and animals. Perhaps as early as twenty thousand years ago

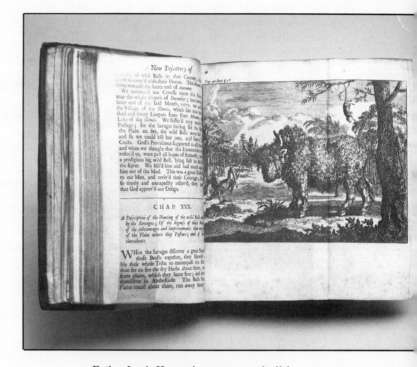

Father Louis Hennepin never saw a buffalo on the Niagara Frontier. He drew this one in 1698 to represent animals that he encountered on the Illinois prairie. Etymologists have disputed the origin of the name for the city of Buffalo for more than a century. The most pleasing (but least likely) is that Buffalo is a corruption of "belle fleuve," beautiful river in French. A more plausible explanation is that "buffalo" was a scribe's error, a mistranslation of the Seneca word for "beaver creek." Whatever the origin, artists and advertisers have been fortunate that this is the only major American city which shares a name with a large land mammal. From the Collections, courtesy Buffalo and Erie County Historical Society

(certainly by ten thousand years ago) hunters and gatherers first lived nomadic lives in this favorable terrain at the southern rim of the ice. They followed it as it retreated north. There is reason to believe that native peoples from the Laurentian, Lamoka, and Woodland cultures hunted in the Niagara region for many thousands of years since. The record of these societies, however, is broken and incomplete—their languages forever lost. What is known about them rests mainly on the skill and luck of investigators who reconstruct vanished societies from the little bits which remain. Anthropologists have found the leavings of ancient campfires on Grand Island that may be as much as five thousand years old. Surely these men and women knew the land with an intimate and sophisticated familiarity. But as they looked out on their Niagara, did they find it as beautiful and sublime as modern-day Americans do? Who these people were, what they felt and believed, how long they stayed in one place, and how widely they ranged are likely to remain matters of conjecture.

All the more settled cultures which followed (including America's brief tenure) have benefited from the passing of the glaciers. The grinding ice sheets exposed new layers of bedrock to weathering. Glacial soils that formed from this debris are new soils, relatively speaking, and not yet leached of the elements that make things grow. Farther east and to the North, the historically distant Algonkian tribes supported a civilization on maize, squash, and beans. More recently and closer to Erie County the Iroquois cultivated large orchards full of peaches, plums, apples, pears and other fruits brought here from Europe. Agriculturalists continue to turn this fertility to their advantage.

The legacy of the glaciers on land and water has long determined how people would get from one place to another in Western New York. In the northern and southern parts of Erie County one can find terminal moraines—those winding mounds of debris gouged up and deposited at the end of melting glaciers. The escarpments trace the routes of ancient footpaths and modern roads. Still much traveled, one of these begins at Buffalo Creek, and follows Main Street through Williamsville, to Clarence Hollow, Akron and then Batavia. Limestone ridges running east and west were scoured and scraped bare by glaciers. They also became convenient tracks. The Iroquois ranged in and out of Western New York on these paths hunting and fishing according to the season. Peter Wilson, a chief of the Cayugas, put it this way in 1849. "Americans" he said, traveled "trails worn so deep by the feet of Iroquois that they became your roads."

Water has also served as a natural highway which brought people and prosperity to the region. Canoes transported native Americans, Jesuit explorers, and English pioneers. British warships confronted the fleet of a young American nation. Teams of oxen (the "horn breeze") dragged commercial vessels up river and canal. Their holds full of enormous measures of grain, these ships sailed out of the west to Buffalo, and the cargo was transshipped east on canal and rail line. Ore boats brought the raw material of big steel to Erie County. By the turn of the twentieth century the Buffalo area was second only to Chicago in its port transshipment business.

Archeological dig in Erie County.
Courtesy Frances R. Pickin

A winding road through Erie County countryside. Courtesy Eden Historical Society

Steam locomotives. Porterfield Collection, courtesy Buffalo and Erie County Historical Society

Some of the evidence for the success of Native American agriculture is indirect. The record of a punitive expedition against the Iroquois ordered by General George Washington and conducted by Sullivan in 1779 includes the tally of some sixty thousand bushels of grain destroyed. Twenty thousand were consumed in the spectacular torching of one granary alone. Troops also burned orchards. And by the end of the war they destroyed twenty-eight of thirty Iroquois villages. Norris's sketch of a war club or "death maul" appears here. Acts of individual courage and ferocity did not long avail the Iroquois once a scorch-and-burn policy became real. In the winter of 1780 refugees huddled on the banks of the Niagara. British rations kept them from starving. *From the Collections, courtesy Buffalo and Erie County Historical Society*

A popular subject, the "maid of the mist" sacrificed. These first Americans are known only a little from the more durable of the artifacts they left behind, and from the lore which survives in much changed forms. Because what can be known about these vanished cultures is so limited, myths have been created about them: the Indian as noble, innocent, sentimental, or treacherous. Unable to understand native people on their terms, the new Americans fashioned these legends in their own image. Americans of the last century admired the Iroquois for their strength and eloquence, and compared them to another group of conquerers, the ancient Romans. But more often, the life of Native Americans has been understood as "savage," and then identified with humankind's own darker side. *From the Collections, courtesy Buffalo and Erie County Historical Society*

*By the art of navigation we obtain a
knowledge of different countries, regions
and realms. By it we attract and bring to
our own land all kinds of riches. By it the
idolatry of paganism is overthrown....*
—Samuel de Champlain
From Voyages of Samuel de Champlain

Chapter Two

Frontier Days

by Joseph A. Grande

The first Europeans to see Western New York were French explorers and missionaries who sought to annex the area and its inhabitants for King Louis XIV and for the Church. Samuel de Champlain was the first of the explorers to write about the Niagara region. He described the original inhabitants in a book, *Des Sauvages*, written in 1604. Though the Indians often prided themselves for their ferocity in hunting and war, they were, in some respects, more "civilized" than the white colonizers proved to be over the next two hundred years. Contact with this advance guard of Europeans in the seventeenth century began a process of change and disruption of Native American life which continues today.

Most is known about the confederation of nations called the Iroquois, who ranged in and out of Western New York. The Iroquois Confederation was composed first of five nations—the Mohawks, the Oneidas, the Onondagas, the Cayugas, and the Senecas, who inhabited Western New York and were later joined by the Tuscaroras. Of all the Native American groups, the Iroquois were best prepared to meet the challenge posed by the influx of Europeans. They were sophisticated politicians long before contact with the white man. Perhaps as early as the 1400s, a loosely knit Iroquois League was organized to keep peace between the member nations, settle disputes within the tribes, and regulate ties of family and kinship. The League was as skillful and delicate a mechanism of compromise as human society has yet invented.

Situated between the frontier of New France and New England, the Iroquois were in a position to use their political skill to play one global super power against the other. They staved off the worst aspects of the conquest of America for two hundred years. But with the British victory in the French and Indian War, the Iroquois lost their bargaining chip. The American Revolution was another turning point for them as well. For the most part, they allied themselves with the British, and the British lost the struggle. With the rise of the new American nation, Iroquois power dwindled.

White settlement in Erie County and all of Western New York did not begin in earnest until the last decade of the eighteenth century. There were many complications which first needed to be resolved. For one, the government of the United States recognized the rights of the Iroquois to the lands of the entire area. Additionally the states of

Massachusetts and New York claimed the region based on ambiguous language in colonial charters granted by the King of England over a century before. And finally, continued presence of British troops at Fort Niagara, in violation of the 1783 peace treaty, and their close ties with the Indians, discouraged westward movement by settlers.

Starting in 1786, these problems were resolved one by one. Representatives of Massachusetts and New York met at Hartford, Connecticut, and forged an agreement whereby the area was recognized as part of New York politically, but land, or preemption, rights were retained by Massachusetts. Subsequently a company organized by New England financiers Oliver Phelps and Nathanial Gorham obtained the right to the land in Western New York from Massachusetts. When they failed to keep up their payments, the right to purchase most of the land was awarded in 1791 to Pennsylvanian Robert Morris, who had served as superintendent of finance of the United States during the War for Independence. Two years later Morris, pressed by debts, sold his over three million acres to a group of Dutch merchants and financiers from Amsterdam.

Five Dutch banking houses joined together to establish the Holland Land Company with a general agent headquartered in Philadelphia and additional lands in central New York and northwestern Pennsylvania. Before any lands could be sold, the Holland Land company had to extinguish Indian title to its Western New York holdings, called the Holland Land Purchase. The desirability of those lands was greatly enhanced in 1796 by the withdrawal of British troops from Fort Niagara as a result of Jay's Treaty. In the summer of 1797, representatives of the federal government and the Holland Company met with Iroquois chiefs and persuaded them to cede their land rights to the Holland Company except for two hundred thousand acres set aside for reservation.

The Holland Land Company was now ready to begin the immense task of surveying and selling the wilderness acres of the Purchase. A tall, rugged Pennsylvanian, Joseph Ellicott, was chosen to supervise the survey. He had been trained by an older brother, Andrew, and had assisted him in surveying the new city of Washington, D.C. Ellicott had also done survey work in Georgia and northwestern Pennsylvania, and had been employed by the federal government to clarify the New York-Pennsylvania boundary. The chief surveyor and his crew of 150 men

moved about the forests and woods laying out townships, six square miles, and subdividing them into lots of 320 acres. This huge undertaking was completed with great speed and efficiency.

It was no surprise when in 1800 the Holland Land Company appointed Joseph Ellicott as its resident agent on the Holland Land Purchase. By this time, the company's general agent in Philadelphia was Italian-born Paul Busti, an urbane, retired businessman from Amsterdam who was anxious to develop Western New York by increasing land sales, and thereby, his company's profits. Busti believed Ellicott was ideally suited to carry out the company's objectives, and the two men became close friends and frequent correspondents. Land sales began in 1801 and the permanent land office was placed at Batavia, a central location on the Purchase given a Dutch name as a gesture to the company owners. Subagencies were set up in the southern areas of the Purchase as well as at the new western settlement of Buffalo on the shores of Lake Erie.

Ellicott was a realistic businessman who hoped to attract settlers by a generous system of credit. He had no illusions about the financial capabilities of the poor settlers who moved west in hopes of greater opportunity. Company policies requiring four-to six-year contracts and 10 to 15 percent down payments were, in his eyes, a serious obstacle to land sales. More attractive terms were available in other parts of Western New York and across the Niagara River in Upper Canada. To surmount these obstacles, the resident agent allowed purchasers to pay the down payment by helping build roads and sawmills for the company. A system of conditional sales was also developed, giving the buyer six months to make some improvement on the land and to raise the down payment. In 1803 Ellicott convinced Busti to extend the credit period to ten years, and by 1810, as sales improved, it was again changed to eight years, where it remained.

Ellicott's actions grew out of his understanding of the frontier and its problems. Settlers arrived on the Holland Purchase with little or no money. Even those with money were concerned with saving enough to live on during the first year. Trees needed to be cleared, a home built, and the land placed under cultivation before the first crops, usually only enough to provide for the family, were harvested. Even when there was a surplus to be sold, there were few or no roads, transportation costs were high, and markets were far away on the eastern seaboard. The local market was very limited in the first years of settlement. Settlers understandably put pressure on the Holland Company to speed building of roads and such other necessary im- provements as gristmills and sawmills. Thus Ellicott undertook an extensive road-building program including roads to Lake Erie, the Niagara River, and Lake Ontario. Settlers who worked on these projects for the company were paid in land and cash.

The resident agent's many efforts to increase land sales were only partially successful because of circum- stances beyond his control. The United States' cool relations with Great Britain, the former mother country, deteriorated badly after 1807, when the British ship

La Salle's dreams of a trading empire around the Great Lakes led him to return to France for royal permission for the venture from Louis XIV and to recruit followers to assist him. Upon return to New France, he plunged into preparations for pursuing his scheme. An eighteen-man advance party proceeded to the Niagara region in November 1678, soon to be joined by La Salle and his lieutenant, Enrico Tonti, an Italian adventurer and soldier known as "the Man with the Iron Hand." On January 22, 1679, the expedition climbed the Niagara Escarpment to move twelve miles south to Cayuga Creek, in present-day Niagara Falls, where construction began on the first sailing vessel on the Great Lakes above Niagara Falls. Named the Griffon in honor of Count Frontenac, the governor of New France, the ship was launched into the Niagara River as soon as it was seaworthy and towed up to Squaw Island in present-day Buffalo, where finishing touches were added. On August 7, 1679, the Griffon sailed into Lake Erie carrying La Salle and his men westward on the first leg of their expedition down the Mississippi. On the return journey to Niagara, laden with furs, the ship mysteriously disappeared without a trace and thus has been dubbed "the Ghost Ship of the Great Lakes." Roy W. Nagle Collection, courtesy Buffalo and Erie County Historical Society

Leopard used force to seize sailors off the American frigate *Chesapeake,* as it sailed out of Norfolk, Virginia, enroute to the Mediterranean Sea. President Thomas Jefferson resisted war hysteria which swept the country by adopting a program of economic retaliation, cutting off trade with Europe and European colonies. The fragile economy of Western New York received a severe jolt as trade across the Niagara to Upper Canada was banned and the possibility of war openly discussed. Such circumstances were not conducive to attracting settlers to the Niagara Frontier.

Continued efforts at economic warfare against Britain under President James Madison adversely affected the American economy and the fortunes of the Holland Land Company. The English, engaged in a life-and-death struggle with France's Napoleon Bonaparte, showed little evidence of a willingness to cease their policy of impressing American seamen and seizing American ships and cargo for trading with French-dominated Europe. While there was widespread anti-British feeling across the nation, opinion in Western New York was seriously divided. Illegal trade or smuggling across the Niagara was common and could only be ended, according to Buffalo's customs collector, Erastus Granger, by sending a large number of federal troops to the border.

Western New York's militant congressman, Peter B. Porter, gained notoriety as a "War Hawk" on the floor of the House of Representatives by blistering attacks on the British. He and his fellow War Hawks—men like Henry Clay of Kentucky, John C. Calhoun of South Carolina, and Felix Grundy of Pennsylvania—were willing if necessary to forsake economic warfare for military action against England by seizing Canada, thereby expelling the British from North America. The security of the Niagara Frontier was of deep concern to Porter and settlers who protested the lack of action on defense preparations in Washington. Porter voted to increase military spending, and he demanded passage of laws to strengthen national defenses and build an effective fighting force capable of taking Canada. He urged creation of a naval force on Lake Erie and grew impatient with the slow pace of military preparations. He worried that the British might attack American territory in the Niagara country before defense measures were completed.

In April 1812, Porter was summoned home by

15

The Iroquois (Mohawk, Onondaga, Seneca, Oneida and Cayuga) thought of themselves as the "People of the Longhouse." Those bark-covered structures served as the symbol of cooperation and mutual interest for the Iroquois League. Politically the people of the Five Nations dwelt under one roof. Their confederation was the most durable and effective Native American government in the Northeast. With the addition of the Tuscarora in 1713 the Five Nations became Six. Because of their oratorical skill, martial values, and military success, writers of the nineteenth century often compared the Iroquois to another group of conquerers, the Romans. The reconstructed longhouse dwelling pictured here has the added detail of statuary. Our appreciation of Indian life has long been frozen into poses of heroics and savagery. Porterfield Collection, courtesy Buffalo and Erie County Historical Society

Governor Daniel D. Tompkins of New York to serve as quartermaster general of the state militia. He strenuously directed efforts to supply, equip, transport, and house thirteen thousand militiamen ordered into service to defend the New York-Canadian border. When Congress, at the behest of President James Madison, declared war on Great Britain in mid-June, several thousand militiamen had already arrived in Western New York, and by fall, a force of two thousand regular troops joined the six thousand militia gathered along the Niagara River between Lakes Erie and Ontario.

The people of Erie County experienced the first taste of war when, on July 11, 1813, a force of British Redcoats struck across the river at Black Rock to destroy the navy yard and naval supplies. A hastily recruited army of three hundred regulars, militia, and Indians commanded by General Porter launched a determined counterattack and drove the invaders back across the river. After long delays, an American army then invaded Canada, capturing strategic Fort George at the juncture of the Niagara River and Lake Ontario. When the American commander, General George McClure, decided to evacuate the fort in mid-December 1813, he foolishly ordered the burning of the nearby village of Newark, now Niagara-on-the-Lake, leaving four hundred people homeless in the winter snows. Reaction on both sides of the border was one of outrage.

News of the despicable act hastened the advance of a large British army which quickly moved across the border, seizing Fort Niagara and torching all settlements north of Niagara Falls. The British army then recrossed the border, to the relief of the settlers at Black Rock and Buffalo. However, early in the morning of December 30, 1813, a force of over a thousand enemy invaders landed north of Black Rock, setting fire to the settlement and marching quickly toward Buffalo. Fleeing militiamen and panicky settlers streamed eastward, and when the British arrived at Buffalo, they found the village nearly deserted. Redcoats proceeded to scurry up and down the streets setting fire to buildings. By the night of January 1, 1814, the whole settlement lay in ashes except for the home of Mrs. Gamaliel St. John, a blacksmith shop, and a small stone jail. Their vengeance now satisfied, the British returned to Canada.

The war dragged on as the settlers gradually returned to rebuild their homes along the border. In July 1814, a new American invasion resulted in the capture of Fort Erie, but efforts to recapture Fort George and threaten York, now Toronto, the capital of Upper Canada, were unsuccessful as the enemy despatched fresh troops into the battle. By winter, the war had come to a halt as American forces left Canadian soil. Rumors of peace were confirmed when news arrived in early 1815 of the ratification of the Treaty of Ghent. The settlers of what would become Erie County six years later could now turn their attention to building for the future with a sense of hope and expectation.

This famous work by John Mix Stanley portrays the trial in 1802 of Red Jacket, a Seneca chief at Buffalo Creek. Accused of witchcraft by a rival named Cornplanter (seated at right), Red Jacket spoke eloquently (and successfully) in his own defense for three hours. Lawyerly and noble in this painting, the real Red Jacket was independent, mischievous and cantankerous— jealously protecting Indian religious tradition against white encroachment. An ally of Cornplanter, Handsome Lake (standing at left) became the founder and prophet of a revealed religion that blended traditional Iroquois elements with aspects of Christianity. From the Collections, courtesy Buffalo and Erie County Historical Society

Paul Busti was general agent for the Holland Land Company for all its holdings in western Pennsylvania as well as Central and Western New York. Born Paolo Busti in Milan, Italy, he migrated to Amsterdam, Holland, where he pursued a successful business career. When he retired, the owners of the Holland Land Company persuaded him to go to Philadelphia in 1797 to straighten out their troubled American operations. He was instrumental in the selection of Ellicott as resident agent in Western New York and worked closely with him in approving the development of a plan for the village of Buffalo. He also authorized a large donation of company lands to push the construction of the Erie Canal by the state of New York. The saddest of his rare visits from the Philadelphia headquarters to Western New York came in 1821 when he traveled there to convince an ailing Ellicott to relinquish the office of resident agent. Busti died in Philadelphia in 1824 while still serving as general agent of the Holland Land Company. Roy W. Nagle Collection courtesy Buffalo and Erie County Historical Society

17

Joseph Ellicott spent a quarter of a century serving the interests of the Holland Land Company in Western New York. He directed the survey of the 3 million-acre Holland Land Purchase and faithfully labored as resident agent to attract settlers to buy the land. Much of his attention was devoted to politics in an effort to minimize land taxes, influence county government to enact measures to promote the company's interests, and support state politicians like

DeWitt Clinton, "Father of the Erie Canal," whose programs would help land sales on the Niagara Frontier. He reaped great rewards in fostering the Erie Canal, which provided easy access to the Purchase by settlers from the east. His long career came to a sad end when he retired because of illness in 1821, the very same year Erie County was divided from Niagara County as a separate entity. Courtesy Old Amherst Colony Museum

Life for the early pioneers in heavily forested Erie County was not an easy one. They were usually poor people and used primitive farm practices, which made the task of clearing trees and planting crops difficult. Hunting skills were vital to survival, and life was one of long days of hard work and nagging loneliness. Travelers were warmly welcomed to help settlers overcome the isolation of the wilderness. The first structures erected by new settlers were very crude, frequently mere log cabins made with small logs which could be handled alone by a pioneer builder. Roofs were of bark and floors of earth, though some better homes had split log floors. Courtesy of John W. Percy, Tonawanda, The Way It Was: A History of the Town of Tonawanda From 1805-1903

Furnishings in primitive log cabins were equally primitive. Families often arrived behind a yoke of oxen, bringing with them a featherbed, but seldom a bedstead or even chairs. These items, as well as tables and wooden utensils for the home and the fields, had to be shaped from the ample logs cut to clear the land for planting. Finishing touches were made to log cabins as blankets were replaced by board doors at entrances, oiled paper windows were added, and stone fireplaces built. Women worked alongside their husbands tending to usual domestic duties like cooking and making clothes. They milked cows, churned butter, and tended chickens and geese. Courtesy John W. Percy, Tonawanda, The Way It Was

The farm pictured was in the Buffalo area along Main Street about 1805. Coming from the east, Main Street was then a mere path through the heavily forested wilderness. Pioneer settlers bought their lands, usually on credit, from the Holland Land Company at prices that ranged from three to four dollars an acre in the outlying areas to two hundred dollars for a lot near the center of the new village of Buffalo. Clearings were then cut out of the woods, log cabins built, and crude wooden plows fashioned to plant crops in the rich virgin soil. Wooden fences were soon erected to enclose the livestock, usually cows and pigs. Roy W. Nagle Collection, courtesy Buffalo and Erie County Historical Society

An early settler of Buffalo was Martin Middaugh, a German cooper who, with his daughter and son-in-law, arrived in Buffalo after first settling unsuccessfully in Lewiston and in Chippewa, Ontario. Chippewa, with its many Loyalist refugees, did not welcome the Middaugh family very warmly since Ezekiel Lane, Middaugh's son-in-law, was a veteran of the American army during the War for Independence. As shown in the print, the family lived in 1797 on a peninsula at the foot of Main Street in a double log house. The house was located on property given to Captain William Johnson, Buffalo's first settler, by his Seneca Indian wife's relatives. Roy W. Nagle Collection, courtesy Buffalo and Erie County Historical Society

The arrival of settlers in Erie County made the construction of roads a high priority. Area leaders sought government assistance, and area settlers demanded that the Holland Land Company use some of its profits to build them. Military considerations also played a role, since Western New York was located along an international border with British Canada at a time when British-American relations were unstable. In 1801, General Moses Porter, commander at Fort Niagara, was ordered by the federal government to build a military road with army soldiers to improve communications between Lakes Erie and Ontario. Fort Niagara was connected with present-day Erie County by Military Road, pictured in the rendition. The road, surveyed by Joseph Ellicott, cut through the woods to connect Lewiston in Niagara County with Black Rock in Erie County by 1802. It was completed in 1809 after the settlement of a federal-state dispute over who would pay for surfacing costs. Courtesy Tonawanda-Kenmore Historical Society

Williamsville was the rendezvous for American regular troops and militia volunteers during the War of 1812. Brig. Gen. Winfield Scott, at thirty years old the beau-ideal of a gallant soldier, for a short time used as his headquarters the Evans homestead shown here, which originally stood at the southwest corner of Main Street and Oakgrove Drive. He established a garrison with a long row of barracks along the main street and a hospital a mile or so away. Roy W. Nagle Collection, courtesy Buffalo and Erie County Historical Society

The burning of Buffalo resulted from American Gen. George McClure's burning of the village of Newark, now Niagara-on-the-Lake, as he retreated late in 1813 from Fort George on the Canadian side of the border at the juncture of Lake Ontario and the Niagara River. Some 150 houses were put to the torch, leaving the helpless inhabitants, mostly women and children, out in the bitter mid-December cold and snow. A large British army quickly struck across the river, seizing Fort Niagara and marching southward to Lewiston and Manchester, now Niagara Falls, destroying the settlements. The citizens of Buffalo and Black Rock waited in terror for the arrival of the vengeful Redcoats, but their fears subsided when the enemy returned to Canadian soil. This move, however, was only temporary, for early on the morning of December 30, over a thousand British troops crossed the Niagara River. Defenders at Black Rock were routed and the village burned. When the British arrived at Buffalo, most defenders and citizens had fled. The enemy then proceeded up and down the streets, setting fire to the buildings. Courtesy Buffalo and Erie County Historical Society

Margaret St. John, born Margaret Kinsman Marsh, was born in Connecticut and married a road builder and farmer, Gamaliel St. John, in 1788. The couple had a dozen or more children. The St. John family moved west into New York State first to Oneida County, then to Cayuga County, and finally to Erie County, where after a brief residence in Williamsville, its members moved to Buffalo in 1810. The St. John family first lived in a crowded, small home in the new village, though a more spacious dwelling was later acquired. The outbreak of the War of 1812 disrupted the family's life and threatened the safety of its members as the specter of British invasion across the Niagara River threatened. Tragedy struck in 1813 when Gamaliel St. John died by drowning, leaving a widow and nine children at home. The widow moved her family eastward to the greater safety of Clarence for a time. Roy W. Nagle Collection, courtesy Buffalo and Erie County Historical Society

Margaret St. John did not remain in Clarence very long. By the Christmas of 1813, she had returned to Buffalo acquiring the modest residence shown in the rendition at left, one and a half stories and not yet completed. It was here that she was living with several of her children in the latter days of December when British troops and their Indian allies approached Buffalo, and militia and citizens alike fled east and south. When the invaders began to burn the village in retribution for the burning of the village of Newark across the river by American forces, Mrs. St. John refused stubbornly to flee. She bravely demanded that British officers provide for the safety of her family and home. By the night of January 1, 1814, the entire settlement of Buffalo was a smoldering mass of ashes except for a blacksmith shop, a small stone jail, and the home of Mrs. Gamaliel St. John, the only residence left standing. Roy W. Nagle Collection, courtesy Buffalo and Erie County Historical Society

Peter Buell Porter of Black Rock played a major role in the War of 1812. In 1795 he migrated from Connecticut to Canandaigua, where he became involved in law, business, and politics. He rose in 1808 to congressman from Western New York, shortly thereafter relocating to Black Rock. After his arrival in New York, he served as an officer in the New York Militia. A member of the militant band of War Hawk nationalists in Congress before the war, he urged Congress to take effective actions to strengthen the nation's ability to fend off British insults to American national honor. Very early he urged in vain that a naval force be built on Lake Erie. When war was declared, he was already active as Quartermaster General of the New York Militia, gathering arms and supplies as well as providing transportation and shelter for the thousands of militiamen ordered into service to protect the New York border with Canada. He led the militia in repelling a force of British troops which invaded across the Niagara at Black Rock on July 11, 1813. During much of the war, he served as a commander of militia and Indian volunteers who accompanied army regulars in the invasion of Canada. When the war ended, this citizen-soldier, "having no idea of adopting permanently the professions of arms," returned to civilian life to resume his business and political pursuits. Roy W. Nagle Collection, courtesy Buffalo and Erie County Historical Society

*In 1913 the Buffalo Yacht Club, founded
in 1860 and located at the foot of Buffalo's
Porter Avenue, played host to Oliver
Hazard Perry's flagship, the* Niagara,
*famed for its exploits on Lake Erie during
the War of 1812. It was from the deck of
this ship that Perry, upon defeating the
British on September 10, 1813, uttered the
famous words, "We have met the enemy
and they are ours." The hulk of the*
Niagara *lay at the bottom of Misery Bay in
Erie, Pennsylvania, for many years until it
was raised, refitted and commissioned to
observe the hundredth anniversary of the
Battle of Lake Erie. Buffalo was chosen for
the celebration, and the* Niagara *arrived at
the Buffalo Yacht Club to bask in the limelight of the gala celebrations of the American victory a century before, a victory
which did much to discourage further
British invasions across the lakes into
American territory. Courtesy Buffalo
Yacht Club,* The First 125 Years: History
and Lore of the Buffalo Yacht Club

Louis LeCouteulx was a French nobleman who fled the violence of the French Revolution to come to the United States and in 1804 settle in the new village of Buffalo. This colorful Frenchman gave the frontier settlement a unique air of elegance. He walked the streets carrying a jeweled snuffbox given him by King Louis XVI. He dressed in silver-buckled shoes, knee britches, and long stockings, and wore his hair in a braided ponytail tied with a bright ribbon. He worked as a pharmacist but listed himself as a gentleman. He was a public benefactor who donated land for what became St. Louis Church, the first Roman Catholic church in Western New York. Courtesy Buffalo and Erie County Historical Society

Chapter Three

Settlement and Boom

by Joseph A. Grande

In the long run, war did little to hamper the development of Erie County. The seeds of progress planted in the early years of the nineteenth century began to bloom as people streamed in, communities were founded, and the foundations of prosperity were laid.

In 1797 while surveying the Holland Land Purchase, Joseph Ellicott had first arrived at the juncture of Buffalo Creek and Lake Erie to find a group of settlers already established. Captain William Johnston and his family, granted land by his wife's Seneca Indian relatives, had arrived eight years earlier to become the first permanent settlers in what would become the city of Buffalo. Nearby were Indian trader Cornelius Winney and German cooper Martin Middaugh as well as black trading-store proprietor Joseph Hodge.

This site at the eastern end of Lake Erie attracted Ellicott's excited attention because he dreamed of a great commercial center arising here to handle trade between the east coast and the growing West along the Hudson-Mohawk Gap outlet through the Appalachians from the Atlantic. He hoped to lay out a town site, although he encountered difficulties in convincing the owners of the Holland Company to let the project go forward. Ellicott and general agent Paul Busti finally won approval for the town in 1802, and Ellicott acted quickly to draw up plans. Having worked with his brother Andrew on designs for the new federal capital at Washington, he adopted a similar scheme, with the hub at the Lake Erie waterfront and streets radiating north, east, and south like spokes on a wheel.

New settlers soon arrived. Louis LeCouteulx, a refugee from the French Revolution, built the first frame house in the settlement in 1804 and ran a pharmacy from its front room. The settlement's first doctor, Cyrenius Chapin, moved with his family into their newly completed home a year later. Indian Commissioner Erastus Granger, well connected in Washington through his cousin Gideon, a member of President Thomas Jefferson's cabinet, also took up residence and became postmaster of the "District of Buffalo Creek." By 1806, the town had the appearance of a permanent community, with over a dozen dwellings, a drugstore, several other stores, and two taverns. Two years later, it had a school and by 1812, a church and a courthouse.

Meanwhile settlers were also taking up land and founding other communities in the area of the future Erie County. On the north, John Hershey, John King, and Alexander Logan bought farmlands along the Tonawanda Creek affording them easy access to local markets in a region where roads were scarce. Loyalist Henry Anguish returned to the new United States in 1808 from nearby Fort Erie, Canada, to make his home at the mouth of Tonawanda Creek, where it empties into the Niagara River. Three years later he opened a tavern and was soon joined by others to lay the foundations of the village, now the city, of Tonawanda. Further south in the Tonawandas, Adam Zimmerman bought one hundred acres from the Holland Company, and with several brothers, established a hamlet not surprisingly called the Zimmerman Settlement in what now is the town of Tonawanda.

The 1840 home shown is that of William A. Zimmerman, son of pioneer Adam Zimmerman who, in 1813, bought from the Holland Land Company a hundred-acre farm for $350. It stands on the same site as Adam Zimmerman's log house along what is now Delaware Road in the town of Tonawanda. In that log house, Adam and his family lived alone in the wilderness for five years before his four brothers took up land nearby. Thus developed one of the first hamlets in the town of Tonawanda, the Zimmerman Settlement, where resided the families of Adam, Conrad, Jacob, Peter and William. The Zimmerman farms were prosperous enterprises devoted mainly to dairying and raising hay for the Buffalo market. Adam Zimmerman died in 1839, the year before his son built the house shown. Courtesy John W. Percy, Tonawanda, The Way It Was

Eastward from the Tonawandas, silversmith Asa Ransom abandoned Buffalo Creek in 1799 to build a tavern at Clarence Hollow at the behest of the Holland Land Company. In the same year, three hundred acres were sold to John Thompson and Benjamin Ellicott, the land agent's brother, in nearby Amherst. The land contained a prime mill site where a mill and blockhouse were erected in 1801 but were soon abandoned. Other settlers followed, among them Samuel Kelsey, William Lewis, William Maltby and Timothy Hopkins. Jonas Williams, a clerk in the Holland Company's office in Batavia, purchased land at the excellent waterpower site on Eleven Mile Creek near the Buffalo Road. Here he rebuilt the abandoned sawmill, attracted new settlers, and founded a village first called Williams' Mills but which soon was called Williamsville, as it is now known.

To the south in the "land of the crabapple"—Cheektowaga—a Connecticut man, Appollos Hitchcock, purchased land on both sides of the Batavia Road in 1809. There he built a sawmill, gristmill, and distillery to convert Indian corn into liquor. Other New Englanders sank roots nearby. Alanson Eggleston and the Woodward brothers took up land along Ellicott Creek in the Bowmansville area of present-day Lancaster. Didymus Kinney and his family acquired a homestead at Chestnut Ridge in what is now Orchard Park. Jabez Hammond bought 1,734 acres in 1804 in Aurora, where he cleared the land, built a log cabin, and planted wheat. To Wales came William and Ethan Allen, grandsons of the Vermont hero of the American Revolution. Jonas Van Wey settled in Alden, where he was joined by others who farmed or founded stores or taverns.

Another Vermonter, Arthur Humphrey, bought land in the valley area of the Holland Hills. Shortly thereafter, Ezekiel and Nathan Colby settled east of the valley on

what came to be called Vermont Hill. Pioneer George Richmond, of similar origins, moved farther south into Sardinia. Deacon Samuel Tubbs and his family went farther west into the Eden valley, where he was joined by Dr. John Marsh from New Hampshire. Charles and Oliver Johnson bought land in the Boston valley, and New Englander John Cummings settled in Hamburg, where on Eighteen Mile Creek he established the first gristmill south of Buffalo. In Collins, Jacob Taylor built a Quaker mission to minister to the Indians on the nearby reservation. Christopher Stone and John Albro settled in the Springville area of Concord while Jonathan Townsend constructed a gristmill, distillery and small hotel in the Waterville area.

These people and many others migrated to Erie County to work hard farming the land and building communities where they could realize their dreams of a happy and prosperous life. They were the type of people Joseph Ellicott yearned to attract to develop the area around what he dreamed would become the commercial hub of the eastern end of the Great Lakes, a town he planned to call New Amsterdam in honor of the Dutch owners of the Holland Land Company. That expectation, however, was not to be achieved because the settlers stubbornly refused to use the name, preferring instead "Buffalo Creek" and later simply "Buffalo."

If the flap over a name for his town irritated Ellicott, plans for a rival town two miles north at Black Rock on the Niagara River proved a source of great concern. The chief architect of that scheme was Peter B. Porter, the energetic Connecticut Yankee who emigrated to Canandaigua in 1795, where he quickly became a prominent attorney and businessman. His business endeavors were centered in Porter, Barton and Company, a trading firm which obtained the portage monopoly around Niagara Falls from New York State. The northern anchor of the portage below

Shown is the Jonas Williams home as it looked in 1914 after site repositioning and additions. Jonas Williams, after whom the village of Williamsville was named, came to Western New York from Pennsylvania to work for the Holland Land Company. A considerable inheritance allowed him to buy large tracts of land in Erie County, which included an abandoned mill on the west bank of Ellicott Creek near Main Street. His log cabin was expanded several times and is actually the front section of the house shown. Williams was buried on the southeast corner of the lot on which the house stood before it was demolished to make way for town parking. Courtesy Old Amherst Colony Museum

The Williamsville Water Mills still operate today, over a century and a half later, on Jonas Williams' original site of 1811. It was built when Williams abandoned his first mill on the east side of Ellicott Creek to erect the present mill on the west side. A stone dam was also constructed, and a stone-lined raceway carried the water from a mill pond to the mill. The mill passed through a number of owners over the years, serving at times as a gristmill or a cement mill. For many years, the mill was owned in part or totally by Timothy Hopkins. Carefully reconditioned and restored in the late 1940s and early 1950s it was selling, among other things, stone-ground grains and cereals. Courtesy Old Amherst Colony Museum

the falls was at Lewiston and the southern anchor above the falls at Black Rock with its "safe and commodious" natural harbor. Here Porter purchased state lands and planned to lay out a town as well as build warehouses and other trading facilities.

Efforts to frustrate the Black Rock project were undertaken by Ellicott and Paul Busti. Ellicott urged the Holland Land Company to buy several thousand acres of state land near Black Rock to prevent future Porter purchases. Failing at that, he got authority to lend money to anyone willing to buy lands between Buffalo and Black Rock for the same purpose. As the Black Rock project moved ahead, Busti emphasized the need to push Buffalo's interests by using an aggressive sales campaign and political pressure in Albany.

Political influence was one lever to which Porter had easy access. Venturing into politics as early as 1797, he rose from county clerk to state assemblyman, and in 1808 to

27

United States congressman. In Washington he moved into a leadership position with influence which reached into the presidential mansion. Black Rock became his residence in 1810, and at the nation's capital, he acted swiftly to relocate the customshouse, then at Buffalo, to his new home village.

This action triggered a conflict with another Western New Yorker with influence in the high echelons of the federal government, Erastus Granger, who was then the collector of customs. Granger opposed Porter's proposal, refuting the latter's contention that most ships carrying trade west docked at Black Rock. Buffalo had a fine harbor, he said, and was a fast-growing community with forty-three families and a core of professional men and young merchants who conducted most of the trade across the border. Black Rock, on the other hand, had only four families, a tavern, a store and a ferry house serving travelers crossing to Canada. Despite Granger's efforts, the congressman from Black Rock won the day when President James Madison, proclaiming what appeared to be a compromise, awarded Black Rock the customshouse during the shipping season from April to November, and located it at Buffalo during the rest of the year, namely, the winter months.

Hostilities between Buffalo and Black Rock ceased temporarily during the War of 1812. Citizens and leaders in both villages cooperated in the face of the threat of British invasion. Porter, a militia general, organized volunteers to repel invasion, and he led them in several assaults on Canada. After the infamous burning of the Niagara Frontier during the winter of 1813-1814, a new American incursion into Canada was launched. When the momentum of the campaign bogged down, the militia volunteers played an important role in checking the British advance on American-held Fort Erie, across from Buffalo. Consequently the British withdrew toward York, now Toronto, ending the danger to Black Rock and Buffalo. After the war, leaders in both villages worked together to obtain federal and state funds to compensate the "Niagara sufferers," those civilians whose property had been damaged or destroyed during British invasions of American soil.

This cooperation did not mask the conflicting purposes and objectives of leaders in both communities. Porter, with his heavy investments at Black Rock, did not hesitate to advocate its interests out of civic pride and personal gain. Add to this the aspirations of a new Buffalo emerging from the ashes of war, and one can appreciate the bitter tone of the rivalry reflected in speeches, newspaper editorials, and pamphlet wars. The struggle was even more intense because Buffalo's leaders—businessman Samuel Wilkeson, lawyer Albert H. Tracy, editor David Day, new customs collector Oliver Forward—allied themselves with DeWitt Clinton while Porter and his friends belonged to the anti-Clinton Bucktail Party. When smuggling and profiteering charges led to Forward's dismissal, Porter was denounced for instigating the purge because he was a man of "avaricious ambition"

who used his "wicked zeal" against anyone who opposed his interests.

Conflicting ideas on a canal system to connect the Great Lakes and Atlantic Ocean also divided the general and Buffalo's village fathers. Porter wanted a system with two canals, one joining the Hudson with Lake Ontario and another around Niagara Falls joining Lakes Erie and Ontario. Buffalo's leaders united with Joseph Ellicott to support DeWitt Clinton's proposal to dig a canal west from Albany to Lake Erie, thus keeping the canal totally within New York State. Porter's influence in Albany and Washington, where he pressured for federal aid, was feared. When Clinton became governor in 1817, the state legislature endorsed his route and authorized the canal's construction with state funds.

The Black Rock-Buffalo struggle now shifted to winning the prized designation as western terminus of the Erie Canal. It was well understood that that prize would make the victor the urban commercial center of Western New York. Black Rock touted its expanded natural harbor located down the Niagara River, away from the turbulent winds and swells which came across Lake Erie from the west. At Buffalo, Wilkeson, Forward, and businessman Charles Townsend labored with determination to make their village the canal's western terminus. Assisted by Clinton and Ellicott, they embarked upon building a good harbor out of range of the British cannons on the Canadian shore, which endangered the harbor works of Black Rock. DeWitt Clinton predicted correctly in 1816 that "Buffalo is to be the point of beginning [of the Erie Canal from the west], and in 50 years...will be next to New York in wealth and population."

The battle raged from the shores of the Niagara to the state and national capitals in the press, in pamphlet wars, and in the words of lobbyists from both villages. Black Rock, its enemies insisted, was too vulnerable to British artillery and too exposed to ice damage. Its leader was a selfish opportunist who misrepresented facts for personal gain. Buffalo was not spared as its rivals emphasized the danger to shipping of sandbars that regularly collected at the mouth of Buffalo Creek. References were made to the "vulgar eyes of the herd in Buffalo" and the bunch of "foul mouthed slanderers" who led the village. Both sides exerted great pressure on the state Canal Commission which, after much hesitation and vacillation, late in 1823 designated Buffalo as the western terminus of the Erie Canal.

Buffalo's 2,412 inhabitants enjoyed an exciting year in 1825 as they awaited the official opening of the canal. Early in June, the venerable Marquis de Lafayette, hero of the American Revolution, arrived to help celebrate the fiftieth anniversary of the outbreak of that war. He arrived in Buffalo's new harbor the morning of June 4 aboard a steamboat from Dunkirk. An assemblage of local dignitaries escorted by a parade of bands and militia units led him to a gaily decorated platform in front of the Eagle Tavern, one of the finest hotels in Western New York. There, facing across a large green which was later named

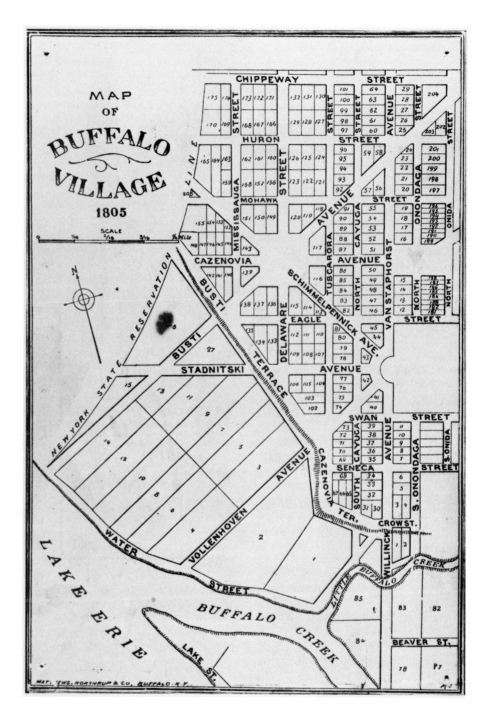

Joseph Ellicott's plans for the village he wished to call New Amsterdam were heavily influenced by the work he had done with his brother Andrew, one of the principal designers of the new federal capital along the Potomac, Washington, D.C. He thought its location ideal on the high banks of Lake Erie at the juncture with Buffalo Creek. A grid street system was used with avenues radiating from a public square like spokes from a hub. The similarity to Washington, D.C., was deliberate. The proposed name, New Amsterdam, was meant to please the owners of the Holland Land Company. Their names—Stadnitski, Schimmelpennick, Vollenhoven, Willinck, and Van Staphorst—as well as that of general agent Paul Busti were attached to many of the principal streets. However, many were renamed, and the only names on the map still listed today are Delaware, Huron, Mohawk, Eagle, Swan, Chippewa, Seneca, Elk, and after a long absence and in a different location, Busti. Roy W. Nagle Collection, courtesy Buffalo and Erie County Historical Society

LaFayette Square, he was welcomed with great ceremony and given the opportunity to address a crowd of excited citizens. A civic dinner and gala ball followed the same evening. The next morning, LaFayette traveled to Black Rock, where he breakfasted at General Porter's home and greeted many of the village's 1,039 inhabitants before departing on the canal packet, the *Seneca Chief,* enroute to Niagara Falls and points east.

Several days after his departure, another assemblage of several thousand gathered at Niagara Square to witness the last public hangings in the area. Executed were three brothers from the Boston valley area: Israel, Isaac, and Nelson Thayer, found guilty of the murder of a Scottish peddler, John Love. Love had disappeared mysteriously late in 1824 and his body was discovered several months later in a frozen shallow grave on a slope near Israel Thayer's cabin.

Four months later, to the cheers of crowds along the entire Erie Canal, the *Seneca Chief,* with Governor Clinton and other dignitaries aboard, led a parade of packets from

Buffalo to New York City. There Lake Erie water was ceremoniously dumped into the harbor, signifying the realization of a great dream, the wedding of the waters of the Atlantic Ocean and the Great Lakes.

The opening of the Erie Canal proved a boon to the development of Erie County. Its population increased 145 percent in the two decades between 1820 and 1840. Five years after the canal's opening, the count surpassed 35,000, surging to 57,594 by 1835 and 62,465 in 1840. The fortunes of the village of Buffalo were similarly spectacular. The number of people there jumped from 2,492 in 1825 to 8,653 in 1830 to 15,661 in 1835 and to 18,213 by 1840. Little wonder that in 1831 the village fathers agreed on the need to incorporate as a city, drawing up a city charter which was approved by the New York State legislature the following year.

The people who settled in Erie County were only one part of a tide of humanity, including Yankees and immigrants from abroad, who streamed along the canal seeking the lush acres and great opportunities to be found in the lands washed by the waters of the Great Lakes. Canal transportation was twice as fast and much more comfortable than stagecoach travel. Loaded canal packets ended their trek at Buffalo, where many settlers boarded lake ships to sail westward to Ohio, Michigan and beyond in their quest for a better life.

There was ample opportunity available in Buffalo and Erie County. The cost of living came down as shipping costs dropped—the Albany-Buffalo rate declined from a hundred dollars per ton to three dollars per ton. Not only did the county's people benefit from the lower costs of goods brought from the east, but farmers enjoyed a boom as well. The lower shipping costs enabled them to send their grain to Albany and New York City, where prices were often three times those of the local market. It is no surprise that around the county the signs of prosperity grew. The county wheat crop, with a yield of twenty to forty bushels per acre, brought in an annual export income of over $6 million. Consequently, pioneer log cabins gave way to neat frame farmhouses from Sardinia in the south to the Tonawandas on the north. New villages and hamlets appeared as taverns, sawmills and gristmills were needed to serve the countryside.

Although agriculture would remain a vital part of the county's economy, diversification became the order of the day as commerce and navigation flourished. Buffalo harbor was alive with excitement as canal packets from Albany and lake steamers from the West exchanged goods and passengers. Wheat shipments from the West rose from 3,640 barrels in 1829 to over a million barrels by 1841, when the harbor also handled sixty-seven thousand barrels of pork, 5 million pounds of butter and lard, three hundred thousand pounds of wool, and seven hundred thousand barrels of "spirits." The increased volume of shipping required the harbor's enlargement within a decade of its completion, and the number of jobs tied to commerce and navigation increased tenfold.

Wharves and warehouses went up along the canal and around the harbor. Manufacturing enterprises jumped 262 percent in the years from 1820 to 1840. Shipyards, stockyards, tanneries, soap factories, flour mills, iron foundries, and lumberyards sprang up to serve the needs of a booming area. Dry-goods and grocery stores, clothing and hat stores, bookshops and printing houses, taverns and brewers, artisans and professional men all felt the effects of this new prosperity. Buffalo's first daily newspaper, the *Commercial Advertiser,* joined the ranks of several weeklies. In 1829, the Bank of the United States established a branch in Buffalo and two years later, the Bank of Buffalo opened for business. Fire and marine insurance agencies appeared about the same time.

Quaker missionaries also came to work among the Indians. So did young, frail John Neumann, a newly ordained priest from Bohemia later declared a saint by his church, who spent four years ministering to his fellow Catholics in the region outside of Buffalo. His parish included mostly German farmers, with a sprinkling of Irish, French, and Scots, and it extended from the Tonawandas on the north to Batavia on the east and Sheldon on the south.

Hope and expectations of prosperity motivated locally born Hiram Pratt, who was instrumental in establishing the Bank of Buffalo and the first flour mills at Buffalo. Similar motivations must have brought Lewis Falley Allen to Buffalo, where he opened the first insurance office and then moved into real estate and timber investments around the county. The lure of opportunity attracted young Millard Fillmore, future president of the United States, first to East Aurora to study and practice law, and then to Buffalo, where his political career advanced from state assemblyman to congressman to state comptroller to vice president and then president of the United States upon the death of Zachary Taylor. These men and many others like them fostered the emergence of Erie County from a rural frontier to a diversified, settled community where people could hope to make a good life for themselves and their families.

The opening of the Erie Canal, for all its positive effects, also had its darker sides. Along the canal came the dreaded cholera which in 1832 struck 184 people in Buffalo. In that newly incorporated city, where the canal emptied into the harbor, there developed one of the "wickedest" streets in the nation, Canal Street, where sailor and canaleer, rich and poor, Yankee and immigrant drank, played, fought, and sometimes died. Canal Street boasted of ninety-three saloons, fifteen dance halls, and numerous bordellos which attracted transients and citizens alike. It could also boast of the young performer, Ned Christy, who created the minstrel show to entertain the rowdy clientele before going on to achieve national fame.

Concern with the immorality of Canal Street was only one facet of the dissatisfaction around the county. Rural citizens protested the Holland Land Company's slow progress in building such public improvements as roads. They banded together in the Agrarian Movement to stop the draining of profits abroad, and demanded that the state tax foreign landowners to construct needed public improvements. Rallies were held in towns and villages across the area, and political campaigns were fought to force the legislature to enact appropriate laws.

Politics again felt the impact of popular movement when an eccentric Western New Yorker, William Morgan, disappeared after threatening to expose the secrets of the Masonic Order. Fear spread of a Masonic conspiracy to control the government and destroy democracy. Demands multiplied for the disbanding of Masonic lodges, and a political party, the Anti-Masonic Party, was born vowing to defeat any Mason who ran for public office. The party's influence spread rapidly westward into Pennsylvania and Ohio, and eastward across the state and into New England. Young, ambitious politicians like Millard Fillmore joined its ranks and reaped the benefits of its power and momentum.

Fear of war with England cropped up in 1837 as a result of a rebellion in Canada called the Patriot War. The rebels, led by William L. MacKenzie, fled to Navy Island near the American shore of the Niagara River, where they set up headquarters. Popular support on the American side of the border was strong as open efforts were made to raise funds and recruit men. The British government naturally demanded action to suppress such flagrant actions. On December 29, a little steamer, the *Caroline*, was hired at Buffalo to ferry goods from the American shore to Navy Island. During the course of the night, several boatloads of armed men crossed the river from Canada. They seized the steamer, killing one man, towed her into the middle of the river, and, setting her afire, sent her blazing down the rapids toward Niagara Falls. The war scare which fol-

lowed resulted in the dispatching of army troops under Gen. Winfield Scott to the border at Buffalo where a military installation, the Poinsett Barracks, was constructed between Allen and North Streets on the east side of Delaware Avenue. It remained there until the 1840s, when it was replaced by a fort on the Niagara River opposite Fort Erie.

The shady dealings of a remarkable Buffalonian, Benjamin Rathbun, mixed with volatile politics and fear of war to unsettle the economy of Erie County. Rathbun was a respected entrepreneur who began his business career as a hotel keeper but soon emerged as a developer and land speculator at a time when land values soared. In 1835 alone, he built ninety-nine buildings, both commercial and residential. He operated stone quarries and brick plants, grocery stores and dry-goods stores as well as stagecoaches and a private bank. Consequently the Buffalo financial community panicked in 1836 when he was arrested and jailed for forgery. It seems he had borrowed beyond his means on the basis of notes to which he forged the signatures of other prominent Buffalonians. An estimated $1.5 million in forged notes was issued, leading to his trial and sentencing to five years in prison. What was even more tragic to the community was the loss of jobs by Rathbun's twenty-five hundred employees when his empire collapsed.

The economic jolt of the Rathbun scandal and the ensuing national depression in 1837 ended the heyday of Erie County's reckless boom. While problems there were, by 1840 the county had undoubtedly progressed immensely in its growth and development, and more could be expected in the future.

Joseph Ellicott found the settlers in the new village of Buffalo obstinate. Not only did they refuse to call the village New Amsterdam as he wished, but they also rejected his plans for a new home. Ellicott had retained for himself a hundred-acre reserve extending back from Main Street between Swan and Eagle Streets. Here he planned a fine home in the middle of a five-street intersection, giving him a view of all that went on in the village. When the village board decided that a main street should run right through the Ellicott reserve, he abruptly moved about forty miles eastward to Batavia, saying "I intend to do all I can for Batavia because the Almighty will look after Buffalo." At Batavia, more centrally located in the Holland Purchase, he erected the building shown here for the company's main land office. The building still stands today, serving as a Holland Land Company museum surrounded by a small park recently named in honor of Ellicott's close associate, Paul Busti. Courtesy Buffalo and Erie County Historical Society

31

The home shown is the residence of Peter B. Porter at Black Rock, built in 1816 after his first home was burned during the War of 1812. It stood on present-day Niagara Street near Ferry on the bluff high above the river, affording a fine view of the area. Here in 1818 Porter brought his new bride, Laetitia Breckenridge Grayson Porter, member of the powerful Kentucky political clan. Here she and the general played host to such illustrious figures in American history as the Marquis de Lafayette, Henry Clay, DeWitt Clinton, James Monroe, and John Quincy Adams, who appointed Porter Secretary of War in 1828. When Porter abandoned Black Rock for a residence at Prospect Point in Niagara Falls in 1837, the home was sold to Buffalo businessman Lewis Falley Allen. It was here that Allen's nephew, Grover Cleveland, resided for a short time after his arrival in Buffalo in the 1850s, by which time Black Rock had been annexed to Buffalo. The house was torn down in 1911 to make way for commercial development. Roy W. Nagle Collection, courtesy Buffalo and Erie County Historical Society

The residence of William A. Bird was built in 1819 in Black Rock at Niagara and Gull streets. Bird, a nephew of Peter B. Porter, for many years worked closely with his uncle's enterprises. He was elected the first supervisor of the town of Black Rock and pursued a successful business career. He donated a lot for the Grace Episcopal Church at Niagara and Penfield streets. Lawn fetes of the church were frequently held on the grounds of his home, which was torn down in 1911 to make way for commercial buildings. Roy W. Nagle Collection, courtesy Buffalo and Erie County Historical Society

Like a phoenix of Egyptian mythology, the devastated village of Buffalo renewed itself from its own ashes following its burning in the winter of 1813-1814. Settlers did not wait until the war was over to start strag-gling back, and buildings again began to rise as they looked with optimism to the future. One of the buildings constructed right after the war was the Phoenix Hotel on Main Street, where large crowds fre-quently gathered to greet the arrival of stagecoaches bringing goods and passengers with news of the outside world. The hotel was razed in 1865 to make way for a more elegant establishment, the Tifft House, which itself came down in 1902 to make way for a department store. Roy W. Nagle Collection, courtesy Buffalo and Erie County Historical Society

Buffalo served as the county seat of Niagara County, and after 1821, the new Erie County. The county courthouse shown was built in 1816 off Main Street eastward across a green, dubbed Courthouse Park. This Greek Revival structure stood there until 1876. Besides legal business, public meetings and county fair activities were held in and around the grounds. In 1825 the area in front of it was renamed in honor of the venerable hero of the Ameri-can Revolution, the Marquis de LaFayette. It was in this park that twenty-three years later the Free Soil Party, predecessor of the Republican Party, held its national conven-tion and nominated former New York governor and president Martin Van Buren for president on a platform opposed to the extension of slavery into the territories. Roy W. Nagle Collection, courtesy Buffalo and Erie County Historical Society

The village of Buffalo had an exciting year in 1825 with the visit of the Marquis de LaFayette, the public execution of the three Thayer brothers, and the opening of the Erie Canal. Its slightly over two thousand citizens lived in a pleasant frontier community which was about to expand at an amazing pace. The 1825 Buffalo scenes shown in the accompanying prints give an idea of how the little town looked just before the boom began. The harbor was already beginning to experience the inevitable effects of being the western terminus of the Erie Canal. A short distance from the harbor was Main at Terrace, one of the business centers of the village. Farther up

Main Street on the west side south of Court Street stood the Eagle Tavern, a spacious three-story brick structure built by entrepreneur Benjamin Rathbun and renowned as the finest hotel in the western part of the state. Roy W. Nagle Collection, courtesy Buffalo and Erie County Historical Society

Samuel Wilkeson was the man most responsible for the building of Buffalo harbor, which became the western terminus of the Erie Canal, securing Buffalo's future. Son of a pioneer farmer in western Pennsylvania, he began as a farmer and then went on to become a shipbuilder, a merchant, and a ship owner. He settled in Buffalo after the War of 1812, serving as justice of the peace. He was an ardent supporter of the construction of the Erie Canal and thus an ally of DeWitt Clinton, who wished to make Buffalo its western terminus. He labored strongly for state assistance in developing Buffalo harbor and personally supervised much of the work. He fought bitterly against the power of Peter B. Porter, who wished to make Black Rock the western terminus of the Erie Canal. When Buffalo's victory was won, he accompanied Governor Clinton aboard the canal packet Seneca Chief, traveling eastward to dump Lake Erie water into New York harbor, signaling the union of the waters of the Atlantic and the Great Lakes. On his return to Buffalo, he brought a cask of ocean water, which after suitable ceremonies, was mingled with the waters of Lake Erie. Courtesy Buffalo and Erie County Historical Society

This elegant house was the home of Samuel Wilkeson, built in 1825 on Niagara Square. Erected the same year the Erie Canal opened, it symbolized the confidence of Buffalo's leaders in future growth and prosperity. Though not a lawyer, Wilkeson served as the first judge of the Erie Common Pleas. He later was elected to the New York State Senate and in 1836, he became mayor of the new city of Buffalo. While active in public service, he also remained a wise and successful businessman. He erected the city's first iron foundry and started the manufacture of steam engines and stoves. His home stood on Niagara Square until 1915, when it was replaced by the city's first drive-in service station. Appropriately, the site was later occupied by the magnificent Buffalo City Hall constructed in the 1930s. Roy W. Nagle Collection, courtesy Buffalo and Erie County Historical Society

The Marquis de LaFayette's visit to
Buffalo on June 4, 1825, was part of a
nationwide tour undertaken at the invitation of Congress to commemorate the
golden anniversary of American independence, a cause he had assisted by his
service in the Continental Army under
Gen. George Washington. Accompanied by
his son, George Washington LaFayette, he
traveled around the land visiting ex-
presidents Jefferson, Madison, and
Monroe, addressing Congress and meeting
the new president, John Quincy Adams.
His journey brought him to Buffalo
enroute to Boston to participate in the
June 17 anniversary of Bunker Hill Day,
Buffalo Village President Oliver Forward
hailed his voluntary sacrifices in support
of liberty and asked him to accept "the
humble tribute of our respect" and that of
"every friend of liberty and of mankind."
The sixty-seven-year-old Frenchman
responded by conveying the "tribute of my
respect to the citizens of Buffalo." After
greeting the people at Black Rock the next
morning, he continued his trek eastward
to New England. Courtesy Buffalo and
Erie County Historical Society

The Eagle House, pictured as it looked in the 1880s, was built around 1830 on the north side of Main Street in the Williamsville settlement east of Buffalo. It was a major stopping-off point for travelers coming from Canandaigua and Batavia enroute to Buffalo. It later served as a station for the Underground Railroad for smuggling runaway slaves to the Niagara River and across into Canada, where slavery had been abolished. With the exception of the porch, the original hotel looked very much as it is pictured. The Eagle House still stands today, serving as a fine restaurant enjoyed by people from around Erie County. Courtesy Old Amherst Colony Museum

Dr. Ebenezer Johnson came to Buffalo in 1809 to open a medical practice in the pioneer settlement. He served as a medical officer during the War of 1812. A baby daughter was born just before the war broke out, and as the British approached the village in 1813 to burn it, his wife Sallie placed the baby on a feather bed in a sleigh and fled to the protection of the army garrison in Williamsville. "Baby Mary" was taken in charge by Gen. Winfield Scott and other officers so that her mother might aid the sick and the wounded. The Johnsons' first dwelling in Buffalo was burned by the British rampage during the winter of 1813-1814. Shown is the new one they built in the early 1830s on Delaware Avenue, known as the Johnson Cottage. It was erected just after Buffalo received a city charter in 1832 and Johnson was elected the first mayor of the new city. Its grounds were surrounded by a high fence and ornamented with rare shrubbery and plants. It eventually came to house the Buffalo Female Academy, now the Buffalo Seminary, and was later torn down. Roy W. Nagle Collection, courtesy Buffalo and Erie County Historical Society

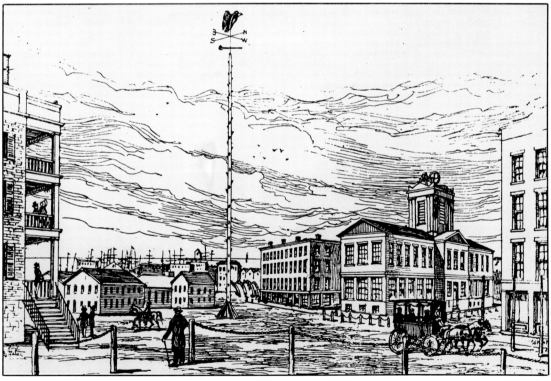

By the mid-1830s, Buffalo's population surpassed fifteen thousand, constituting about one-third of the population of Erie County. Signs of its growth can be seen in the accompanying prints. The 1835 Buffalo harbor scene shows bustling activity passing the historic "Chinaman's" lighthouse, at the entrance to the inner harbor, two years after it was built to replace one erected in 1818 closer to shore. It still stands today, a symbol to the city's history as a great port. The other print depicts a liberty pole raised on July 4, 1838, at Main and Terrace. At right is the two-story Market House with a square belfry on its top containing a great clanging bell which sounded at fire alarms. Roy W. Nagle Collection, courtesy Buffalo and Erie County Historical Society

Religion was very much part of the life of the people of early Buffalo. Fitting houses of worship, some shown in the accompanying prints, were constructed by the many denominations in the area. A drawing of the downtown area as it was in 1838 depicts the homes of two of Buffalo's oldest congregations, the First Presbyterian Church, right, erected in 1823, and St. Paul's Episcopal Church, left, erected in 1819-1820, side by side on Main Street lots separated by what came to be called Church Street. The oldest church building still standing in Buffalo, now devoted to commercial use, was erected in 1831 as the Breckenridge Street Presbyterian Church in what was then the village of Black Rock. A year later, the first Roman Catholic parish received a donation of land at Main and Edward streets and built a humble "Lamb of God" church, later replaced by the more elaborate St. Louis Church. Roy W. Nagle Collection, courtesy Buffalo and Erie County Historical Society

The Jubilee Water Works was one of Buffalo's first water systems. When built in 1830, it replaced the village's "Water John" Kuecherer who for years had gone about the streets on a horse-drawn cart, selling water from Lake Erie to homes without wells in their backyards. Through miles of log pipes, the Water Works delivered water from the Jubilee Springs, located out Delaware Avenue near present-day Gates Circle, to Buffalo and Black Rock. By the 1890s, the city had outgrown the Water Works, and adopted a reservoir system which was filled by pump with Lake Erie water. One such reservoir stood on top of Prospect Hill along Niagara Street, where the Connecticut Street Armory stands today. Just before World War I, a new modern water system came into being with the construction of the Colonel Ward Pumping Station at the foot of Porter Avenue, where Lake Erie and the Niagara River join. Roy W. Nagle Collection, courtesy Buffalo and Erie County Historical Society

The German-speaking Father John Neumann was ordained in New York City and was sent as a missionary to the thousands of immigrants, many of them German-speaking, who had settled in Western New York. Headquartered first at Williamsville and then at North Bush, he ministerd to the people in a fifteen-mile radius, where four hundred families were busy taming the thick wilderness forests and cultivating the land for farming. For four years he crisscrossed his large parish on foot or by horse in snow, rain or heat. A student of botany, he classified the flora of the wilderness forests. After months of exhausting work, he collapsed, and while he regained his health, decided to enter the Redemptorist Order. In 1840 he left Erie County, going on to Baltimore and eventually to Philadelphia where, in 1852 he became bishop. When he died in 1860, he left behind an inspiring reputation for spirituality and an amazing record in the establishment of a parochial school system in his diocese. *Courtesy John W. Percy, Tonawanda, The Way It Was*

About 1837, the settlers in the North Bush section of what is now the town of Tonawanda gave Father John Neumann a five-acre plot on which to build a home and plant a garden to provide his food. Here he built a log chapel where local Catholics worshipped until increased attendance rendered it too small. A squabble ensued over the location of a new church, and one group of the congregation left to form St. Joseph's parish in the University Heights area of present-day north Buffalo. The remaining people of North Bush built a new fieldstone church, completing it in 1850. The North Bush Chapel, as it is called today, still stands on the grounds of St. John the Baptist Parish in the town of Tonawanda, serving as a shrine to the man who, since 1977, has been called St. John Neumann by official declaration of the Roman Catholic Church. *Courtesy John W. Percy, Tonawanda, The Way It Was*

Rebellion broke out in British Canada in 1837. The armed uprising in Lower Canada, now Quebec, was suppressed at considerable cost in blood and money. In Upper Canada, now Ontario, an ex-member of the Provincial Parliament, William Lyon Mackenzie, led the uprising. After an unsuccessful uprising north of Toronto, he fled to Buffalo in December 1837, to enlist support from a sympathetic public south of the border. His "patriot" forces established themselves on British Navy Island close to the American shore off Grand Island. To British consternation, American volunteers joined the rebels, and William Wells' little steamer, the Caroline, ferried men and supplies between Navy Island and the American shore. When American authorities were slow in preventing such unneutral actions, the British sent forces across the Niagara River under cover of darkness, seizing the Caroline, killing one man, and cutting the ship loose to sail down the river ablaze to sure destruction in the treacherous rapids and Niagara Falls. The print shown is a rendition of the ship going over the falls, though it may actually have been smashed to pieces by the rapids before it ever reached the falls. Roy W. Nagle Collection, courtesy Buffalo and Erie County Historical Society

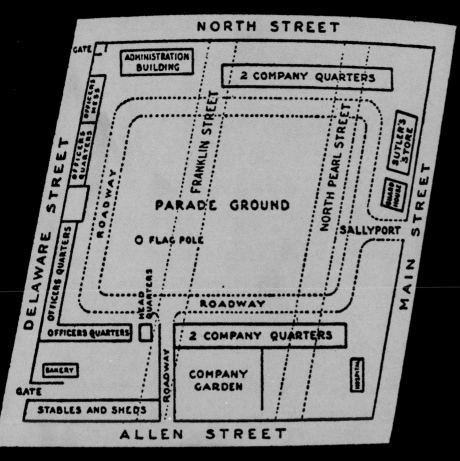

The crisis occasioned by the burning of the Caroline *threatened to bring the United States and Great Britain to war. A force of American troops was sent to the border under Gen. Winfield Scott, who had served in the area during the War of 1812. Construction of a military post, called the Poinsett Barracks, was begun to house Scott's command. In 1839, President Martin Van Buren journeyed to Buffalo to dedicate the post. The Poinsett Barracks served as an active military post until the mid-1840s when a fort, dedicated to the memory of Gen. Peter B. Porter, who had just died, rose on the high ground near the shore overlooking the juncture of Lake Erie and the Niagara River. The post was then dismantled, leaving only one of the original buildings standing near the corner of Delaware Avenue and North Street. That building became the residence of prominent Buffalo attorney and civic leader Ansley Wilcox, and Theodore Roosevelt took the presidential oath there in 1901 upon the assassination of William McKinley. Roy W. Nagle Collection, courtesy Buffalo and Erie County Historical Society*

Benjamin Rathbun was one of the most colorful figures in the history of early Western New York. A daring entrepreneur, his stagecoaches rumbled through the streets and roads of Erie County. He bought a three-story Georgian-style tavern from one Gaius Kibbe and renamed it the Eagle Tavern, making it one of the finest stagecoach stops and public gathering places in the state west of New York City. In the 1830s he constructed many of the city's commercial, residential, and religious buildings, operating stores and a bank at the same time. His conviction for forgery in 1837 shook the foundations of the entire business community, bringing an end to an era of reckless boom. After serving a jail sentence, he took his talents to New York City to recoup his fortunes. Roy W. Nagle Collection, courtesy Buffalo and Erie County Historical Society

Many of the early roads built in Erie County to tie communities together were constructed by private companies chartered by New York State. To recoup their investments and make a profit, these companies charged tolls for the use of their roads. This toll booth was erected at Main Street and Getzville Road in what is now the Snyder area of the Town of Amherst. Carriages and coaches going eastward toward Clarence and Batavia paid their tolls here until the booth was abandoned near the end of the nineteenth century. Roy W. Nagle Collection, courtesy Buffalo and Erie County Historical Society

Chapter Four

In Pursuit of Greatness

by Joseph A. Grande

In the three decades after 1840, Erie County underwent continued agricultural expansion, a boom in commerce and trade, the beginning of industry, and the trauma of the Civil War. Buffalo's growth advanced as it annexed Black Rock, drew up a new charter, and took on the aura of a prosperous urban center composed of a mosaic now including more and more foreign immigrants as well as New England Yankees and other groups of old American stock. The nearby Indian presence was lessened as the Buffalo Creek Reservation was sold and its settlers moved to other area reservations or out West. Also extinguished by 1840 were the last holdings of the Holland Land Company, which sold its remaining acres to various American land speculators.

The Holland Land Company had been instrumental in bringing thousands of farm families to Erie County, where agricultural enterprise remained a strong element of the regional economy. The county included forty thousand farmers and their families, and much of the landscape was dotted with well cultivated farms and neat frame farmhouses. As the population increased in nearby towns and in the urban hub at Buffalo, ample markets were easily accessible as were more distant markets via the Erie Canal and the growing number of railroads. Farmers produced hay and feed for the Buffalo market. Northern towns focused on wheat and southern towns on oats. The southern towns like Eden, Boston, Collins, Concord, and Evans began to move into dairying to provision Buffalo with such

staples as cheese and butter. Farmers also raised some beef cattle for the Philadelphia market.

While farm families were the mainstay of the agricultural economy, leading Buffalo businessmen acquired farms in such towns as Aurora and Grand Island. There they directed various kinds of agricultural activities. Lewis Falley Allen, for example, purchased Allenton, a 600-acre

This toll gate, photographed in the late 1800s, stood at Orchard Park and Ridge Roads in the town of West Seneca. Courtesy James J. Ciesla, West Seneca Town Historian

One vehicle frequently passing the toll gate at Main Street and Getzville Road was the stagecoach, shown here in a rare photo taken in the 1860s, which ran between Buffalo and Williamsville. Courtesy Old Amherst Colony Museum

farm on Grand Island. There experimentation was conducted with cows to improve milk production and with swine to improve meat production. Orchards of apple, pear, and cherry trees were planted as were grapevines, pioneering endeavors in fruit growing, which became an important element of the regional agricultural economy.

Men like Allen joined with their fellow citizens in the countryside and in communities such as Hamburg, Aurora, Holland, Wales, Eden, Boston and Amherst to organize the Erie County Agricultural Society, which sponsored an Erie County fair. In October 1841, Buffalo hosted the fair, which was held in and behind the courthouse near present-day Lafayette Square. A livestock show featured horses, sheep and swine. Displays in the courthouse included prize vegetables, fruit and cheeses, as well as homemade food and crafts.

Seven years later, the New York State Fair came to the city, where it was held near the Poinsett Barracks on Delaware Avenue, with the governors of New York and Michigan in attendance. A joint Erie-Cattaraugus County fair, the Union Agricultural Fair, was held at Springville in 1851. In other years, the county fair rotated between such towns as Aurora, Hamburg, and Lancaster until 1868, when the Hamburg Driving Park Association invited the fair to its grounds. This location eventually became the permanent site of the annual event.

Located along the Erie Canal as it went southward paralleling the Niagara River was the Cherry Farm. Hamilton Cherry arrived in what is now the town of Tonawanda in 1832 from Newfoundland. He acquired a 300-acre farm, where he built a log cabin which was rebuilt and expanded over the years to look as it does in these late nineteenth-century photos. The people seated in the carriage are members of the Cherry family. The old farmhouse served at various times as a tavern, a school and a church. It was demolished about 1950, by which time the area around it had become industrial. Courtesy Tonawanda-Kenmore Historical Society

Two Salisbury families settled in what is now the village of Blasdell in the town of Hamburg in the nineteenth century. Smith Salisbury came from Vermont to erect a home on Milestrip Road. His son, Oliver Cromwell Salisbury, later served as fire chief and village president. Charles Salisbury, no relation to Smith, moved to the area in 1850. Two of his many children, Maurice and Warren, opened a general store and called it the Blasdell Park Store, shown here as it looked in the late nineteenth century. A number of businesses were located in the building over the years until it burned in 1935. Courtesy Nina M. Brown, Blasdell Village Historian

The Maurice Osborn homestead was built in 1841 in what is now the Village of Blasdell in the town of Hamburg. Osborn came from Connecticut in 1812, as did many of the other early settlers in Erie County. And like many other pioneers he first erected a log cabin and a sawmill. As the years passed he improved on his homestead to develop one of the finest in the area. The children remaining in the area received a farm and similar houses from their father. Courtesy Nina M. Brown, Blasdell Village Historian

Lewis F. Allen was born in Westfield, Massachusetts, in 1800. He entered business early, working in Connecticut, New York City, and Ohio. In April 1827, he came to Buffalo to serve as secretary and financial manager of the Western Insurance Company. With him came his bride of two years, the former Margaret Cleveland, whose nephew, Stephen Grover Cleveland, would one day be president of the United States. Allen's successful business career branched out into real estate and other areas. In association with businessmen from New England, he handled the Boston Lumber Company's purchases on Grand Island and oversaw the development of enterprises there. When the company sold its holdings on the island, he acquired several hundred acres, where he experimented with livestock breeding and fruit raising. He and his associates purchased the interests of Gen. Peter B. Porter at Black Rock, and he moved into the Porter home overlooking the Niagara River. He later convinced Grover Cleveland, on his way to Ohio, to remain in Buffalo to pursue a legal career which led to politics and the White House. Roy W. Nagle Collection, courtesy Buffalo and Erie County Historical Society

The East Boston Lumber Company bought sixteen thousand acres of land on Grand Island in 1833. Just eight years before Mordecai Noah had failed in his dream to make the island a homeland for the Jews. Now East Boston Company employees began to fell the white oak forests, and a sawmill was built on the eastern shore opposite Tonawanda. At this settlement called Whitheaven, lumber was cut to be shipped along the Erie Canal to the company's shipyard in Boston, Massachusetts. There the lumber was used to build the magnificent American multisail clipper ships which plied the world's sea lanes in great numbers in the middle of the nineteenth century. When Grand Island's white oak forests were exhausted in the 1850s, company operations ceased and the Whitehaven settlement was eventually abandoned. Roy W. Nagle Collection, courtesy Buffalo and Erie County Historical Society

Closely related to agriculture was the rise of the lumber industry. Local firms supplying local needs from local forests were nothing new. Erie County, however, soon became involved with lumbering on a national scale, exploiting not only local forests but also those farther west and across the border in Canada. In 1833, the East Boston Lumber Company of Massachusetts purchased sixteen thousand forest acres on Grand Island. Lumber was badly needed for clipper ship construction at its shipyards on Noodle Island in Boston harbor. Across from Tonawanda, the Whitehaven settlement was established with a saw-mill, a store, a church, and a school. From a comfortable home on nearby Tonawanda Island, company president Stephen White directed the enterprise, which sent fine white oak eastward to Massachusetts. The similar move-ment of lumber—by ship, by canal, and by rail—from Michigan and other areas of the Great Lakes, including Southern Ontario, would make Buffalo and the Tona-wandas important lumber centers with an impact far beyond the local area.

The rise of the lumber trade paled when compared to the rapid growth of the grain industry. Gristmills dotted the county from the days of earliest settlement, but no mills were reported at Buffalo and Black Rock until after the Erie Canal opened. Those villages had depended mainly on the mill at Williamsville more than eleven miles away. The Erie Canal and the expansion of grain farming in the developing West changed the pattern in Erie County. Buffalo became a point of transshipment from lake schooners to canal boats as more and more grain passed through the harbor. The volume of grain shipment grew from 2 million bushels in 1841 to 31.5 million in 1860 as the port climbed toward the rank of first grain port in the world. The trade focused on wheat, although by the 1850s a considerable amount of corn was carried, with much smaller amounts of oats and rye.

Western New York's preeminence in the grain trade was further strengthened by the invention of the grain elevator. Invented by Joseph Dart, the elevator used perpendicular conveyor belts strung with a series of buckets which could be lowered into ships' holds. This new system of unloading grain, using steam power, revolutionized the industry, cutting labor costs and unloading time and allowing the harbor to handle the increasing volume of grain shipped eastward. Dart's first elevator, opened in 1842, unloaded over two hundred

The village of Tonawanda grew up at the northwest corner of the town of the same name where Tonawanda Creek flowed into the Niagara River. The Erie Canal was dug westward until it reached the village, where it turned south to parallel the Niagara River as it wended its way to Buffalo harbor. While most of the town remained agricultural, the village developed into a lumber center. First white oak from nearby Grand Island and then white pine from the forests of Michigan, Wisconsin, Minnesota, and Ontario were loaded there on canal boats for shipment to the markets of the east. By the end of the century, Tonawanda and its neighboring village, North Tonawanda, became the largest lumber supply center in the world. On March 23, 1903, Tonawanda incorporated as a city, separating from the rest of the town. A scene of life in the bustling village is shown about 1860 at Niagara Street and the Main Street bridge over the Erie Canal. Courtesy Tonawanda-Kenmore Historical Society

Joseph Dart helped to make Buffalo the busiest grain-transfer port in the nation and the world. He watched grain being unloaded at the Buffalo wharves, laboriously cupped into buckets by hand and then carried on the backs of the Irish dock workers to the warehouse for weighing. This method of unloading the harbor's rapidly growing grain imports allowed the movement of only two thousand bushels a day from the holds of the many lake ships docked in the harbor. Remembering the invention of Oliver Evans, who originated a conveyor belt for use in grain milling, Dart focused his energy on developing a system for unloading grain using the same principle, thereby revolutionizing grain handling. Courtesy Buffalo and Erie County Historical Society

Eight-sided houses were popularized by Orson Squire Fowler in the mid-1800s as ideal homes, easy to build, efficient, and harmonious with nature. They would eliminate useless square corners and provide plenty of window space for light and ventilation. Indian agent Charles Rich admired an octagon house in the Hudson Valley and when he reached the village of Akron in the town of Newstead, he decided to build one. Thus what is now called the Rich-Twinn house, shown here probably in the 1860s, rose in 1849 on Main Street. It is unique in Erie County, and while long used as a residence, it now belongs to the Newstead Historical Society, which is in the process of restoring it. Courtesy Newstead Historical Society

Despite the taunts of skeptics, Joseph Dart constructed a large warehouse on Buffalo Creek, where he installed a perpendicular conveyor belt fitted with buckets that could elevate grain from a ship's hold to the storage bins or to canal boats. The elevator was powered by a steam engine. Fellow grain merchants viewed the mechanical grain elevator dimly because of the initial costs involved. Yet the new system proved an instant success, with the elevator unloading in one hour the two thousand bushels that took a day to move by hand. By 1855, ten towering wooden grain elevators dotted the Buffalo waterfornt, unloading over twenty thousand bushels an hour. For a century following, grain elevators, some shown in the accompanying illustrations, would be a major factor in the Buffalo economy. Roy W. Nagle Collection, courtesy Buffalo and Erie County Historical Society

thousand bushels in the first season. By 1848 there were eight elevators, and seventeen years later, twenty-seven elevators around Buffalo harbor with a storage capacity of 1.5 million bushels. This presence of an abundance of grain made it only natural that flour-milling enterprises should evolve. Hiram Pratt established the first flour mill, and by 1856, there were six mills as Buffalo moved toward becoming a great flour-milling center.

Commerce and trade received even further impetus with the coming of the railroads. Efforts to connect the Hudson River and Lake Erie with a "ribbon of rails" date back to the 1830s. The desire then was for a transportation system to complement the Erie Canal, which closed during the winter months. Even if railroad shipping proved more expensive because of small engines with low freight-haul-

ing capacities, the shipping season would be year-round. The first successful effort in Erie County involved Peter B. Porter and his nephew, William A. Bird, who opened a rail line from Buffalo to Black Rock; the line became the Buffalo and Niagara Falls Railroad when it extended its lines northward through the Tonawandas to Niagara Falls and then eastward to Lockport.

By 1842, another railroad linked Buffalo and Attica through Lancaster and Alden, and it soon gave the area a rail tie to Albany and Boston when it was joined to a Rochester line. Yet another access route to the Atlantic coast arose by 1852, when rail lines from Buffalo met the Erie Railroad at Hornell, tying Erie County to New York City. About the same time, the Buffalo and State Line Railway provided service southward to Pennsylvania and

later connected to Cleveland and to Chicago. Desired ties to Canadian tracks necessitated the construction of the International Bridge in 1870 to replace the rail-car ferry service across the Niagara River. By that time, many of these lines were absorbed into the New York Central system, consolidated through the efforts of Erastus Corning of Albany and Cornelius Vanderbilt of New York City. Thus came the elimination of frequent line changes by passengers and freight. Passengers could now travel

with little interruption and in relative comfort from New York City through Buffalo to Chicago. Fourteen great trunk lines served Buffalo by 1860. As railroad engines were perfected and became more powerful, their freight-hauling capacity increased significantly, making them real competitors to the Erie Canal. The canal's days were now numbered.

The increased pace of commerce and trade made the establishment of an expanded banking system vital to the

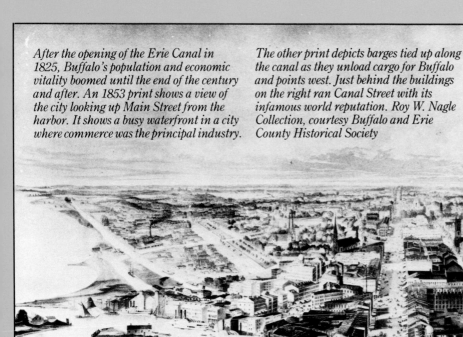

economic health of Erie County. By 1843 the Bank of Attica had moved to Buffalo, where its assets, combined with those of the Farmer and Drovers Bank and Oliver Lee and Company, totaled $192,000. As the growth of population and commerce accelerated, larger banks were needed. In 1846 the Buffalo Savings Bank opened for business and four years later the Marine Bank of Buffalo began with an initial capital of $170,000. The Western Savings Bank, the Erie County Savings Bank and the Farmers and Mechanics Bank followed shortly thereafter. Prominent Buffalo businessmen Pascal Pratt and Bronson Rumsey obtained a charter for the Manufacturers and Traders Bank, which opened for business on August 26, 1856, with initial capital totaling $300,000. From two banks in 1841, Buffalo had a total of fourteen banks by 1860.

These institutions were vital to the prosperity of the area's economy with their heavy investments in railroad expansion and other business ventures. Thus they were vulnerable when the Panic of 1857 sent economic shockwaves across the land. Canal business dropped; railroads like the Erie were driven to the verge of bankruptcy. This jolt to economic confidence caused a run on the banks, forcing the Bank of Buffalo to suspend payment in August and driving small banks like Oliver Lee and Company to ruin. Although in the end, only three banks failed, profits at the others dropped sharply, with Buffalo's biggest institution, the Marine Bank, barely staying out of the red.

It became apparent after the panic of 1857 that a heavy dependence on national commercial ties exposed the area's economy too greatly to national cycles of boom and bust. Consequently, it was important that the business community act in concert to push the expansion of industry. Cooperative action was nothing new, as evidenced by the establishment of the Board of Trade in 1844 to foster goodwill among the merchants, promote honest business practices, and agitate for harbor expansion, canal improvement and better navigational facilities around the Great Lakes. Fourteen years later, with the decline of the canal and its adverse impact on the forwarding trade, the Association for the Encouragement of Manufactories was established to promote a permanent industrial base independent of the canal, the lake or railroads. Buffalo, with only 5 percent of the work force employed in manufacturing, lagged behind other cities like Rochester and Syracuse, where 10 percent were industrial workers. In 1869, the Mechanics Association sponsored the first annual Industrial Exposition to highlight the opportunities possible with an expanded industrial base.

While extensive industrial expansion occurred after 1870, healthy beginnings had been made by that year. In a heavily agricultural area, the rise of the tanning and leather industry was a natural result. Tanneries were common in small towns around the county with access to

Pascal Paoli Pratt, born in 1819, was one of the area's most remarkable nineteenth-century entrepreneurs. A third-generation Buffalonian, he began his business career at the age of sixteen as a clerk in his brother's hardware store. He soon became a partner in the expanding enterprise, and it was not long before he branched out into industry, where he concentrated his efforts in directing companies involved in manufacturing iron products. Additionally he dabbled in banking as a director for the Bank of Buffalo and the Bank of Attica. At the age of sixty-four, he took over as president of the Manufacturers and Traders Bank, which he had helped found three decades earlier. During his busy life, he found time to serve as first president of the board of trustees of the YMCA, as first president of the Buffalo Park Commission, established in 1869, and as a trustee of other civic and educational institutions. Roy W. Nagle Collection, courtesy Buffalo and Erie County Historical Society

The Marine Bank, one of many supporting Buffalo's expanding industry and rail network, was organized on July 8, 1850, by a group of men including Buffalonian George Palmer and James Wadsworth of Geneseo, both of whom had railroad connections. The two had financial interests in and served as directors of the Attica and Hornell Railroad, while Palmer had links also with the Buffalo and State Line Railroad. Their new bank opened for business on August 15, 1850, at 79 Main Street. It has evolved over the years into the far-flung Marine Midland banking empire under the leadership of men with such famous Buffalo-area names as Knox, Rand, and Schoellkopf. Roy W. Nagle Collection, courtesy Buffalo and Erie County Historical Society

cheap hides and heavy stands of hemlock. However, the rapid growth of Buffalo's population and ample access to lake and canal shipping opened up greater opportunities on a larger scale. Aaron Rumsey opened tanneries in Aurora, Holland, and Buffalo, while Myron Bushe and George Howard centered their business in Lancaster. Jacob Schoellkopf ran tanneries in Hamburg and in Buffalo, where he founded the first leather retail outlet, and later expanded to Chicago and Milwaukee. The first shoe factory began production in 1853, and by the end of the decade there were more than a dozen tanneries with an investment of over $1 million involving over five hundred workers.

Attempts were also undertaken to build a textile industry in the county with much less success. A cotton mill operated in Buffalo as early as 1846, and woolen mills were soon found in Buffalo, Alden, and Springville. This agriculturally related industry never took root, in contrast to shipbuilding, which served the brisk lakes and canal trade. In 1855, thirty-eight ships were built totaling 17,271 tons, valued at $1 million and involving two thousand workers. Two years later, the area could count eight shipyards, the largest of which was Bidwell and Banta. Canal Boats and lake boats, steamers and schooners, freight boats and passenger ships all were produced to serve the commerce of the region. Because of overbuilding and the loss of passenger service to the railroads, there was by the 1870s a shift to building schooners to haul cargo between Buffalo and the ports of the western Great Lakes.

Shipbuilding was naturally centered on the shores around Buffalo, but other manufacturing enterprises operated out in the towns. With the coming of the railroads and easier access to raw materials, a glass factory opened in Lancaster in 1847, augmenting the county's production begun four years earlier by a glass factory in Buffalo. The Lancaster enterprise, founded by eight glass blowers from Pittsburgh, produced railroad flasks and medicine bottles which reached markets beyond the local area. In Clarence, there were two potash plants and brick factories. The discovery of limestone strata in Newstead made the village of Akron a center of cement production, much of it used in enlarging the Erie Canal.

Crucial to the coming of heavy industry to the county were the beginnings of iron and steel production. The Erie Canal, Lake Erie, and later the railroads made access to raw materials easy and routes to local and more distant markets convenient. Prior to the discovery of iron ore near Lake Superior, Adirondack iron was shipped cheaply on the Erie Canal to Buffalo and Black Rock. Part of it then went to foundries in Springville, Lancaster and Aurora to make plows and other farm implements. Iron enterprises took firm root in Buffalo by the 1840s. A rolling mill joined several iron foundries to serve as the core of a thriving industry.

The efforts of hardware merchant Pascal Pratt played a major role in the continued development of the industry. He sold bar iron, iron tools, and iron coach and saddle ware. Soon he joined William Letchworth to form Pratt and Letchworth, a firm which pioneered in the open-hearth system of steel-making. It was not long before old enterprises were expanded into the Buffalo Malleable Iron works and a new foundry, the Buffalo Steel Company, was established. Pratt's companies also included the Buffalo Nail and Iron Works, the largest iron factory in the area, employing over two hundred men.

There were other companies as well—Niagara Forge, the Buffalo Steam Engine Works, Shepard's Iron Works, and the Union Iron Works, which began smelting operations in Buffalo in 1860. There were machine shops and boiler factories as well as the Jewett and Root stove factory

Western New Yorkers generally perceive Buffalo's Delaware Avenue as a thoroughfare devoted to light commercial or residential use. Few are aware that there was a time in the nineteenth century when it was dotted by heavy business enterprises.

One such enterprise was S. G. Cornell and Son White Lead Manufacturers built in 1865 at the corner of Delaware Avenue and Virginia Street and razed in 1889. The two-acre cornell lead works had a capacity of five tons of white lead per day with an

equal amount of leader bar, pipe and sheet. It was the last of many factories and cabinet ships along Delaware Avenue. Roy W. Nagle Collection, courtesy Buffalo and Erie County Historical Society

which, in the 1850s, produced ninety different stoves. Finished iron products also included screws, iron verandas, bells, locks, fireproof vaults, and various types of agricultural machinery, such as John A. Pitt's thresher-cleaner and Pratt and Company's feed cutter. Added to these enterprises must be bridge and scale manufacturing and the increased volume of rail traffic bringing anthracite coal from eastern Pennsylvania and bituminous coal from the western part of that state.

As early as 1854, the iron and steel industry employed over sixteen hundred workers producing nine thousand tons of iron a year. This was a large percentage of all workers employed in all types of industry. In 1859 that figure was reported as six thousand, including furniture factories, lead factories, and what became the world-famous Birge Wallpaper Company. Area businessmen by 1860 had invested nearly $5 million in over five hundred manufacturing firms with an annual production value at $8.5 million. A firm foundation had been laid for future industrial expansion.

Economic growth was only one part of the story of Erie County's development in the three decades prior to 1870. The entire story involves a group of remarkable men who frequently assumed leadership roles in several areas of endeavor. Pascal Pratt had interests in banking as well as the iron industry. Dry-goods merchant Cicero Jabez Hamlin, later president of the Buffalo Grape Sugar Company, bought a farm in East Aurora, where he specialized in breeding trotting horses. Lawyer Elbridge Gerry Spaulding actively promoted banking expansion and went on into politics, serving as city alderman, mayor, and congressman. He spent much of his time pushing harbor improvement, better fire protection, and an improved sewage system. Spaulding was also instrumental in founding the Buffalo Gaslight Company, which established the first manufactured-gas plant in the nation in 1848. Similarly William Fargo came to Buffalo, and along with Henry Wells and William Livingston, developed an express business, eventually American Express, providing service from coast to coast. Like Spaulding, he went into public life and

The Buffalo Gas Light Company was organized on May 8, 1848, and began manufacturing gas on November 7, 1848. Its building complex on West Genesee Street near the Erie Canal was the first gas-manufacturing facility in the United States. Its location along the Erie Canal shortly before the canal entered Buffalo harbor was selected to take advantage of the cheap cost of transporting fuel from which gas was to be manufactured. A canal slip was dug at the rear of the works and named in honor of Judge Samuel Wilkeson. The company was led by men of vision beginning with its first president, Samuel Pratt, who worked hard to make the enterprise a success because he felt its services were vital to a booming city. Lawyer, banker, and former Congressman E. G. Spaulding later assumed leadership of the company's activities. In 1859, renowned Buffalo architect John Selkirk was retained to remodel the facility. He created a distinctive, architecturally unique plant, remodeling the works as a castle combining the Italianate style with the Medieval Revival style. Using

brick with a locally quarried limestone facing, he produced one of the area's most interesting industrial showcases. Roy W.

Nagle Collection, courtesy Buffalo and Erie County Historical Society

William G. Fargo, born in 1818 near Syracuse, was the son of a veteran of the War of 1812 who had seen service on the Niagara Frontier. Fargo won fame as a self-made businessman who, at the age of thirteen, carried mail on horseback in a forty-mile circuit around his home. After working as a hotel and grocery store clerk, he hired on as a messenger for Pomeroy and Company, which had established an express line between Albany and Buffalo.

In 1843, he was appointed company agent in Buffalo, where he began a long business association with Henry Wells. These two men were instrumental in founding the American Express Company and in 1851 in establishing Wells, Fargo and Company to provide express service between New York City and San Francisco via the Isthmus of Panama as well as to operate interior lines on the Pacific coast. He served as mayor for two terms during the Civil War. Following

the war, he built an elegant new home on a beautiful estate on Buffalo's West Side, bounded by West, Jersey, and Pennsylvania streets as well as Fargo Avenue. The mansard-roofed mansion stood until it was demolished in 1900, when the estate was divided into city lots for real estate development. Roy W. Nagle Collection, courtesy Buffalo and Erie County Historical Society

Dr. James Platt White received his medical degree from Jefferson College in Philadelphia. He worked under the tutelage of Dr. Josiah Trowbridge in Buffalo, specializing in surgery, and became active in the Erie County Medical Society. He soon changed his field of specialty to obstetrics and gynecology, where he focused the remainder of his career. In 1846, he was instrumental in obtaining from the state legislature a charter for the University of Buffalo, which opened its doors in the following year as a medical college. He taught the first class of eighty-nine men as professor of obstetrics, gaining in the years that followed great repute as a teacher. He actively cooperated with Catholic Bishop John Timon in founding Buffalo's first hospital conducted by the Sisters of Charity. Platt played a major role later in the establishment of a hospital for the mentally ill at Buffalo near Delaware Park, the Buffalo State Hospital, now the Buffalo Psychiatric Center. Courtesy Buffalo and Erie County Historical Society

served as mayor in the 1860s. Added to these should be men like George W. Clinton, Millard Fillmore and his partner Nathan Hall. They made a major contribution by serving on boards of directors of various institutions, occupying public office, and engaging in philanthropic and educational endeavors.

Leadership also came from several remarkable doctors, namely, James Platt White, Austin Flint, and Frank Hastings Hamilton. In 1845, Flint founded the *Buffalo Medical Journal* while White and Hamilton organized the Buffalo Medical Association. They were active in the Youngmen's Association along with Pratt, Hall, Fillmore and Spaulding. That group collected artifacts and a library, and it sponsored lectures, some of them by men of national acclaim. The three men acted to establish a medical school in 1846, and with Hall's assistance in the state assembly, a charter was granted for a university of which the medical school would be but the first part. A subscription campaign to raise a hundred thousand dollars drew support from doctors, lawyers, businessmen and editors. The new University of Buffalo began with the opening of its medical school in 1847 with Millard Fillmore as its first chancellor. A year later the Sisters of Charity opened a hospital nearby, and in 1858, the Buffalo General Hospital was founded, both affording medical students clinical experience. Other educational and cultural institutions with roots in the Youngmen's

Association sprang up, among them the Buffalo Fine Arts Academy and the Buffalo Historical Society in 1862.

Education at all levels had been a concern of Erie County's settlers from the very beginning. Individual teachers opened schools in a number of settlements, and public funds were voted for educational purposes. Private academies were established in Buffalo, Springville, Clarence, Aurora, and Williamsville. The tax-supported "common school" movement made significant strides. In Buffalo, Superintendent Oliver Steele centralized control of the city's common schools and removed the last pretenses of tuition payment, making them totally free. In 1852, a central high school opened for classes, and an evening school was conducted for those who worked during the day. The great experiment in common schools, bringing children of all classes and nationalities together, would create, it was hoped, a better community with active, alert, and informed citizens.

As the organization of schools and hospitals gained momentum, so did the growth of religious congregations. A religious revival was sweeping the land fueled by the preachings of Charles G. Finney, who advocated moral and humanitarian reform. The oldest religious congregations across much of the county were Presbyterian, consistent with the Congregationalist New England stock who were the first settlers. In Buffalo, a number of Episcopalians and Unitarians could also be numbered among their ranks.

The Williamsville Classical Institute, erected in 1853 and opened as a private institution, was one of the early schools in Erie County to go beyond the elementary level. It had a three-year curriculum which included the study of the sciences and classical languages as well as French and German. Special courses were organized for those wishing to prepare as teachers. Each student was expected to attend some place of worship on Sunday and to join one of two literary societies—one for men and one for women. The literary societies held debates on such topics as "Our future husbands should never be allowed to criticize our cooking or say 'Mother made better pie,'" and "It is more beneficial to saw wood before breakfast than to wait until next week." Yearly tuition was charged per course and "board and wash" was available. Courtesy Old Amherst Colony Museum

St. Peter's German Evangelical and Reformed Church was built in 1849 on land donated by Philip Knoche who owned a fifty-acre farm facing on a road which now bears his name. The church continued to serve the congregation until 1967, when it was turned over to the town of Tonawanda to serve as a museum for the Tonawanda-Kenmore Historical Society. The oldest church in the town, it is surrounded by a cemetery in which are buried members of the original German families who settled in the area. Among them were the Kuhn family, whose name is visible on the large marker. A 113-acre farm was run by Heinrich Kuhn and his descendants south of the Knoche property along Military Road. Courtesy Tonawanda-Kenmore Historical Society

On April 23, 1847, the Roman Catholic Diocese of Buffalo was established, and John Timon was appointed its first bishop. Born in a log cabin in Pennsylvania in 1797, he had spent most of his priestly life as a missionary up and down the Mississippi Valley, in the American heartland. He arrived in Buffalo in October 1847, to assume office as leader of the forty-six hundred Roman Catholics in his twenty-county diocese, most of them concentrated around Buffalo. In the entire diocese, he found only four schools, sixteen priests, and sixteen churches, many of them mere huts or shanties. He began by visiting all parts of the diocese, holding services in barns, halls, homes, or courthouses where necessary. He established a seminary to train priests and brought the Sisters of Charity to the diocese, where they founded the first hospital in Buffalo in 1848. Other religious orders soon followed to establish schools, orphanages, and homes for the elderly. To get money to build a cathedral, he went to Europe, where he received a donation of two thousand dollars from Pope Pius IX. Other funds were given by such prominent non-Catholics as President Millard Fillmore, with whom Timon lunched in the White House on several occasions. When Timon died in 1867, he passed on to his successors St. Joseph's Cathedral, a fitting bishop's church in a growing diocese now inhabited by tens of thousands of Roman Catholics. *Courtesy of Buffalo and Erie County Historical Society*

Soon Methodist and Baptist preachers arrived, giving rise to the birth of new congregations.

The influx of German immigrants in the towns as well as in Buffalo resulted in the formation of churches ranging from the German Evangelical and Reformed to the Lutheran and Roman Catholic. With the arrival of the Irish came more Catholic churches and the founding of parochial schools. Catholic numbers in the county and nearby area were great enough to warrant the creation of the Catholic Diocese of Buffalo in 1847 with John Timon as the first bishop. Several years later, a sprinkling of German Jews in Buffalo established their first synagogue. Quakers could be found in Orchard Park and German Ebenezers in what became West Seneca, where they practiced Christian communal living until the growth of Buffalo and the coming of the railroad destroyed their isolation and drove most of them further west to Iowa.

Religion had a powerful influence on society. The visible signs of its impact could be seen as a few Romanesque but mostly Gothic churches rose in Buffalo and in smaller communities where simpler churches modeled on the New England meetinghouse dominated. Community leaders maintained visible congregational ties and did not hesitate to assist in such charitable ventures as the Sailor's Home, the Buffalo Orphan Asylum, the Church Charity Foundation or the Young Men's Christian Association.

The construction of impressive churches accompanied the erection of comfortable residences as more and more people attained affluence. In the city, narrow three-story townhouses side by side and close to the street rose in the 1840s as did larger homes in the Greek Revival style all around the country. A strong desire for individual homes developed in the 1850s, when residences were patterned as Mediterranean villas in the Italianate style or English structures in the Gothic style from the reign of Elizabeth I. In general, wood provided the basic building material, although there were some areas where brick homes were constructed.

New hotels and theaters also rose to join earlier structures as social and entertainment centers. Springville had its American House; Marilla, its Spring Hotel, and in Buffalo there were the Eagle Tavern, the Mansion House, the America Hotel and others. Guests at Buffalo hotels, and local citizens as well, could attend productions at such theaters as the Metropolitan Theater, later the Academy of Music; the Buffalo Opera House, later the Adelphi; or the Eagle Street Theater.

Theater attractions in early Buffalo were
staged in the county courthouse and even in
a riding academy, but soon theaters were
built to accommodate them. The Eagle
Street Theater opened in 1835 at the corner
of Eagle and Court streets, and the
Academy of Music opened at 245 Main
Street as the Metropolitan Theater in 1852
serving as a legitimate stage and eventually
a movie house until 1957. Shakespearean
productions as well as more recent drama
and music programs were presented,
starring such eminent figures as Junius
Booth, Jenny Lind, Lola Montez and
Fanny Kemble. These theaters were also
used for patriotic pageants on holidays,
public meetings, and lectures on various
reform causes such as abolition and
women's rights. Lectures were given by
such prominent women's rights advocates
as Fanny Wright, Lucy Stone, and
England's Mary Wollstonecraft. Roy W.
Nagle Collection, courtesy Buffalo and Erie
County Historical Society

The building shown, located at the corner
of Franklin and West Eagle, is closely
connected with the life of Millard Fillmore.
Erected in 1833, it served until 1880 as the
home of the Unitarian Church of Our
Father, and numbered Fillmore among its
congregation. In February 1861, the
ex-president brought President-elect
Abraham Lincoln here to attend services
before he continued his journey to Washington, where he would be inaugurated on
March 4. After the Unitarian Church
moved to new quarters, it housed the
Buffalo Fine Arts Academy. The Academy
came into being in 1862 and prospered in
part because of Fillmore's support as a
contributor and member of the governing
board. Roy W. Nagle Collection, courtesy
Buffalo and Erie County Historical Society

63

In 1822, a young Millard Fillmore traveled west from Cayuga County in central New York to the tiny village of East Aurora in Erie County. After reading law and being admitted to the bar, he opened his law offices there and soon married Abigail Powers, the sweetheart he had left behind in Cayuga County. He prospered in his law practice and took an active part in public affairs. He advocated the building of the Erie Canal and supported the Agrarian Movement, a protest movement by settlers

against the policies of the Holland Land Company. He was elected to the state assembly on the Anti-Masonic ticket as protest spread across the state against the alleged undue Masonic influence in government. In 1830 he moved to Buffalo to practice law with Solomon Haven and Nathan K. Hall, a family friend who had studied law in his East Aurora office. It was not long before Fillmore went to Washington as a member of the House of Representatives, where he served until

1843. Four years later, the popular Buffalonian was elected New York State comptroller and in 1848 vice-president of the United States on the Whig Party ticket with Gen. Zachary Taylor. With President Taylor's untimely death in 1850, Millard Fillmore became the thirteenth president of the United States. Roy W. Nagle Collection, courtesy Buffalo and Erie County Historical Society

The son of a pioneer farmer, Millard Fillmore was born in a log cabin and was trained to be a farmer and a mill worker. However, he developed a thirst for broader learning, attending school when work allowed and reading voraciously. After serving as a teacher and a law clerk near his home, he migrated to East Aurora to accept a school position. Fillmore's initial stay in East Aurora was short-lived. He soon went to nearby Buffalo where he taught in the Cold Spring schoolhouse, shown in its last days, and read law to prepare for admission to the bar. Once admitted to the bar, he abandoned teaching and returned to the lawyerless East Aurora to begin his legal career. Roy W. Nagle Collection, courtesy Buffalo and Erie County Historical Society

While residing in East Aurora, Millard and Abigail Fillmore lived in a modest one-and-a-half story clapboard plank house. It was here that the elder of their two children, Powers, was born in 1828. In Buffalo, where they moved two years later, they inhabited a two-story white house in the affluent Franklin Street section of the city. When he retired from the presidency in March 1853, Fillmore returned to Buffalo, where he devoted the rest of his life

philanthropic needs. After Abigail's death, he married Caroline McIntosh, the wealthy widow of a Troy merchant. They purchased the elegant mansion shown here, located at 52 Niagara Square and sometimes called the "House of Seven Gables." Until the former president died in 1874, he lived here serving as an elder statesman and assisting in the establishment of a host of community institutions such as the Buffalo Club, the Buffalo Fine Arts Academy, the

General Hospital. The Fillmore mansion became one of society's most gracious social and cultural centers, and it was here that the prominent couple hosted such visiting dignitaries as the Japanese ambassador, English royalty, and two American presidents. The site is now occupied by the former Statler Hotel, now the Statler Towers. Roy W. Nagle Collection, courtesy Buffalo and Erie County Historical Society

The abolitionist movement used drama as but one weapon to denounce slavery. Quakers like Benjamin Baker of Orchard Park assisted the Underground Railroad by receiving runaway slaves from Warsaw and hiding them in wagonloads of grain to transport them toward the Canadian border and freedom. Lectures by such prominent abolitionists as Theodore Dwight and black orator Samuel Ward were frequent as they toured the county from Buffalo to Williamsville, Clarence, Aurora, Lancaster, Holland, Eden, Alden, Evans and Sardinia. The antislavery Liberty party, after holding its first presidential nominating convention in Warsaw, chose Buffalo as the site of its convention in 1844. Four years later, an estimated ten thousand people, Liberty Party men along with antislave Democrats and Whigs, joined to form the Free Soil Party, which met in Buffalo to nominate its national ticket. Headquartered at the Mansion House, the convention delegates gathered in Court House Park, Now Lafayette Square, to nominate New York's own ex-President Martin Van Buren as its candidate for the White House.

The election of 1848 produced a victory for Gen. Zachary Taylor and his vice-presidential running mate, Erie County's Millard Fillmore. Taylor died during the debate over the Compromise of 1850, which admitted California as a free state and abolished the slave trade in the District of Columbia. Thus Fillmore, now president, had to decide whether to endorse the compromise, which included a strong law to assist in the recovery of runaway slaves. Despite local abolitionist Samuel Addington's urgings that Fillmore should veto the measures, he signed the compromise bills with the support of such newspapers as the *Commercial Advertiser* and the *Daily Courier*. The relative calm following the enactment of the Compromise of 1850 was shattered with the passage of the Kansas-Nebraska Act. That 1854 law repealed the Missouri Compromise of 1820, which had excluded slavery from much of the American heartland between the Mississippi River and the Rocky Mountains. County newspapers denounced the measure and on March 4, 1854, a Buffalo gathering of three hundred people of all political faiths protested its enactment.

Antislavery Whigs, Democrats, and Free Soilers now came together to form the Republican Party. Every town in Erie County sent delegates to the party's first convention at Kremlin Hall in Buffalo in September 1855. In the spring elections the following year, the Republicans enjoyed limited success by electing supervisors in Clarence, Collins and West Seneca. The 1856 election showed even greater support when the first Republican presidential ticket lost the county to the Democrats by a vote of sixty-seven hundred to seventy-five hundred. However, Republicans carried ten towns, including Aurora, Concord, Evans, Newstead, North Collins, Sardinia, and Wales. Republican momentum carried the new party to victory nationally in 1860 with the election of Abraham Lincoln as president.

Lincoln paused at Buffalo in February 1861, enroute to his inauguration. Former President Fillmore greeted him at the train station, and a procession of militia with a band playing escorted him to the American Hotel. There from the balcony, the President-elect addressed the people cautiously, promising to be consistent with the Constitution and to respect states' rights. An evening reception followed, and the presidient-elect left the next day, Sunday, after attending religious services at the Unitarian Church with Fillmore. The people of the area would not directly pay him homage again until after his assassination in the spring of 1865, when the coffin carrying his remains came to Buffalo on the way to his beloved Springfield, Illinois, for burial.

The assassination of President Lincoln by Confederate sympathizer John Wilkes Booth at Ford's Theater in Washington on April 15, 1865, stunned the citizens of Erie County as well as the rest of the nation. The Lincoln funeral cortege followed the same route returning his body for burial in Springfield, Illinois, as he had taken to his inauguration some four years before. Mayor William Fargo chaired the local arrangements committee handling preparations to receive the funeral procession. He issued a proclamation urging the people to wear badges of mourning, and he asked that dwellings and public places be appropriately draped. Throngs of Western New Yorkers flocked to watch the cortege as it made its way down Main Street to St. James Hall at Washington and Eagle streets on April 27, 1865. There thousands more paid their respects as Lincoln's body lay in state, attended by honor guards from the Union Continentals and the 74th Regiment of the New York Militia. Roy W. Nagle Collection, courtesy Buffalo and Erie County Historical Society

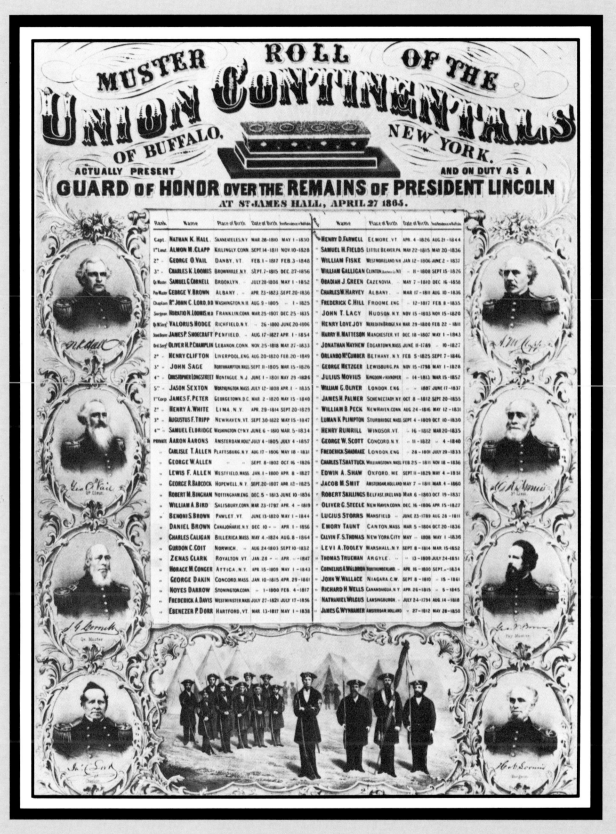

The Civil War had its inevitable impact on the citizens of Erie County. Volunteers were solicited for the Union cause by flyers promising bonuses and land. Area leaders like ex-President Fillmore organized the "Union Continentals," mostly retired militia officers too old to bear arms. Resplendent in elegant uniforms, they escorted departing troops to the railroad stations, provided honor guards at funerals, and marched in Independence Day parades. One of the saddest occasions of their service was providing the honor guard for the remains of assassinated President Abraham Lincoln enroute through Buffalo on April 27, 1865, to burial in Springfield, Illinois. Courtesy Buffalo and Erie County Historical Society

Erie County provided over twenty-thousand
men for the Union Army during the Civil
War and suffered over four thousand
casualties either killed, wounded, or
missing in action. Among the units which
saw action in either the lower Mississippi
Valley or on the Virginia front were the
21st New York Volunteer Infantry, the first
to depart; the 49th New York Infantry,
commanded by Major Daniel Bidwell of
Buffalo; and the 8th New York Heavy
Artillery, the most famous military unit,
led by Colonel Peter A. Porter, son of Peter
B. Porter of War of 1812 fame. Pictured
are Colonel Porter, center, and his staff at
Fort Federal Hill in Baltimore. In 1864,
he fell mortally wounded at the Battle of
Cold Harbor as the Army of the Potomac
slugged its way toward Richmond, Virginia, the Confederate capital. Also pictured are unidentified western New
Yorkers from Company D of the 74th
Regiment who were among the many sent
to the battlefronts during the Civil War.
Courtesy Buffalo and Erie County
Historical Society

The southern states left the Union following Lincoln's election, and the bombardment of Fort Sumter in April 1861 brought the outbreak of Civil War. The president immediately issued a call for seventy-five thousand volunteers to put down the rebellion. Thousands gathered in front of the American Hotel in Buffalo on April 15 to hear a call for "minutemen" volunteers. Millard Fillmore presided over another rally the next night, and on April 18, Erie County's first volunteer company was organized. Young men from the outlying villages and towns traveled to the city to help fill the ranks of such units as the 21st New York Infantry and the 100th New York Infantry, whose over nine-hundred men represented every town in the county. Towns like Concord and Tonawanda provided an entire company to the regiment. There were also individuals who enlisted in the Navy and Marines as well as Canadians who crossed the Niagara River to join the Union Army.

If recruiting went smoothly right after Fort Sumter, early Union defeats made it more difficult to attract volunteers later on. Governments at all levels offered bounties for enlistments and sometimes bonuses for reenlistments. Erie County alone expended over $2 million. When local quotas could not be reached by volunteers, the draft enacted by Congress was applied reluctantly in Erie County. News of draft riots elsewhere caused apprehension as a five-day selection period began at Fort Porter in August 1863. Using a "wheel of fortune," names of eligible men were drawn and published in the newspapers. Advertisements for substitutes, whose enlistments could be purchased for three hundred dollars, also appeared in the press. After the fifth day, the draft moved into the towns. Thus Erie County, whether through volunteers or draftees, contributed over twenty thousand men to the war effort, and it sustained more than forty-seven hundred casualties killed, wounded, or missing.

The Civil War contributed to the prosperity of the Buffalo area economy not so much through war contracts to industry as to increased commerce on the Great Lakes. With the Mississippi River outlet closed to the West during much of the war, area shipyards were busy constructing lakers and canal boats to handle the larger volume of trade. Storage rates rose as record amounts of grain passed through enroute to the east coast and Europe. Local shipyards produced tugs for the Union Navy, and the Niagara Steam Forge made parts for the ironclad U.S.S. *Monitor* which met its Confederate counterpart, the *Merrimac,* at Hampton Roads. Tanneries made leather for the horse-and-mule-drawn Union Army while iron foundries produced castings, steam engines, stoves and agricultural machinery. While industry thrived, even if its expansion was limited, the cost of living rose to the detriment of wage earners, whose pay did not keep pace. Consequently, strikes occurred here as elsewhere in protest against this uneven sharing of the new wealth.

To prevent the deterioration of morale, citizens across the county engaged in a host of activities to help the war effort. A branch of the United States Sanitary Commission, the Ladies General Aid Society, was formed. It received donations from such sources as the Board of Trade and even Pope Pius IX who, through Bishop Timon, sent a gift of five hundred dollars. By 1864, it had raised over fifty-two thousand dollars, a large portion of which went to finance a "Soldiers Rest" near the Exchange Street railroad station. There a dining room, kitchen, and thirty beds were provided free to traveling servicemen. Generous donations of money, beds, and food enabled the society to house nearly six thousand men and serve over sixteen thousand meals during the course of the war.

Concerted action largely by the women of Erie County resulted in the collection of large amounts of hospital supplies, 9,380 pairs of socks, and 5,588 bandages destined for use at the battlefronts. Fairs and festivals raised funds to expend on the war effort. The Great Union Festival in July 1862 attracted eighteen thousand people and raised over ten thousand dollars. There was also a Children's Fair and in 1864, a Strawberry Festival at Fort Porter.

The enthusiasm generated by those patriotic activities was tempered not only by labor unrest but also by rumors of Confederate raids from Canada across the border. The harbor, the shipyards and the federal arsenal served as obvious targets of Confederate conspiracies to terrorize the North and destroy morale. A war scare in 1861 followed the Union Navy's seizure of the *Trent,* a British ship carrying Confederate agents. Cries went up locally to build up armed defenses and a Committee of Public Defense, led by Fillmore and Mayor William Fargo, pressured for state and federal action. The reactivation of Fort Porter did not satisfy the community, and dissatisfaction with the conduct of the war resulted in Lincoln's loss of Erie County by a close vote in the election of 1864.

That year, rumors of a Confederate plot persisted, rumors based on solid evidence that conspirators in Toronto planned to seize the only armed vessel on Lake Erie, the *Michigan,* and then free Confederate prisoners-of-war at Sandusky, Ohio. The plot included an attack on the harbor and arsenal at Buffalo. City leaders posted round-the-clock guards at strategic points, and the Board of Trade armed tugs to patrol the waterfront. Police and federal Secret Service agents kept careful vigil at area hotels to detect the arrival of suspicious travelers. A few Confederate agents did arrive undetected, but when they realized the extent of precautions, they left the city to journey southward in hopes of derailing trains on the Lakeshore line. Failing this, they returned to Toronto, and danger passed as the war drew to a close.

Once the Civil War was over, American protests against Confederate activities in Canada were replaced by British protests against the activities of the Irish Fenians along the southern side of the Canadian border. Having failed to pull off a successful revolt in Ireland, Fenian leaders crossed the ocean to recruit Irish-American Civil War veterans for an assault in Canada. Canada, once taken, could be a pawn for Irish independence. American authorities moved slowly despite British complaints because they felt the danger exaggerated. Thus men and arms found their way to border points like Buffalo, from which a major assault was planned. Arms arrived at such places as the O'Day house on Pearl Street, while members of the Fenian Sisterhood, in their homes on the West Side near the river, sewed Fenian Flags for the Seventh Fenian Regiment. By the end of May 1866, thousands of Fenians were ready at Buffalo to cross the river and take the strategic Welland Canal.

Tugs and canal boats were seized to carry the invaders across the river. When the United States government issued orders to prevent any crossing, half the Fenian force had already landed on Canadian soil. Fort Erie was easily secured and the invaders performed well during an encounter with an equal number of Canadian

The Fenians planned to capture Canada as ransom for the freedom of Ireland from British rule. Buffalo became a major rendezvous for hundreds of Irish-American Civil War veterans who volunteered to aid the conspiracy. On the night of May 31, 1866, squads of men and wagons loaded with munitions streamed toward Black Rock, where canal boats towed by steam tugs awaited them. Government authorities acted too late to prevent the crossing of invaders. The steamer Michigan *came down to Niagara River to prevent any more crossings on the morning of June 1. News of the invasion lured crowds of local citizens to the river shore and to Black Rock. The invaders marched as far as Ridgeway where, after an encounter on June 2 (shown here) they retreated toward Buffalo. U.S. government vessels took many of the invaders into custody as they tried to cross the river to the American side. Fenians continued to stream into the city and hold defiant meetings until regular troops were sent to Fort Porter and the arrest of all connected with the Fenians was ordered by the attorney general of the United States. The situation was further defused when Fenians taken prisoner by American authorities were released from custody. Roy W. Nagle Collection, courtesy Buffalo and Erie County Historical Society*

defenders at Ridgeway. With reinforcements cut off by federal orders, and the threat of the arrival of more units of Canadian defenders, the Fenians withdrew to the river shore, where they scrambled on to the skiffs, dories, and canal boats to recross the river. A few were captured and tried at Toronto, where their sentences to hanging were commuted to prison terms. A much larger number were arrested by American authorities and eventually released on promises to end their illegal activities. As the 1870s dawned, calm returned to Erie County, freeing its 178,699 citizens to continue their labors in pursuit of prosperity and a better life. In its hub at Buffalo, the populace, now numbering 117,714, stood on the threshold of a golden age of progress.

Even when we might think that immigrants could be natural allies, as in the case of co-religionists, groups often clashed because of the traditions they brought with them. St. Louis Church, Buffalo's first Roman Catholic parish (founded 1829), was also the area's largest in the decades before the Civil War. Originally multiethnic, the Church became more and more German as the Irish departed, complaining of harassment. St. Louis was the scene of a hard-fought struggle between the Irish hierarchy and the German-Alsatian laity. In Germany, and in Eastern Europe, individual churches were owned by the members of a parish. But in America the diocese held title to the buildings and the land. In 1852, four hundred parishioners who wished to maintain control of their church petitioned Pope Pius IX to intervene against Buffalo's Irish bishop, John Timon. Bishop Timon saw the lay demand for control as an act of mutiny. Parishioners saw only a threat to their cultural identity. The pope knew the gravity of the situation and dispatched a personal emissary. St. Louis was placed under an interdict. The dispute ended in the excommunication of the church trustees, and their eventual capitulation to diocesan control. St. Louis Church. Courtesy Buffalo and Erie County Historical Society

Chapter Five

Neighbors: The People of Erie County

by Scott Eberle

Of the one million people of Erie County, all but the original inhabitants, the Native Americans, are the descendants of immigrants. Nearly a third of this million continue to have a familiarity with the language of their ancestors. Where people live, where they work and worship, how they speak, and even what they eat is still much influenced by their backgrounds.

One historian has said that Buffalo consisted of a "ring of ethnic neighborhoods." While the suburbs often have meant escape from such ties, the city has maintained this special character. Attachment to the neighborhood, the church, the tavern, the particular group, is a feature that separates Buffalo from many other cities of its size. South Buffalo is still recognizably Irish, and the west side Italian. Black-Americans live on the east side. Poles live to the east and north, and in Cheektowaga. Other Eastern European groups live farther north into Tonawanda. Hispanics live on the lower west side. The strength and persistence of immigrant ways in the Buffalo area challenges the notion that America was a melting pot of immigrant groups.

The image of the melting pot, long a symbol for the American ethnic mix, has also been a national article of faith and hope. Although immigrant groups arrive with distinct traditions of language, politics, and religion, although they are different in their occupations, their dress and their diet, they eventually begin to lose the distinctiveness they brought with them, melt into the main mass, amalgamate, and finally, "Americanize."

This hopeful vision was often framed as a response to those who feared that foreigners would change the character of American society. Something basic would be lost as others came. The idea of society as a melting pot bears the apologetic stamp (and the limitation) of that rejoinder. In the sweep of local and national history immigrants have nothing to apologize for. The traditions that these peoples brought, and the changes that resulted made Buffalo and Erie County vibrate. Life would never have been so interesting or prosperous without them. In time, of course, "they" became "us." If we wish to describe the real lives of immigrants for the nineteenth century and much of the twentieth, we might be better off picking another metaphor. Instead of "melting pot," one scholar suggested "plum pudding." The parts make their individual contributions, but remain separate. The whole

sticks together somehow.

People left their homes for Erie County because they were both pushed and pulled. Forced to leave by famine, war or religious persecution, they were also drawn here by opportunity. Some were actively recruited. Many came at the invitation of relatives already living in the Buffalo area. An invisible chain linked old country and new, and drew immigrants from the European countryside to settled urban ethnic neighborhoods.

Had Erie County not received waves of immigrants, there might have been little to distinguish the people on either side of the Niagara River. Separated by a political boundary, Americans and English-speaking Canadians in the early nineteenth century still shared a close heritage. In large part they still do. The differences between neighbors, though subtle, are important. As the American heritage across the Niagara was broadened and enriched by the immigrants, the two cultures diverged.

The Irish

The first wave of non-Yankee immigrants arrived in the 1820s from poor and overpopulated Ireland to build one of the wonders of the world, the Erie Canal. Logically the Irish settlement began at the terminus of the canal, in the area to the south of Buffalo. It was there that they stayed. Many of these people in the first generation, before 1835, were farmers or artisans displaced by troubles at home. As sailors and ship carpenters, cartmen and teamsters, furnace workers and watchmen, Irish laborers often worked intermittently once they got to Buffalo.

As a transshipment center, Buffalo demanded a great deal of labor. The Irish filled the need. When Joseph Dart installed his revolutionary grain elevators, a skeptic derided the technology by disparaging the Irish. "Irishmen's backs," he said, "are the cheapest elevators ever built." Handling shipments of grain and freight was seasonal work which came to an end as the water froze. Workers spent long winters mostly idle, doing odd jobs.

In the crowded and poorly drained Irish neighborhoods, housing was unimaginably squalid. When disease epidemics struck, they struck first here. A visiting physician, Dr. Bryant Burwell, described the house of one of his patients. It was twelve feet on a side, and he shared it with a hen and a dozen chicks, a cat, and, when the weather was cold, a dog and some pigs. He noted that though it was chillier outside, the air was healthier. Canal Street and the adjacent areas were filled with single men who lived in boarding houses. The area became notorious for its bars, its brawls, and its brothels. Saloon owners doubled as hotel keepers and labor contractors.

Irish women left their homeland in larger proportion than women of other immigrant groups. They often made the difficult trip alone. Poverty in Ireland had forced many to find work outside the home. This may have contributed to a tradition of independent-mindedness that is behind the stereotype of the feisty Irish serving girl. As live-in domestic servants, their circumstances were more settled than men's. Even if they were relegated to the attics and kitchen anterooms of their employers' households, their material surroundings were more comfortable. Pay was low, fifty-nine cents a day on average, and domestic work could be dreary. But demand for their services was high in the boom years. Quitting a less-indulgent employer did not usually mean a long stretch out of work. They began such work early, sometimes at the age of eleven. By twenty-one years of age, nearly all were working away from home. By age twenty-five most were married, raising a family, and no longer working as servants. Despite the pressure of discrimination and poverty, these families remained very stable.

By the 1840s a new generation of desperately poor Irish arrived in Buffalo and Erie County. This time they were forced to leave by famine, crop failure, and foreign domination. In the nineteenth century the Irish economy was a virtual monoculture. In this instance the seeds of destruction were sown quite literally in the fields. Potatoes supported six million people (or more) in that tiny island nation. However benevolent, this crop was also vulnerable.

Imported from the new world, the potato had no resistance to old world plant diseases. When the inevitable blight arrived, the crop rotted in field after field. British land policy, taxation, mass eviction, and reluctance to give relief increased the burden. Two million starved. Two million stayed. Two million left. In the late 1840s and 1850s most of these desperate people came to America.

In the midst of famine and foreign political domination Catholics in Ireland found the church to be their only dependable anchor. They became fiercely loyal Catholics. American society exerted a considerable pressure on all immigrants to assimilate. In this case Roman Catholicism acted as the glue that held the group together. It also helped to keep them separate.

At mid-century the Irish in Buffalo still fell at the bottom of all social measures. They occupied the poorest paying jobs. Only one in four owned a house. They worked well beyond the usual retirement age. Irish immigrants shared the English language (though in a lilting and accented form) with the mainstream. They endured more than their share of prejudice and discrimination, but speaking English gave them one advantage that other immigrants did not enjoy.

Once in America, Irishmen came to dominate the clergy. In succeeding decades, they exercised considerable authority over the Catholic immigrants arriving from other parts of Europe. The relationship was often uneasy.

One of the best examples of the conflicts that arose between immigrant groups took place in the mid-nineteenth century at the St. Louis Church. In a struggle that lasted two decades, Alsatians and Germans resisted the efforts of Buffalo's Irish-American bishop John Timon to control church affairs. It took the personal intervention of the pope to bring the parishioners into compliance.

Plenary councils in 1852 and 1884 first urged, then required each American bishop to establish a separate (parochial) school system for its Catholic children. Bishop Timon built no fewer than thirty seven elementary schools. Though the diocesan authorities remained in Irish-American hands, other ethnic Catholic groups were able to maintain their identification with the old country through schools that preserved the original language. Courtesy Buffalo and Erie County Historical Society

Anglo-American prejudice made Buffalo's Irish aware of their separateness from the first. A steady stream of new immigrants carried tales of British oppression, which continually reinfused the community with a sense of purpose, and the determination that, somehow, the British would be punished for their depredations. A number of Irish-American Civil War veterans joined the 1866 raid on Canada (see Chapter Four). One of the raiders carried this club. From the Collections, courtesy Buffalo and Erie County Historical Society

Schooled in the hard experience of centuries of political conquest and domination, the Irish took an especially keen interest in American politics. Unvaryingly, they were Democrats. Buffalo's William Sheehan is the very type of the Irish party boss and ward heeler of the 1890s. He dispensed patronage through his lieutenants, the street commissioner, and the superintendent of public works, who also were Irish. The public school system hired large numbers of Irish women. The police force was dominated by the Irish. Irish-American writer Jimmy Breslin has noted that these lifetime jobs which have so appealed to the Irish left a legacy of "lost possibilities." Whatever is lost, though, must be balanced against a sense of belonging and stability which persists in South Buffalo today. Courtesy Buffalo and Erie County Historical Society

At the St. Patricks Day Parade In the city of Buffalo, political loyalties are still often ethnic loyalties. Poles in the Broadway-Fillmore area, Italians on the West Side, and South Buffalo Irish have chosen to remain in the city living together in the neighborhoods that their ancestors first settled. There are political and cultural advantages. Jimmy Griffin, a scrappy political maverick, was first elected mayor of the city in 1978. Now the longest tenured of any of Buffalo's mayors, he draws from a stronghold in South Buffalo. Politics, in fact, probably plays a larger role than culture in holding this group together. While the ties to Ireland become more attenuated year by year, the St. Patrick's Day Parade remains a grand opportunity for politicking. By the middle of March, winter-weary Buffalonians are ready for a break. In a sense, history has made it possible for the Irish to come to the rescue.

When they arrived in Western New York in the nineteenth century, the Irish brought with them a freer, more spontaneous life than the indigenous Victorian culture would allow. The St. Patrick's Day Parade certainly is the best party of the springtime. Mayor Griffin (left) is enjoying this one fully. Photograph by Joe Traver, Courier-Express Collection, courtesy Buffalo and Erie County Historical Society

The Germans

Germans began to arrive in numbers as early as the 1820s. At the instigation of Joseph Ellicott, Lancaster (just to the east of Buffalo) was settled with Germans from Lancaster, Pennsylvania. Other enclaves with a recognizably German ancestry are scattered in the county. Hamburg, Eggertsville, and Snyder were all settled by Germans. By the 1830s Germans were moving to the southern end of Main Street. Another German area was just to the north in the rocky "Buffalo plains" that the settlers called the *Jammerthal,* the "valley of woe." Nearly seven thousand were already living in Buffalo at mid-century, slightly more, in fact, than there were Irish. By 1855 (if the Alsatians are counted) the city was nearly half German. At that time one of every one hundred German immigrants in this country lived in the quiet residential neighborhoods on Buffalo's east side. More followed.

Germans responded to the same push and pull that brought other immigrant groups. Opportunity lured some, trouble at home pushed more away. Germany of the mid-nineteenth century was not a single country, but a patchwork quilt of minor states, principalities, dukedoms, and free cities. As the Buffalo journal *Der Weltberger* put it, "Germany is ruled by thirty-four monarchs, oppressed by hordes of official servants, robbed of the freedom of its press and the means of giving its inhabitants the desired enlightenment, and is altogether in a deplorable political condition."

Famine in 1846 and 1847 had a further unsettling effect. When the revolutions of 1848 swept through Europe, the German states were particularly disturbed. Failed revolutions not only increased the pressure to move, but made it harder for the homesick to return. Because political refugees were often intellectuals, and always energetic, the immigration of the forty-eighters invigorated cultural life for Buffalo's Germans. One result was the founding of a singing society called the *Buffalo Liedertafel.* German theater was so vital in Buffalo that even Christmas did not interrupt performances. Despite the rapid influx, this was an extraordinarily stable community. And it grew. Though other immigrants swelled the city's population, by the 1880s the city of Buffalo was two-fifths German.

The Germans who came to Erie County arrived, by and large, not as uprooted peasants turned urbanites, but with considerable skills and good preparation for living in the commercial world of nineteenth-century Buffalo. In contemporary accounts the Germans were invariably called "hard working." As bootmakers, tinsmiths, clockmakers, butchers, bakers, brewers, and stonecutters, working class Germans lived considerably more prosperous and settled lives than the Irish. Not a few were grocers who also kept back-room grog shops. These emerged as the center of neighborliness. This was the kind of patient business that, while not wildly profitable, yielded a lifetime of respectable income. A few parlayed their skills and steady work into fortunes. Louis Fuhrmann (who was eventually responsible for the cattle drives down Main Street) began modestly as a butcher. Jacob Schoellkopf started with a small tanning shop on Mohawk Street. His prudent investment in Niagara Falls hydropower in 1877 generated a long term reward.

The Schoellkopf Power Station (Niagara Mohawk), 1925. Courtesy Buffalo and Erie County Historical Society

Solomon Scheu, mayor of Buffalo, 1878-1879. Courtesy Buffalo and Erie County Historical Society

If there was no real political unity in Germany, Germans who came to Buffalo formed a cultural group that remained close-knit into the first decades of the twentieth century. Ethnic Germans consciously wished not to melt into the mainstream of American culture. An emblem of difference, language was also a binding force and a carrier of tradition. Children of immigrants remained bilingual, often more fluent in German than English. A simple measure helps to gauge the vitality of the German-American community of the last century. Currently the Buffalo area is able to support only one major newspaper; one hundred years ago *several* German language newspapers thrived, representing a variety of political viewpoints. German voluntary associations, like the popular singing societies and drinking guilds, perpetuated the use of the language and helped maintain the community's solidarity.

Solid economic successes helped the Germans become a potent political force in the city. Cultural unity did not restrain the lively politics of the German community. Two of Buffalo's mayors in the 1870s were born in Bavaria—the first a Republican and a Roman Catholic, the second a Democrat and a Lutheran. They faced each other in the election of 1877. Philip Becker, a wealthy insurance broker to the German community (who began as a grocer), became the first German-American mayor of Buffalo in 1876. Solomon Scheu, a baker turned successful grocer, defeated Becker in his bid for a second term. Becker served again for two more terms starting in 1886.

A surge of cultural nationalism was the natural consequence of the growing political power of the Germans. Established groups did not fail to notice this. Anti-German feeling is an obscure prejudice now, but in the 1870s, demands to teach the German language in Buffalo's high schools met with strong nativist suspicion and hostility. When the Common Council hired ten teachers for this purpose in 1874, public school colleagues were some of the loudest grumblers. When the number of births was tallied for the year 1878, and it was revealed that of the thirty-seven hundred children born nearly two thousand were German, one Buffalo newspaper warned "Americans to scan these figures, and realize in what a contemptible minority they are in this Teutonic city."

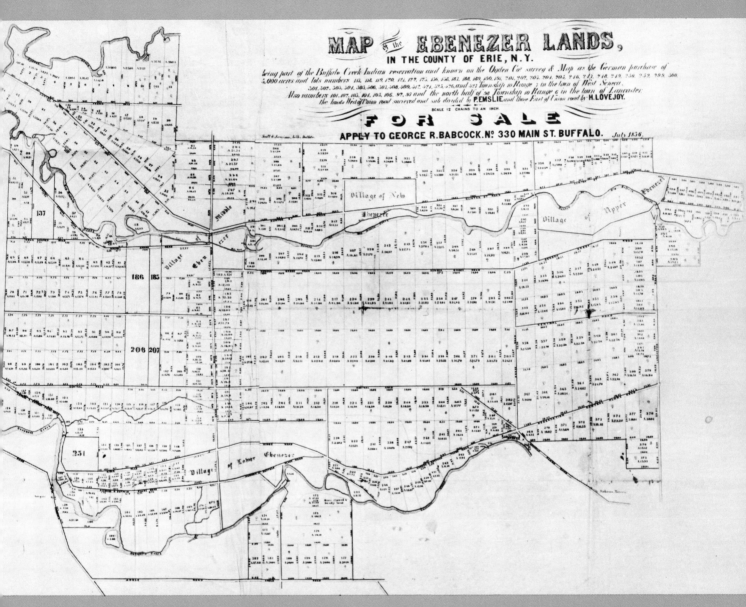

The dispute that created the Ebenezer Society stretches back to the conflicts of the Reformation in Germany. In the early eighteenth century a sect of dissident Lutherans who called themselves the "Community of True Inspiration" came to believe that the mainstream church had retreated from the strictness of the original Protestant values. This Pietist quest for perfection and serene removal from a spiritually contaminated society eventually led them to America, to settle in West Seneca (Ebenezer) in 1842. The society was self-sufficient. Farming, tanning, knitting, lumbering, brewing, and manufacturing operations were organized along communal lines. The group dined in communal halls. Property was held in common. Women held equal status with men. Each Inspirationist contributed according to his means, and took according to his needs.

Little irritations plagued the Ebenezers.

The colony was too small for twelve hundred people; a dam upstream left little power for water mills. But the real problem was temptation. Buffalo and its exuberant German-speaking community was only six miles away. The Ebenezers left for Iowa in 1856 making yet another move because they feared the encroachment of the secular society. *Courtesy Buffalo and Erie County Historical Society*

West Seneca underwent considerable change by the turn of the twentieth century. If the Ebenezer Society settled there in the 1840s because of its isolation, the breakdown of that isolation later drove the Ebenezers to Iowa. The photograph shown was a home for the elderly taken about 1900. The building, located at Indian Church and Union Roads was originally constructed by the Ebenezers as a general store and is now used as an apartment house. Courtesy James J. Ciesla, West Seneca Town Historian

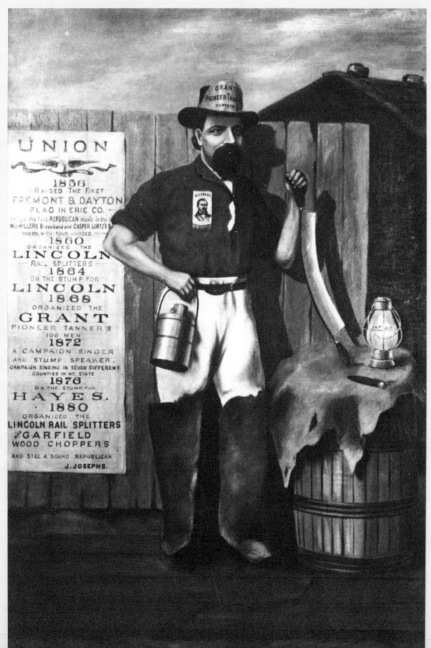

Joe Josephs, sign painter, sometime artist, and Liedertafel singer, was one of Buffalo's authentic characters. Like many of his fellow Protestant Germans in the post-Civil War era, he was also staunchly Republican. Josephs understood the publicity stunt. He was captain of the local rail-splitting team for two Republican presidential candidates. Lincoln in 1860 and Garfield in 1880. His shop at the foot of Exchange St. in Buffalo was decorated top to bottom with visual word puzzles and pictures of elephants. A publicity wizard, Elephant Joe could (as the saying went) make people "see an elephant" where there was none.

German language newspapers of the nineteenth century record the volatility of German-American politics. Founded in 1837 Der Weltberger ("The Cosmopolitan") was the first of the German-language newspapers, and the only nonpartisan paper of the 1830s and 1840s. It did not long remain so. Der Weltburger later became the Demokrat, and espoused the principles of the Democratic party. The Democrats' principal opponent was the Whig party, which was a bastion of nativism. For a short time the Whigs published a German-language newspaper, but it had little appeal. During the political turbulence of the 1850s Protestant Germans shifted toward the Republican Party. Roman Catholic Germans tended to remain Democrats. Courtesy Buffalo and Erie County Historical Society

Der Weltbürger.

Eine literarische und politische Zeitung.

Herausgegeben von G. Zahm, Buchdrucker und Buchhändler, No. 290 Mainstraße, Buffalo.

Jahrsgang I. Buffalo, den 2. Dezember 1837. No. 1.

[Bedi]ngungen. Diese Zeitung erscheint wöchentlich jeden Samstag um $2.50 das Jahr für diejenigen Subscribenten, denen die Zeitung auf Kosten des Herausgebers zugestellt wird, und um $2 für jene, welche sie durch die Post erhalten. Die Bezahlung des Subscriptionspreises geschieht halbjährig im Voraus. Wer den ganzen Jahrgang im Voraus bezahlt, dem wird 25 Cents Abzug bewilligt. Für Einrückungen werden die hier üblichen Preise berechnet. Zusendungen werden portofrei erwartet.

Ankündigung.

Der Weltbürger.

Eine literarische und politische Zeitung.

Die Anzahl der deutschen Bevölkerung von Buffalo hat sich in den letzten vier oder fünf Jahren so bedeutend gemehrt, und die kommerziellen sowohl als politischen Verhältnisse dieser Stadt erhielten für die da wohnenden Deutschen eine so hohe Bedeutung, daß man das Erscheinen einer Zeitung in deutscher Sprache längst schon als dringendes Bedürfniß fühlte.

Der wiederholt ausgesprochene Wunsch der Deutschen von Buffalo, eine deutsche Presse zu errichten, hat den Unterzeichneten veranlaßt, sich diesem Unternehmen zu unterziehen, und er legt hiemit den Plan zur Herausgabe einer deutschen Zeitung vor.

Sie soll wöchentlich unter dem Titel: "der Weltbürger" erscheinen. Ihr Zweck ist Belehrung der Deutschen über die Politik des Landes und Mittheilung der wichtigsten amerikanischen und europäischen Begebenheiten. Da Belehrung der Leser einer ihrer Hauptrücksichten ist, so wird sie sich keiner besonderen Partei anschließen, sondern unabhängig und unparteiisch jene Grundsätze zu entwickeln suchen, welche zur Aufrechthaltung der Verfassung nothwendig sind. In wichtigeren politischen Fragen sollen die Ansichten beider Parteien mitgetheilt werden, um die Leser in den Stand zu setzen, ihr eigenes Urtheil zu fällen. Entschieden wird sie sich gegen die ungerechten Verfolgungen der eingewanderten Europäer erklären, und dieselben auf jene Rechte aufmerksam machen, welche ihnen Verfassung und Gesetze zugesichert haben.

Während so die Zeitung dahin abzweckt, die Deutschen zu nützlichen amerikanischen Bürgern zu bilden, wird sie sich bemühen, auch den übrigen Anforderungen an eine Zeitung möglichst zu entsprechen. Sie wird gelungene Erzählungen aus deutschen und amerikanischen Schriftstellern liefern, und vorzüglich die für Buffalo und die angränzenden Counties wissenswerthen Nachrichten sammeln, die interessantesten Tagesneuigkeiten mittheilen, von Woche zu Woche regelmäßig die Marktpreise aufnehmen, die, für die deutschen Einwanderer besonders, wichtigen Verhältnisse des Westens erörtern, und aus dem Gebiete der Kunst und Wissenschaften solche Auszüge geben, welche gleich geeignet zur Unterhaltung und Belehrung sind.

Die Zeitung soll regelmäßig jeden Samstag erscheinen, und die erste Nummer am ersten Samstag im Dezember ausgegeben werden. Der Subscriptionspreis für das Jahr beträgt $2, 50 für diejenigen Subskribenten, denen die Zeitung auf Kosten des Herausgebers zugestellt wird, und $2 für jene, welche sie durch die Post erhalten. Die Bezahlung des Subkriptionspreises geschieht halbjährig im Voraus. Einrückungen werden für die hier üblichen Preise aufgenommen.

Die Offizin der Zeitung befindet sich Nr. 290 Main Straße über zwei Stiegen.

Der Einfluß geistiger Beschäftigungen auf den menschlichen Charakter.

Wer kann in der Welt sich umsehen und ihre verschiedene Gestalt in verschiedenen Zeiträumen ihrer Geschichte betrachten, ohne von der Ueberzeugung durchdrungen zu werden, daß die Fortschritte wissenschaftlicher Bildung zur Verfeinerung und Veredlung des Charakters führen? Es ist ein Ausspruch der Alten: "Gründliche Forschung der Wissenschaften sänftigt die Sitten und wirkt der Verwilderung entgegen." Dies ist in hohem Grade in Hinsicht auf Völker und Volksgemeinden der Fall. Betrachtet man den Menschen in dem Zustande der rohen und zuchtlosen Natur, nicht etwa wie er einsam und abgeschieden wohnt, sondern wie er sich zu seinen Stammgenossen gesellt, welche eben so wild als er sind und sich nur durch ihre Gestalt von den Thieren unterscheiden, die sie in den Wäldern jagen. Was sind seine Beschäftigungen? Nicht seine Fähigkeiten zu auf ein edles und nützliches Streben zu richten, nicht seine geistigen Kräfte auf die Erforschung der Wahrheit, auf die Betrachtung des Schönen in ihrer weiten Schöpfung und in ihren unermeßlichen Schätzen zu wenden, nicht seine physischen Kräfte in einer heilsamen und sinnreichen Arbeit anzustrengen. Dies sind Bestrebungen, die ihm fremd sind, zu fein und zu schwierig für seine Fassungskraft. Was sind seine Vergnügen? Nicht die hohen Genüsse, die aus dem Verkehr der Geister, aus dem Austausche der Gedanken, aus der Mittheilung von Kenntnissen, aus einem verfeinerten geselligen Leben entstehen, nicht die reinen und edeln Freuden, die aus der Erfüllung häuslicher und verwandtschaftlicher Pflichten entspringen. Dies sind Genüsse, die er so wenig kennt, als er von den Bestrebungen und Beschäftigungen der Bewohner anderer Planeten weiß. Die Befriedigung der rohesten Begierden, oft bis zu einem der Gesundheit, selbst dem Leben verderblichen Uebermaße, verrätherische und betrügerische Anschläge, worin sich ein angeborener Scharfsinn zeigt, die wilden und grausamen Aeußerungen eines natürlichen Muthes, Metzeleien und Verheerungen und blutige Rache bei den Beleidigungen eines Nachbarstammes, das sind die einzigen Beschäftigungen, die ihn erfreuen, die einzigen Vortheile, die er kennt. Ein afrikanischer Häuptling, der die Wände seiner Wohnung mit den Schädelhäuten seiner besiegten Feinde ziert, kann als ein Bild der Gewohnheiten und Gesinnungen eines Menschen im Zustande der unwissenden, ungebildeten Natur gelten. Weit entfernt, daß dies ein Bild wäre, weches nur auf ungewohnliche Beispiele von Grausamkeit paßte, kann man sicher behaupten, daß jedes Volk auf Erden, ehe es von dem Lichte der Gesittung erleuchtet wurde, mit sehr unbedeutenden Veränderungen, in jenem ursprunglichen Zustande war. Das Licht der Wahrheit, dessen Strahlen allmählig die Uebel der Unwissenheit und des Irrthums zerstreuen, entwickelte die schlummernden Fähigkeiten, die den Menschen in Stand setzen, die eigentlichen Zwecke der Menschheit zu erfüllen.

Es gibt aber einen Zustand der Unwissenheit, der wesentlich verschieden von der geistigen Rohheit der wilden Natur ist, aber doch nur wenige der schönen Züge der Menschheit auf der Stufe höherer Gesittung und Geistesbildung zeigt. Freilich ist selbst der gesittetste gesellschaftliche Zustand nicht ohne seine Laster; Ueppigkeit, wollüstige Verfeinerung und Ausschweifung gesellen sich oft zu bedeutender wissenschaftlicher Bildung und feinem Geschmacke, und das Gemuth ist zuweilen mit den verdorbenen Neigungen der menschlichen Natur verbunden und wirft einen täuschenden Schein auf die Kanäle, welche dem Charakter sittliche Entwürdigung in der Gestalt geistiger Vorzüge mittheilen; freilich zeigt die menschliche Natur, selbst wenn wissenschaftliche Bildung und Philosophie sie von den Schlacken der Sinnlichkeit gereinigt haben, noch zu viel Hinneigung zu dem Verderbnisse, zu viel Wahlverwandtschaft zu Allem, was in den moralischen Elementen, die sie umgeben, schlecht und unwürdig ist; aber mitten in der rohen Unwissenheit, wo die Vernunft noch nie versucht hat, ihre Würde und Unabhängigkeit zu behaupten und ihre Ueberlegenheit über die niedern Naturkräfte in Anspruch zu nehmen, wo physische Kräfte und Neigungen, die, wie durch einen mechanischen Antrieb, ohne eine heilsame Hemmung wirken, für das Ganze der Menschen gelten, da werden die ursprunglichen bösen Neigungen des menschlichen Charakters sich in noch gehässigern und empörendern Gestalten zeigen. Wir haben zwar von dem Zustande einer arkadischen Unschuld gelesen, wo die unverdorbene Natur, ohne den Beistand der Wissenschaft und Kunst, Alles gewährte, was zu menschlicher Glückseligkeit nöthig war; wer aber Gelegenheit gehabt hat, sich mit dem wirklichen Charakter des Menschen in jenen Zufluchtsstätten abgeschiedener Unwissenheit bekannt zu machen, weiß, daß das Gemälde eine Täuschung ist; er weiß, daß diese Zustände unwissender Unschuld und ländlicher Glückseligkeit nur im Gebiete der Dichtung ein Dasein haben, und daß rohe Unwissenheit nur ein anderer Ausdruck für einen Zustand von lasterhafter Verderbniß und in vielen Fällen von thierischer Wildheit ist. In einem solchen gesellschaftlichen Zustande sucht man vergebens strenge Grundsätze, edles Ehrgefühl, Gesinnungen und Gewohnheiten, welche durch geistige Bildung und Streben nach Kenntnissen erzeugt und genährt werden; man sucht vergebens, ausgenommen in sehr seltenen Fällen, jene zarten Pflichten, die das häusliche Leben verschönern und die Glieder einer Familie aneinander knüpfen, jenes freie Benehmen, jene Höflichkeit im Verkehr, welche die Atmosphäre der menschlichen Gesellschaft erheitern. Die fruchtbarsten Gebiete der geistigen Menschennatur sind in jenen Fällen ganz unangebaut, ein wilder, ungelichteter Wald, in welchen nie eine edle höhere Idee sich verliert, aber wo böse Leidenschaften frei umherschweifen und zu furchtbarer Größe gedeihen. Gegenseitige Erbitterung, die bei der geringsten Herausfoderung in wilde Rache übergeht, Kraftanstrengungen, welche jedes Gefühl für Tugend und Menschlichkeit beleidigend, vielleicht zur Befriedigung einer schaulustigen Menge geübt werden, Grausamkeit gegen Thiere, die zuweilen bis zu rohem Muthwillen geht, dies sind die vorherrschenden Züge in dem Charakter einer unwissenden und ungebildeten Menschengesellschaft. Wenn die Verbreitung des Lichts der Kenntnisse, abgesehen von ihren höhern Wirkungen, auch nur etwas von dieser anstoßenden Rohheit hinwegnähme, so würde ein wichtiger Schritt geschehen sein, die gesellschaftlichen Gewohnheiten zu verbessern und ein Volk auf eine höhere moralische Stufe zu heben.

Ist der Charakter auf diese Weise zur Menschlichkeit gesänftigt und für den geselligen Verkehr gesittigt, so ist er für einen andern, aus der Pflege der Wissenschaft hervorgehenden wichtigen Einfluß empfänglich, der zur Befestigung in sittlichen Gewohnheiten führt; der Mensch lernt den Werth und den rechten Gebrauch der Zeit kennen. Es liegt am Tage, daß Jeder, dessen Beruf angestrengte Thätigkeit fodert, doch immer noch Zeit übrig hat. Jedes Geschäft, jedes gewerbliche Berufsleben hat mehr oder weniger Mußestunden; manche Gewerbe können nicht zu allen Zeiten fortgeführt werden, und überdies ist es der Fall, das selbst der fleißigste und thätigste Mensch zuweilen in seinem Gewerbe nicht volle und regelmäßige Beschäftigung findet und viel Zeit übrig hat. Wer wird nun diese Mußestunden am nützlichsten anwenden! Derjenige, dessen Seele von jeder über blos physische Beschäftigungen hinausgehende Idee leer ist, oder Derjenige, dessen Geist eine höhere Ausbildung und Empfänglichkeit erhalten hat? Jener wird in dem Augenblicke, wo er von den Fesseln seines Tagwerkes befreit ist, sich in lärmende und aufregende Vergnügungen stürzen oder vielleicht einer herabwürdigenden Trägheit sich hingeben, sich selber eine Last; er wird jeder Versuchung zugänglich sein und leicht eine Beute schlechter Gesellschaft werden. Haben Trägheit und Unwissenheit ihn zur Liederlichkeit verführt, so ist es ein Glück, wenn er sich nicht zu strafwürdigen Vergehen verleiten läßt. Allerdings kann in vielen Fällen mit einem sehr beschränkten Ideenkreise viel gute Gesinnung verbunden sein, und es gibt wenige Erscheinungen im Menschenleben, die man so gern betrachtet, als einen solchen Triumph unfreiwilliger geistiger Armuth über alle Nachtheile ihrer Lagen; aber wir reden hier von den Wirkungen, die eine gedankenlose Unwissenheit in sehr vielen Fällen bei dem Mangel besserer Grundsätze haben wird. Vergleiche man nun mit den in solchen Fällen hervortretenden Wirkungen den Menschen, dem die Wissenschaft ihre Schätze zu öffnen angefangen hat. Er wird jede Gelegenheit benützen, seine geistigen Fähigkeiten auszubilden und sich freuen, wenn sein Beruf ihm dazu Muße gibt; er wird fühlen, daß er seine Zeit nicht mehr verschwenden kann, und der Gedanke, daß er nur wenig Mußestunden übrig hat, wird ihn darauf bedacht machen, keine ungenützt vorüber gehen zu lassen, und so werden seine Stunden zwischen den Pflichten seines Berufs und der Ausbildung seines Geistes und Charakters getheilt sein. Man kann die moralische Wichtigkeit der geschäftlosen Stunden in dem Leben selbst des arbeitsamsten Menschen nicht hoch genug anschlagen. Sie sind gerade die Zeit, wo sittliches Verderben sich leicht Eingang verschafft, und es ist daher höchst wichtig, sich durch heilsame Beschäftigung gegen sie zu sichern.

Die buckligen Musikanten.

[Eine Sage.]

Am Tage St. Mathäi, im Jahre nach des Welterlösers Geburt 1549, kam ein armer buckliger Spielmann spät in der Nacht nach Aachen von einem Dorfe zurück, woselbst er bei einer Hochzeit aufgespielt hatte. Halb im Taumel, bekümmerte ihn weder Zeit noch Ort, und so ging er denn wohlgemuthet am Münster vorbei, als eben die Thurmglocke Mitternacht brummte. Da aber erschrack er auch um so mehr, als er nun hörte, wie spät es in der Nacht sey, und dazu sich in der Luft ein seltsames Geschwirre, wie von Eulen- und Fledermäusflügeln, vernehmen ließ. Schnellen Schrittes eilte er, dem Graus der Geisterstunde und ihrem Spucke zu entfliehen, und beugte schüchtern in die Schmiedestraße ein, um durch dieselbe zu seiner Wohnung zu gelangen, welche in der Jakobstraße lag. Was begegnete ihm aber, als er den Fischmarkt betrat? Alle Fischbänke schimmerten von unzähligen Lichtern, welche weithin die dunkle Nacht erhellten; köstliche Speisen waren in goldenen und silbernen Schüsseln aufgetragen, und perlender Wein blinkte in großen Krystallkrügen. Um alles herum saßen eine Menge der reichgekleidetsten Damen und ließen es sich trefflich schmecken. Erschrocken setzte sich der Spielmann in eine Ecke, denn nun erinnerte er sich entsetzt der Quatember-Nacht und ihres Herenspucks. — Doch, es war zu spät, eine der zunächst sitzenden Damen hatte ihn bereits bemerkt, und führte ihn zu Tische. Dann aber sprach sie zu dem Spielmanne, der mit vor Angst klappernden Zähnen und schlotternden Knieen dastand: "Fürchte Dich nicht, und spiele uns eine lustige Weise auf; wir werden Dir dessen Dank wissen." Und indem sie so sprach, reichte sie dem Zagenden einen Pokal mit würzigem Wein gefüllt. Dieser ermuthigte wunderbar den Spielmann dergestalt, daß, sobald er den Becher bis auf die Nagelprobe geleert hatte, er seine Geige zur Hand nahm und lustig zu fiedeln begann.

Da wurden eilig die Bänke mit Allem, was darauf stand bei Seite geschafft, und die Damen, unter denen er manche vornehme Frau aus der Stadt zu erkennen glaubte, erhoben sich allzumal bei dem Tone seiner Geige, und bald wirbelten die Paare durcheinander. Nun aber ging es immer schneller und schneller, und der Spielmann geigte, wie von unsichtbarer Hand getrieben, immer toller darauf los, so daß er mehrmals vermeinte, die Saiten müßten in tausend Stücke zerspringen und ihm Hören und Sehen vergehen.— Indessen sausten die Paare noch immer durcheinander, während sein Arm kräftig den Bogen führte, und sein Spiel von selbst aus einer Weise in die andere überging, und oft so stark wurde, daß es ihn bedünkte, als sey ein ganzes Konzert von Geigen und gellenden Flöten hinter ihm aufgestellt, welche alle in seine Töne einstimmten, und ihm das Ganze wie ein verwirrter Traum vorkam. Da summte endlich die Thurmuhr drei Viertel auf Eins, und plötzlich hielten die Paare in sichtbarer Erschöpfung inne. Alles wurde wieder mit einem Male ruhig und in seine vorige Ordnung gerückt. Unentschlossen stand aber der Spielmann da, nicht wissend, ob er bleiben müsse oder scheiden dürfe. Da trat die frühere Dame wieder zu ihm heran, und sprach: "Braver Spielmann, Du hast uns wacker vergnügt, darum soll Dir auch nun des Lohnes werden." Und damit hatte sie ihm bereits sein Wamms ausgezogen, und ehe er noch recht zur Besinnung kommen konnte, war sie schon hinter ihn getreten, und hatte ihm mit einem Griffe seinen Höcker abgenommen. Wer war froher als unser erleichterter Geiger! Dankdurchdrungen wollte er niederfallen vor seiner Wohlthäterin, da aber schlug es Eins, und Damen, Lichter und Schüsseln waren verschwunden, und der Spielmann stand noch allein in der dunkeln Nacht. Da aber fühlte er abermals nach seinem Rücken; denn ihm war es noch immer zu Muthe, als sey sein ganzes Abenteuer ein wirrer Traum gewesen. Doch nein, es war Wirklichkeit, er war gerade und schlank, und sein Höcker verschwunden. Wer vermöchte wohl die Freude seines Herzens zu beschreiben, in welcher er nun nach seinem Wamms griff, das vor ihm auf der Erde liegen geblieben! Doch noch eine zweite sollte ihm beschieden seyn; denn als er dasselbe aufnahm, kam es ihm ungewöhnlich schwer vor, und als er nach der Ursache dieser außerordentlichen Gewichtigkeit forschte, fand er dessen beide Taschen mit Gold gefüllt, und eilte als ein zwiefach glücklicher Mann nach seiner Wohnung.

Dort aber erkannte die harrende Frau ihren verwandelten Mann fast nicht mehr wieder, bis ihr seine Erzählung von dem Begegnisse der Nacht

The Lake View Brewing Company, which once stood at the foot of Porter Avenue, was one of the many breweries in Buffalo in the nineteenth century. Its president, Philip G. Schaefer, was trained in the classics at Canisius College. The litany of brewery owners shows how successful Germans were in this business. Jacob Roos opened the first one in the 1840s. Roos was followed by Schanzlin, Hoffman, Friedman, Lang, Beck, Baumgartner, Born, Weppner, Heizer, Kuhn, Rochevot, Timmerman, Pankow, Trapp and Beck, and many others. Courtesy Buffalo and Erie County Historical Society

Because they were cautious savers many Germans lost their money in the bank failures of 1857. But the community rebounded. One gauge of the success of the German population is the founding of the German-American Bank in 1882. The structure at Main and Court was one of five banks capitalized with German investment. The German-American bank casts light on a later phase of social history—the impact of World War I in hastening the decline of ethnic identification with the old country. In 1918 amidst the sharp reaction to anything German, hamburger became Salisbury steak, daschunds became "liberty pups," and the German-American Bank took the name we know it by today, Liberty Bank. Roy W. Nagle Collection, courtesy Buffalo and Erie County Historical Society

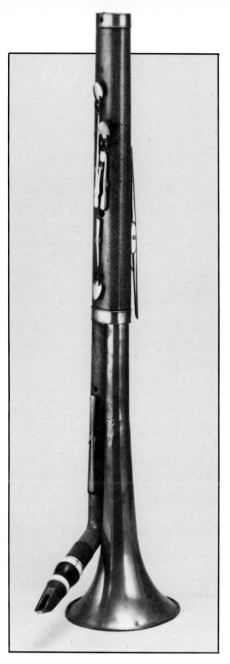

The oldest of the sociable German singing clubs was the Liedertafel, *founded in 1848. The* Saengerbund, *organized in 1855, was another of the groups that promoted good cheer and* gemeutlichkeit. *One historian has cited the singing clubs as an example of "the Germans' unfortunate tendency to dissipate their social energies in ever smaller groups." This undervalues their contribution. The singing societies persisted into the twentieth century, which helped to preserve the German language, and so also helped to promote and assert the unity of* German culture. No ethnic consciousness lasts forever though. By the time this competitive *saengerfest took place in 1932 at Buffalo's centennial, the groups' enthusiasm already had the air of nostalgia. Buffalo's Germans had largely assimilated and lost their separateness by then. The Americanization campaigns of the first world war began the process. World War II and suburbanization would complete it. Program Booklet, First National Saengerfest, Courtesy Buffalo and Erie County Historical Society*

The rich tones of this clarion (a kind of low register clarinet) accompanied the singers in the Liedertafel, a nineteenth-century German-American cultural group. For the Germans, small houses and large families severely taxed the special cultural need for order and domestic tranquility. Historian Andrew Yox recalls the "vigilant supression of capricious remarks and horseplay," in German households. No such restraint prevailed in the social clubs. If not quite the embodiment of spontaneous expression, the clubs nevertheless sanctioned boisterous release. Dating from 1811, the instrument is now held in the permanent collection of the Buffalo and Erie County Historical Society. From the Collections, courtesy Buffalo and Erie County Historical Society

Physical fitness was a mainstay of German culture at home and in America. The Turnverein, *originally a collection of amateur gymnasts, singers, painters and sharpshooters, also tumbled into politics. Many of the young Turners had been galvanized by the failed European revolutions of 1848. In the 1850s the Turners attached themselves to liberal American* causes, the abolition of slavery and the promotion of women's rights. If today we could imagine an amateur softball league which also organized to protest apartheid, we might have a feel for the Turners. The Turners were still active in the twentieth century, and the organization survived into the 1980s as an athletic club. As late as 1910 there were 150 German organizations in Buffalo. The appeal of German cultural groups suffered during the two world wars, but the process of assimilation had even more to do with the decline of a separate German culture in the Buffalo area. Courtesy Buffalo and Erie County Historical Society

The Poles

Poles now constitute the largest ethnic group in the metropolitan area. Their history is an important component of the history of this county. Investigation of Polish immigration is somewhat hampered, though, because the various census documents list immigrants by their country of origin. In the unhappy history of Poland the country was conquered and reconquered, its territory partitioned and occupied by its powerful neighbors to the east, south, and west. In the earliest immigrations, since there were so few from Poland, and the population so distinctive, the task is easier. The census of 1850 lists only fifty people born in Poland, and these were not the Roman Catholic peasants we most often think of as Polish immigrants, but Yiddish-speaking Jews who fled persecution and discrimination in the Russian-Polish pale of control. Czar Nicholas I broke his covenant not to draft Jews into the Russian army before they were granted civil rights, and this prompted others to leave.

After 1830 the Niagara Frontier settled rapidly. The population of Buffalo, for instance, doubled, doubled, and then doubled again in the first three decades after it was incorporated. The county experienced growth that was only slightly less dramatic. The many new households demanded all the little useful utensils, "Yankee notions," and modest fineries that elevated material life in a frontier and boom town. The invention of the department store was decades off, so peddlers supplied these needs. Many of the peddlers were Jews.

With a small investment in goods, and a sturdy pair of shoes, (later, perhaps, a wagon) peddlers on the Niagara Frontier looked forward to quick returns. Historian David Gerber notes that these were the same people that Germans called *luftmenschen* because they seemed to be able to live on nothing but air. However profitable, this life was not easy. It required a great deal of time away from home. Peddlers also faced continual small disappointments and the larger uncertainties of nineteenth-century business. Jewish peddlers endured anti-Semitism that denied them credit (a special disadvantage to peddlers). Nevertheless Jewish immigrants from Poland prospered in this occupation. Over time they established a stable community.

This stone is all the physical evidence we have to remind us of the quixotic scheme hatched in 1825 by Mordecai Manuel Noah to found the state of Israel on Grand Island. Noah, a playwright and impresario, soldier, adventurer, and diplomat, acquired over two thousand acres on the island opposite Tonawanda. Expansively he invited all Jews to be part of the new nation, and appointed himself a "judge" of a reconstituted Zion. American Indians, whom he regarded as one of the lost tribes of Israel, also would have a part. The idea sounds preposterous. Selig Adler, historian of the Niagara region's Jewish experience, pointed out that the plan was "not quite as chimerical" as it seemed. The terminus to the Erie Canal was not far away. Grand Island also sits between two peaceful countries. Jewish communities worldwide might have contributed capital, settlers, and labor, but there was little enthusiasm and much ridicule. In any case, Noah was better at dreaming than managing. Bad weather kept him from holding dedication ceremonies on Grand Island, and he left without ever having gotten there. Roy W. Nagle Collection, courtesy Buffalo and Erie County Historical Society

Russian Jewish immigrants brought this samovar, and their custom of drinking tea from a glass, to Buffalo in the nineteenth century. Immigrant Jews often spent long convivial evenings drinking tea, discussing business, recalling the old country, disputing the Torah. The samovar kept a reserve of boiling water for refills, and for additional guests. Photograph Courtesy Mortimer Spiller

Wearing a cloak and the striped tallifth, this student of the violin came from an Orthodox Jewish family. Westphal Collection, courtesy Buffalo and Erie County Historical Society

Objects long cherished in families provide us with a tangible link to the past. Brought to Buffalo by Polish Jews in the nineteenth century, this menorah recalls the devotion and piety of these immigrants. A Hebrew inscription on the face reads, "to kindle the Sabbath light." Menorahs usually held seven candles, this one holds five. Courtesy Mortimer Spiller

While other communities have suburbanized and melted (to varying degrees) into the main, the Polish settlements in Buffalo, in Black Rock, and in Cheektowaga largely have resisted the pressures to lose what is distinctive about their communities. Religious continuity has been the most important factor in this extraordinary persistence.

Religious holidays are also feasts that bind families across generations. The Broadway Market has long served as the centerpiece of the Polish community in the Broadway-Fillmore neighborhood. It has also helped to preserve Polish cuisine. The vendor pictured here advertises the main ingredient of czernina, the delicious, dark and rich duck's blood soup traditional to Polish cooking. At Christmas and Eastertime the market becomes the major secular gathering place of the Polish-American community.

It is the oldest survivor of the nineteenth-century public market system that meant to centralize facilities, regulate weights, ensure the quality of foods, and more efficiently handle waste. Though the market now caters to a diverse neighbor-

Most Poles who came to Buffalo came decades later when industrial growth created an enormous demand for unskilled labor. Poland was rural and not industrialized. The land could not be endlessly subdivided when the population grew. Peasants were forced to emigrate. The city was such unfamiliar territory that the mere existence of industrial jobs was not enough to pull Poles here, however desperate their need to leave their homeland. Poles who came to America bypassed Buffalo until St. Stanislaus Church was established in 1874. The current of immigration became so swift that eighteen years later five more new churches served the Polish community.

More than mere distance separated Polish immigrants from their former lives. Whatever the rigors of the Atlantic crossing, they crossed a greater psychological gulf between the peasant villages and the crowded industrial neighborhoods north and east of Buffalo. Polish immigrants were no strangers to hard work, of course. But factories are different from farms. Day-to-day work in the iron foundries and in the clothing industry was regulated by the whistle and the time clock. This was a way of life alien to the natural rhythms of farming.

Communication was a special and difficult problem because Polish is at a greater distance from English than German or the romance languages of other immigrants. Though religious ceremonies were conducted in the Latin common to all Roman Catholics, the parish life of a devout community still needed ministering in its mother tongue. A resident Polish priest was a prerequisite to the further settlement of Poles in Buffalo. Their adjustment was made immeasurably easier when an energetic young Polish seminarian named John Pitass was sent from Rome to minister to the community. Fr. Pitass helped create an important bastion of Polish-American culture in Buffalo.

hood, one can still hear the distinctive accents and cadences which echo a Polish heritage held close. To this day, business is often conducted in Polish. Photograph by George J. Butler, Courier-Express *Collection, courtesy Buffalo and Erie County Historical Society*

Haggling at the Chippewa Market. Photographs bring us closer to history, but they still must be animated and brought to life. If we can imagine the bustle, the many accents, the cackling, and the fragrance *of nineteenth-century markets, we begin to appreciate the richness of our past. From the Collections, courtesy Buffalo and Erie County Historical Society*

St. Stanislaus School
Courtesy Buffalo and Erie County
Historical Society

St. Stanislaus School which Fr. John Pitass established, emphasized the Polish heritage. Pitass himself taught in the school, and he was the first to bring the Felician nuns to teach. Strict discipline and commitment overcame most of the difficulties of the very large class sizes. Ironically, the education denied the Polish peasant, that sense of a common cultural past, was more available here than in Poland. Conquering powers believed that education in the mother tongue encouraged Polish nationalism, and nationalism led to revolt. In Austria, Prussia, and Russia, the authorities actively discouraged education in Polish. Even though plagued by high dropout rates, church schools in Buffalo taught the children of immigrants more of Polish literature and history, and a more careful grammar than their parents knew. The children also escaped the class divisions of society within Poland. In Buffalo, belonging to "Polonia" had more to do with being Polish than with one's economic station.

Parish churches and parish schools provided a refuge which drew this community together, countering the prejudice that all new groups faced, and that the Poles faced especially. The price of cultural unity though is sometimes measured in the distance away from the mainstream, or in access to the upward mobility of the larger society. Drawing together has also meant drawing inward. Few progressed from the bilingual parochial grade schools to the public high schools. As a group they mistrusted secular institutions like universities. In 1920, for example, there were only thirty-one physicians and fifteen dentists of Polish extraction in the Buffalo area. The church, the parish school, and the singing society could provide an encompassing world.

Tensions with other ethnic groups, particularly the Germans, are an important feature of the history of Poles in Buffalo. This animosity was rooted in the German conquest of Poland, and reinforced in the streets of Buffalo. Sentiment had real effects. Early on, Polish voters leaned toward the Democratic party, in large part because the Germans were consistently Republican. Polish workers justly complained of discriminatory treatment by German foremen. Unjustified rumors that the Germans were behind plots to expel the Polish population, or to tax church property, spread periodically (and easily) throughout Polonia. Poles endured ethnic taunts. Street fights between German and Polish children punctuated these tensions.

Brought to Buffalo from Rome as a seminarian (and later ordained by Bishop Ryan) John Pitass in time came to be known as the Patriarch of Polonia. From his base at St. Stanislaus parish Fr. Pitass shaped the direction of the Polish community, held it together, and helped it grow. He established a school, a cemetery, and a Polish-language newspaper, and he became involved in the development of real estate near his parish. Small, wooden-frame cottages on inexpensive lots soon surrounded the church. Polish immigrants placed a high value on home ownership. For a twenty-five dollar down payment all but the poorest could begin to live in their own home. In 1886 alone, associates of Pitass built three hundred homes, and sold six hundred lots. In the following year they tripled that figure. His work drew Polish immigrants to the St. Stanislas area like a magnet. By 1890 there were twenty thousand poles in Buffalo. By 1910, St. Stanislaus was baptizing twelve hundred infants per year. By 1920 Buffalo was one quarter Polish. Courtesy Buffalo and Erie County Historical Society

St. Stanislas Church

Neighborhoods sprang up where the work was. Often these neighborhoods took on an ethnic cast. In 1903 Bethlehem Steel attracted 250 Polish families. By 1920 the expanding neighborhood had three churches. The Polish National Catholic Church (an American institution which splintered from Roman Catholicism over parish autonomy rather than doctrine) established a parish in Lackawanna in 1929. Courtesy Buffalo and Erie County Historical Society

Dr. Francis Fronczak was a prominent member of the Polish community. He held undergraduate and graduate degrees from Canisius, and both a medical and a law degree from the University of Buffalo. He led a very public life as a member of the Assembly and the Charter Revision Commission, and especially as public health commissioner beginning in 1910. Fronczak became an ambassador of Polish culture to the rest of Buffalo.

Family members seized the last opportunity to photograph "Droga Babcia," a dear Polish grandmother. For Poles, it was particularly important that family ritual should mark all life's passages. While deeply Roman Catholic, the remnants of folk religion, such as the veneration of saints' personalities, and adoration at special Easter altars, was never far from the surface of Polish piety. Folklorist Katherine Koperski argues that rituals, such as this Corpus Cristi procession which took place in the 1920s, "still serve as an important affirmation of Polish-American community identity." Photographs by Joseph E. Koperski

While the world of Polish-Americans was mostly urban, the tie to the land remained strong, and may help account for the mass move straight eastward down Broadway to the wide-open spaces of postwar Cheektowaga. It requires an act of imagination to picture how an area looked before it was built up, or to recapture its appeal. Orderly suburban developments now give us little hint of their former wildness. This family from the densely populated Polish east side traveled to their relative's Getzville farm in the late 1920s. The district is hardly rural now. Photograph by Joseph E. Koperski

Much of the "infrastructure"—the bridges, roads, and water systems—of Erie County were constructed with immigrant muscle. Here Italian workers erect a bridge in Eden (c. 1897). Courtesy Eden Historical Society

The Italians

The forces that pushed and pulled immigrants from the various European countries were uneven. The misfortunes of war, famine, persecution, population growth, and economic collapse did not happen everywhere in Europe at once. This is why immigrants tended to arrive in waves, nationality by nationality. In Italy drought and crop failure combined with heavy taxation to force people to leave. Fourteen thousand came to Buffalo in the last two decades of the nineteenth century.

The opportunities that attracted immigrants often depended on some prior settlement. For the Poles, establishing a church was the crucial ingredient. For the Italians who came to the Buffalo area, it was more often the case that someone from a local village needed to blaze a trail before others would follow. It is estimated that (after 1901) as many as fifteen hundred passages to Buffalo per year were financed by relatives.

As a rule men came first to do heavy labor in industry, to toil on the docks or work in construction. They sent for their families later, when they had gotten a stake. The inrush of Italians to Buffalo was extraordinarily swift. Only seven appeared on the census of 1850. In the early 1890s there were just twenty-five hundred (though unofficial estimates were four times that). By 1920, however, only Poles and Germans outnumbered Italians in the city of Buffalo.

These people did heavy work outdoors. Often their labor was contracted for by the *padrone.* As a "patron" the *padrone* eased the transition to American industrial society. Labor organizers charged that often the patron became an exploiter who found jobs in construction or industry, but levied extortionate fees for his services. One sympathetic newspaperman estimated that "nine tenths of the failures of the Italian people in this country are due to the systems of these self-possessed friends of the working class." At best the work that they could get for their clients was not steady. Most could spend half of a typical year unemployed. Partly out of necessity, but one suspects, in large part out of choice, Italian-Americans moved into family enterprises. They were particularly successful on the margins of Buffalo's industrial economy, in selling food, fruits and vegetables, or pasta products, and very occasionally as street musicians. Many later found success as barbers, greengrocers, cobblers and restauranteurs. Eventually these enterprises were a passport to the middle class.

On the fringe their time was their own. They could preserve more of the traditional family relationships even in the midst of a new and unfamiliar industrial economy that caused so much disruption elsewhere. Because they venerated old age, patriarchs emerged in large families. Italian women, wives and daughters, often worked under the direction of relatives. Sometimes they earned extra money by seeing to the needs of boarders in their own homes. Unlike women of other ethnic groups, they did not often work outside the home. (Polish women were ten times more likely to do so). When they did venture out, it might be as migrant labor in the farms, canneries, and vineyards in Eden Center, or Fredonia. A respite from the crowded city, this was also work that could be done as part of a family group. This way the traditional authority of the male head of the family could be sustained.

Women had always worked seasonally in the fields in Italy, tending their children at the same time. Work was never allowed to interfere with the task of raising children. Children, in fact, could contribute to the family's support at an early age. Custom long tested in Italy was replicated here. The result was an extraordinarily stable homelife. Whatever had been lost in the potential of greater freedom and latitude for women (or for educational advancement for children) was gained in family stability. Divorce, desertion, and abandonment were very rare in Buffalo Italian society.

Italian immigration coincided with the worst nativist period in American history. Prejudice against these

transcended locality, Italian settlement in the city recalled the intensely local character of the old country. No fewer than five distinct colonies emerged in Buffalo. Newcomers from Sicily, virtually a separate island nation, settled a neighborhood called The Hooks close to Canal Street on the crowded Lower West Side. Calabrians, isolated at the toe of the Italian boot, regrouped in South Buffalo. The Campanese, who hailed from Naples, lived closer to downtown. Another, the Abruzzi, lived on East Delavan. In this group (somewhat surpising) there were a small number of Italian Protestants. Immigrants from central southern Italy, the Campobassese, settled in the Lovejoy-William area.

Small independent enterprises like the Tomasulo family's fruit market on Exchange Street were most typical of Italian businesses at the turn of the century. These were family concerns that already represented a modest prosperity. A decade earlier the fruit may have been sold from a wagon. A woman's face can be seen (just barely) looking out from behind the hand of bananas. Courtesy Buffalo and Erie County Historical Society

Dominic Cocco and his hurdy-gurdy were fixtures of Buffalo's downtown until the 1940s. Italians could be found often at the fringe of the industrial economy. This was the result of both prejudice and preference. From the Collections, courtesy Buffalo and Erie County Historical Society

newcomers ran high. Part of this stemmed from their very success at holding together, part in slipping between the cracks of the new industrial order. If they ingeniously found ways to recycle fabric, they were denounced as rag-pickers. When they spent long days selling fruit, starting early in established neighborhoods, and ending early in their own, they were accused of indolence. Successfully maintaining their community brought nativist charges of clannishness. A front page article in the *Buffalo Express* of 1891 which toured the "Italian haunts" was entitled "Buffalo's Little Italy: Un-American Codes and Modes."

Outsiders in the 1890s (and after) tended to see only an Italian mass. One unfriendly *Buffalo Express* writer noticed "this un-American habit of herding together." The real story in Buffalo is much more complex and interesting. Even though Italy was officially united in 1870, that nation still reflected the divided history of its many feudal strongholds. Where other groups found unity here that

Attachment to the old country remained deep. Even the poorest sent back money. Not a few returned to Italy with a relative fortune. The birth of children in this country helped cement the new bond.

It was true that the Italian neighborhoods were more densely populated than any other. To be sure, the teeming, noisy, and poor Italian neighborhoods had their share of street conflict and violence. Lacking an indigenous tradition of fist-fighting probably had something to do with the frequent charge that Italians fought among themselves with knives. Clashes between Irish and Italian newsboys on Main Street are still part of local lore. To focus on these aspects of a culture obscures the greater strengths, the mutual benefit societies, the religious festivals, the informal organizations that welcomed new immigrants, the lively Italian-language press.

Language of course is not just a matter of the printed word; conversation was a vital part of Italian-American identity. Originally there was a greater separation of dialect in the neighborhoods, but the language still acted as a kind of brotherly code. Elaborate nuances of gesture and body language made possible a special expressiveness of emotion and humor, a subtext that went beyond words. Sometimes history leaves a trace that is audible. Linguists have identified a distinct Buffalo-Italian "ethnolect" that continues to be detectable in contemporary pronunciation. Outsiders are likely to call this the "Buffalo accent." The "a's" are flatter, the tones slightly nasal, and sometimes the grammatical constructions expose Italian or Sicilian roots. If, for most, fluency in the Italian language has long since evaporated, a familiarity lingers. Specialized vocabularies of dining, friendship, and insult hang on the longest.

A journal called Il Coriere, *which began publishing in 1898, was the most solid of the Italian publications. Twice weekly it carried notice of parish events, local crime stories, news from Italy, and serialized romance novels. Lively political journals also flourished; among them,* L'Imparzial *(hardly impartial) and the partisan* La Voce Della Verta *("the voice of truth"). The Italian community briefly supported a fearless lampoon called* Senza Paura, *which after a name change reappeared as* La Vendetta. *It proved to be a little too determined in its satire for what was, after all, a tightly knit community. Courtesy Buffalo and Erie County Historical Society*

The Black Community

Black roots in Buffalo reach as far back in the city's history as white antecedents do. The original non-Indian settlement had at least one black citizen, who was the proprietor of the trading store. Blacks also surveyed with Joseph Ellicott and fought under Commodore Perry. Before 1818, a few blacks were held as slaves in Western New York. Buffalo's black community in the nineteenth century was both the smallest ethnic group and one of the most interesting. Not much survives of a written record, but there are still ways to pry information from the past. A census at mid-century counted only 704 blacks in the city. Among northern cities this was still large enough to rank tenth, and the community was stable and well established. Most blacks had been long-time residents. Heads of families had lived here an average of eleven years, nearly twice as long as the Germans and Irish, who were relative newcomers to the city.

This is a community that has experienced a good deal of change. It has not been easy for historians to reconstruct the past. The picture has built up bit by bit from the information of the periodic census. Sometimes impersonal numbers tell a surprising story. For instance, blacks were not segregated from the rest of the city. In fact to term it a "black community" in the sense that we now use the term to indicate solidarity, black consciousness, and unhappily, ghettoization, would be misleading. Blacks lived in all but three of the city's thirteen wards. None at all lived in the Irish first ward nearest the Erie Canal. Given the condition of the neighborhood, this was almost certainly by choice. Blacks were dispersed mostly in the German neighborhoods.

We have come to think that race is the most important factor to push this community together and to hold it there. On the contrary, the borders between races may have been more permeable then. There were eleven inter-racial marriages in this small group. The most striking feature is family stability. Families were small, and nearly all had a male head—more even than the Irish. Few lived as boarders. Few families took in boarders, or had live-in relatives. The balance between women and men was almost even, another measure of the soundness of the group.

Census takers also asked blacks how they made their living. There were the occupations we expect to find: cooks and porters, waiters and hotel workers, gardeners and laborers—and then there were barbers. Historian Laurence Glasco noticed that blacks worked more often as barbers than they did at other trades. This is curious and important. In later decades racial animosity would not allow blacks and whites to come into such close contact. The distance that later separated the races was not so wide before the Civil War.

This is not to say that antebellum blacks had no difficulty living in the white society of the north. There is no question that they faced disadvantages. Schools were poor and separate. There were black sit-ins as early as the 1830s to protest the conditions of the "African school." It was not until 1872 that the public schools were finally open to blacks. They could not vote, as a rule. Some occupations were unconditionally closed to them. Despite these handicaps the "free negroes" of the pre-Civil War era in Buffalo held their families together as well as whites. Materially they were a little better off than the Irish.

Between 1845 and 1875 the population of Buffalo quadrupled, but the numbers of blacks stayed about the same. There were seven hundred blacks in 1855 and about seven hundred in 1875. Even so, much had changed. These were not the same seven hundred; only one person out of five who had been counted in 1855 remained to be counted in 1875. There were also fewer children among them. In the same twenty years there was a phenomenal business boom, but blacks did not share in this growth either. In 1875 there were fewer carpenters, fewer hotel workers, and fewer barbers. These were the same occupations that brought whites and blacks into close proximity. It is hard to know exactly what this means. But historians have speculated that the loss of these jobs in particular is a measure of an increase in racial prejudice after the Civil War.

By 1890 the black community had grown, but only in a small way. The eleven hundred who lived in Buffalo tended to live in a more restricted area around Michigan and William, or on Vine Street. The population rose to forty-five hundred during World War I. Though this was a quadrupling, blacks still comprised less than 1 percent of the city's population. As the poorest paid of all groups, they moved into neighborhoods already old and declining. Unlike the earlier black settlers, these new immigrants came mostly from the rural South, to serve the needs of industry during World War I. Unions customarily excluded blacks, thus blocking one avenue upward. When they were employed as strikebreakers in the longshoremen's strike of 1916, racial relations deteriorated further.

This charming photograph of mother and daughter dates from about 1900. Their identities are unknown. Westphal Collection, courtesy Buffalo and Erie County Historical Society

The picture of the black community in the 1920's was much changed from the 1850s. Surveys revealed that blacks felt themselves to be sorely discriminated against. The figures bear this out. During this boom period six out of ten worked in unskilled positions. Half of the families took in boarders, more women worked as domestics. The Depression that struck the country in the 1930s was a shattering experience to whites, who had become accustomed to equating hard work with security and success. To blacks who had long lived on the margin of the industrial economy, the experience was not so new.

Though there were fewer than there should have been, black professionals began to serve the black community after World War I. A few doctors and dentists, one lawyer, and several preachers emerged as the leaders of the community in the 1920s. As with other immigrant groups, (and surely these people from the rural South were immigrants) discrimination and prejudice drove them closer. Religious and musical traditions nurtured since the time of slavery tied the generations together.

W.E.B. Du Bois

By the time of her death in 1923 civil rights activist Mary Talbert had become one of the most prominent black women in the United States, and, quite possibly, the world. She had a remarkable career. After graduating from Oberlin College at age nineteen, she became a high school principal. In 1891 she married Buffalo real estate man William H. Talbert. Though higher education for women was still rare, and for black women rarer still, Mary Talbert earned a Ph.D. from the University of Buffalo. She served as president of the National Association of Colored Women's Clubs from 1916 to 1920, and was a delegate to the International Council of Women held in Norway. Where others had failed, Talbert raised the money to restore the Frederick Douglass home in Washington. Talbert was a vice-president and director of the National Association for the Advancement of Colored People. She is remembered most for her campaign against lynching. Organized racial terrorism began after the Civil War and continued in the South through much of the twentieth century. Talbert traveled throughout the country to speak to white and black audiences under the banner "A Million Women United to Suppress Lynching."

Of the many African-American causes that engaged Mary Talbert, one of the most interesting was the Niagara Movement, precursor to the NAACP. Talbert's colleague, the remarkable W. E. B. DuBois, helped found the Niagara Movement. A brilliant polemicist, activist, and sociologist, DuBois spent his long lifetime working on behalf of African-Americans. His last book appeared in 1963, when he was 93 years old. The events surrounding the founding of the Niagara Movement nearly sixty years before wrote an important chapter in the history of the national struggle for civil rights. In July 1905 DuBois called together a group of lawyers, ministers, teachers, and other college-educated people from what he termed the "talented tenth" of the African-American community. They were to meet at Buffalo.

A convention of the fraternal Elks had absorbed all the hotel space in Buffalo, and the delegates were forced to find another place to meet. Mary Talbert offered her home. After finding the hotels in Niagara Falls overflowing with Elks too, the delegates were obliged to cross the Niagara River, as so many fugitive slaves had done before, and convene at Fort Erie. DuBois charged that it was racism and not the Elks which kept them from meeting in Buffalo. The Niagara Movement's "Declaration of Principles" which issued from that meeting agitated for voting rights, free speech, and the repeal of Jim Crow laws. The document spoke forthrightly against the inequality of

economic opportunity that was the most important feature of the lives of American blacks.

The influential conservative black leader Booker T. Washington of Tuskeegee Institute was bitterly opposed to political action of any kind. He had declared that blacks and whites could live harmoniously if they lived separately, "like the fingers of the hand." He did all that he could in the black community to frustrate the aims of

the Niagara Movement. In black papers sympathetic to Booker T. Washington there was no mention of the Niagara Movement. By 1909, plagued by debt and torn by faction in the black community, the Niagara Movement had dissipated. Its successor, the NAACP, founded from the failure of the Niagara Movement, would be more enduring and effective. *Mary B. Talbert Collection, courtesy Buffalo and Erie County Historical Society*

Mary Talbert

Native Americans

The need for a narrative closure in our histories has often meant that Native Americans seem to disappear into the mists. After the years of dramatic conflict with white settlers, there has seemed to be little need to mention Indians save to chronicle the hard process of adjustment to modern life. In fact, Seneca culture is recently enjoying a rebirth.

A council House on the Tonawanda Reservation, near Newstead, 1885. Courtesy Jim Stapleton, Newstead Historical Society

Some Seneca traditions have persisted. Jesse Cornplanter, a descendant of the powerful antagonist Red Jacket, is shown here completing a copy of a false face mask. Real false faces, holy objects carved first into living trees, are invested with the spirits of the Iroquois Longhouse religion. These ceremonial objects continue to play a role in belief and ritual. Porterfield Collection, courtesy Buffalo and Erie County Historical Society

Children's Aid Society Collection, courtesy
Buffalo and Erie County Historical Society

Chapter Six

The Caring Impulse

by Scott Eberle

Civic responsibility was a heartfelt principle for nineteenth-century Americans. Sometimes it arose from professional concern, as, for instance, with physicians who became public health officials. But more often civic responsibility meant "Christian duty" and it coupled with the conviction that material progress was America's divine errand. Established citizens took a proud and paternal interest in the society they watched grow from frontier outpost to bustling hub of commerce and culture. In the Buffalo area these generous impulses created great universities and colleges, hospitals and charitable institutions, fine museums and libraries.

If the paternal activism of the nineteenth century seems careworn today, it is only because governments and courts have assumed responsibility for many areas of life that beforehand were the province of the individual, the family, the church, or a concerned elite. Whatever our complaints about the present though, it would be a mistake to romanticize this past, or try to make it simpler than it actually was. The relationship between caring people and those they care for has been uneasy. The enormous infusion of immigrants meant that helpers and helped often have come from different classes, religions, educational backgrounds or cultures.

In the history of this area it was often literally true that reformers and the people they hoped to reform did not speak the same language. In addition, benevolence in the nineteenth century shared all the earmarks of that time period, all its strengths, all its faults. To those who offered charity, the act was an unalloyed good, but it also imposed a burden.

Philanthropists felt themselves bound by the iron laws of nineteenth-century economics that warned of the moral danger in giving alms. When society's custodians were also reformers, they exerted a double measure of control and guidance. These are complicated relationships. The people helping and the people they help always and everywhere have different notions of the kind of assistance needed. Heartfelt responsibility sometimes earned sincere resentment. These tensions and strains in the social fabric are a vital part of our past.

From the very first, the caring impulse sought to bridge the gulf of language and culture. There were already two centuries of conflict between Europeans and Native Americans before the Revolutionary War. The relationship remained wary long after overt hostilities between Indians and white settlers ended. When the struggle shifted from the fight over control of territory to one of cultural survival, religion became an important battlefield. This is a melancholy story.

In 1792 Red Jacket, the wily Seneca war chief, complained of the encroachment of white missionaries on traditional beliefs. He wondered how they could claim the superiority of one devotion over another when Christians continually squabbled and competed among themselves. "You say there is but one way to worship and serve the great spirit," he said. But "if there is but one religion, why do you white people differ so much about it?" Somewhat mischievously Red Jacket continued, "why are not all agreed, as you can read the Book?" Like Christianity, Iroquois religion also had the force of custom and divine revelation. It was "given to our Fathers, and then handed down to us their children," he said. Red Jacket bitterly suggested that the Iroquois had but one solution: turn the missionaries "neck and heels out of doors." The "only aim of these malicious black coats," he said to a rival (a convert to Christianity named Seneca White) "is to enwrap us with their pretended displays of friendship that they may the more successfully practice their frauds and eventually lay us waste forever."

Though Red Jacket was correct about the erosion of Iroquois culture in the long run, this was not a fair judgment about Quaker missionaries who helped so much in the short term. Missionaries often acted as buffers between sharp-eyed agents like Gen. Peter B. Porter of Black Rock, and the Indian lands which lured them. The Ogden Land Company acquired the right to negotiate for Indian holdings, and in the infamous deal of 1826 gained much territory, including portions of the Buffalo Creek and Tonawanda reservations. One group of Seneca relocated to Kansas, where half their number perished. The rest returned, and others refused to move. Quaker missionaries, long active in the service of the Seneca, led a difficult fight to abrogate this treaty, and achieved a partial success in 1842.

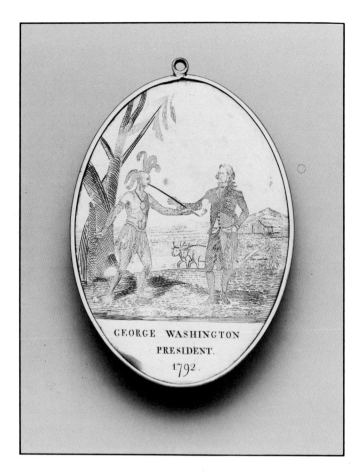

The fondest hope of the founding fathers was for Native Americans to settle and become agriculturalists. The medal that George Washington presented to Red Jacket sketches an ideal future. The transition was not easy. Holding on to Indian land was even more difficult. Courtesy Buffalo and Erie County Historical Society

Beside the constant pressure from land speculators to acquire Indian territory, missionary work was a more subtle threat to Native American tradition and tribal independence. They had extraordinary success in making converts. By 1830 nearly half the Senecas were practicing Christians. At the Seneca Mission at Buffalo Creek, the Rev. Asher Wright was also a conscious agent of change. He hoped to get the Seneca to "act the part of sober and respectable inhabitants of a civilized community." The opposition to conversion occasioned a decades-long tribal dispute that both sides understood as an ingredient of Seneca survival.

Few could have known this wrenching time better than Seneca White. He was an enthusiastic proponent of education and an important convert to Christianity. But he also knew the costs and discontents of civilization. Because change was so painful the Seneca had "been slow to adopt [white] habits of life." Holding on to the old ways, the Seneca were in danger of losing what was theirs. Their land continued to erode. The Treaty of Buffalo Creek ceded the reservation in 1839. White knew how desperate the position of the Iroquois was, and how urgent. He saw clearly that Indian power would shrink as they lost their land. He wrote to a sympathetic Quaker clergyman in 1840: "For a long time you have not ceased to persuade our people to encourage schools among us, you have told us

that our children should be instructed in the arts and the habits of civilized life; and our critical situation now shew us this necessity—for it is most true that we are in a painful dilemma. We fear that we may lose our country and our homes."

The Native Americans of Western New York were kept isolated on reservations by right of conquest, treaty and purchase. Americans of the nineteenth century were also acutely aware of another separate and dependent group, the millions of blacks held in slavery. Americans very often mourned the passing of Native American culture. Scruples over subduing the Indians and removing them from their land, though, rarely much detained Americans from their mission to conquer a continent. But slavery was more troublesome to the national conscience. This "peculiar institution" challenged the political assumptions (and eventually the very survival) of a democratic nation. America was also a deeply religious country, and slavery posed the most difficult moral problems of the last century. In the middle decades of the nineteenth century antislavery activists certainly felt "bound with slaves in their chains," and they wanted an end to slavery. But on what terms? Or whose timetable?

Waves of religious revival swept America in the 1830s. A number of groups expected that the second coming was imminent. In Buffalo, a rough and unholy canal town, prominent evangelists conducted their protracted camp meetings throughout that decade. Rural Erie County was more receptive. It was in the center of the "burned-over district" that the fires of revivalism were particularly intense. This religious sense of purpose, urgency, and seriousness extended also to social reform. Temperance campaigns took shape in the 1830s, as did the movements against prostitution. The antislavery crusade, the most important and longest lasting of these activisms, was a complicated mix.

It is somewhat surprising that most of the abolitionists we know by name (for example, Theodore Dwight Weld, William Lloyd Garrison etc.) began their careers in the 1830s in an organization called the American Colonization Society, which had important ties to Western New York. There is no question that this group believed deeply that slavery was evil and that it must eventually end. Mindful of the consequences of a schism between North and South, the colonizers looked for a solution not in emancipation of slaves, but in their expatriation. For this group there was no place for freed blacks in a post-slave-holding America. The group helped found the colony of Liberia for the purpose of "returning" free blacks to an African homeland most had never seen.

One of the most important local converts to the revivalist Christianity of the 1830s was Judge Samuel Wilkeson. Wilkeson had distinguished himself in the building of Buffalo harbor, and he became mayor of Buffalo in 1836. Already filled with civic spirit, Wilkeson was ignited by the preaching of the famous evangelist Charles Grandison Finney in 1831. He turned his substantial organizational skill and new found religious enthusiasm to rescuing the American Colonization Society from near bankruptcy in 1839. As chairman, Wilkeson also became editor of the *African Repository* where he articulated a benevolent vision (that we now also recognize as racist) of an America free of the scourge of slavery, but also, a country without resident blacks.

Eminent men shared his ideal; James Madison, Henry Clay, John Marshall, Daniel Webster. Like his colleagues in the Colonization Society Wilkeson was wealthy, conserva-tive, well connected, and socially activist. All these men tended to view the world as they viewed their cities, where the remedy for poverty was articulated in personal terms—hard work, upright morals, Christian devotion. They were convinced that Liberia could become an American mis-sionary outpost in Africa that would serve both to "uplift" freed slaves and Christianize the native population. "Everything in Liberia has a tendency to improve the condition of the people," Wilkeson said:

The mind cannot indeed free itself at once from the degrading associations which it has acquired in a condi-tion of slavery, but the *children* of the colonists grow up under the influence of free institutions, with the same consciousness of superiority to the uncivilized natives that the whites of this country feel to the negro.

At the beginning the Colonization Society was able to keep slaveholders and antislavery activists in its ranks. By the late 1830s however, the antislavery impulse was more clearly defined. Radical abolitionists believed slavery to be a grave sin, and declared that there could be no union with slaveholders. Black speakers commanded the attention of white audiences at abolitionist rallies in the North. Though it maintained an appeal for some, Wilkeson's Colonization Society seemed increasingly quaint as civil war seemed more and more a possibility.

Erie County was an important focus of the changed and quickened nationwide antislavery debate. In 1843 a national convention of antislavery activists met in Buffalo under the banner of the Liberty Party and nominated James G. Birney as their presidential candidate. In declaring their unconditional opposition to slavery, Liberty Party activists helped draw out the philosophical issue of slavery in a democracy. This helped to rule out middle-of-the-road solutions. And it predicted the extraordinary political disruptions of the 1850s. In the campaign of 1844 Birney garnered only a small proportion of the vote. But the importance of the Liberty Party does not stop with the election. It was, to use a modern phrase, a consciousness-raising experience.

In Erie County, Liberty Party regulars declared their "eternal hatred of slavery," and took to the stump to spread this work. At a Fourth of July celebration in 1844 in East Aurora the ex-slave Samuel Ringwold Ward was the keynote speaker. The audience later drank a sober cold-water toast to "Erie County: hers is the honor of having furnished the first colored juror and the first colored Fourth of July orator." In the last days of the campaign of 1844, Ward kept a punishing schedule speaking to audiences in Springville, Collins, Eden, Evans, Aurora, Alden, Lancaster, Clarence, Williamsville, Buffalo, Holland and Sardinia.

While the elders of Buffalo feared the political disrup-tion that the fight over slavery would cause, rural people were more likely to fear moral chaos. Quaker influence was strong in Orchard Park, and the Friends were some of the most vocal opponents of slavery. The historian Hilde-garde Graf pointed out that the feeling against slavery was more pronounced in rural Erie County than it was in the city. Erie county farmers were antislavery "almost to a man," she wrote. And to a woman we should add. While nineteenth-century proprieties demanded that women play a less public and political role (even in radical abolitionist circles) they were not without influence, urging their hus-bands, gathering relief supplies and lending their houses to aid fugitive slaves in the Underground Railroad. As guardians of the conscience and morality of nineteenth-century America, women played an essential, and often unsung, behind-the-scenes role.

The countryside of Erie County remained closer to the evangelical spirit that swept the "burned over" district in the 1830s. Evangelical Protestants were likely to consider slavery a sin, and a union with slaveholders sinful. So abolitionist sentiment was more pronounced in the county than it was in the city. The West Shore House in Clarence, built by William Spoor about 1810, served as an Underground Railway stop for fugitive slaves. *Courtesy Rollin C. Miller, Clarence Historical Society*

For fugitive slaves, the Michigan Avenue Baptist Church was the last stop on the Underground Railroad. Sheltered by sympathetic "conductors," fleeing blacks made their dangerous journey by way of Ohio and western Pennsylvania, along the shore of Lake Erie, or through the Southern Tier of counties to converge on the Buffalo area. Sometimes they were pursued by irate owners or slave catchers all the way here. A short ride down Michigan Avenue and the few hundred yards across the Niagara was all that separated them from freedom in Canada. Boat captains concealed and ferried these runaways by the tens of thousands.

On the question of slavery, prominent Buffalonians chose social order over moral fervor. The Rev. John C. Lord, friend of Millard Fillmore, and pastor of Central Presbyterian Church, was a noted opponent of abolitionism.

There is a higher authority for the determination of this question than anything we have yet suggested," Lord wrote. "The existence of domestic slavery was expressly allowed, sanctioned, and regulated by the Supreme Lawgiver in that divine economy which he gave the Hebrew State. Abolitionists must assume that we are wiser and better men than the Savior and the Apostles and that the government of God and the Gospel need revision . . .

Courtesy Buffalo and Erie County Historical Society

A fugitive slave himself, the abolitionist William Wells Brown helped ferry escaped blacks from Cleveland to Buffalo in the 1840s. Brown was also a novelist and playwright. One of his works, an anti-slavery drama, was staged at the Eagle Street Theater in Buffalo. The play was so charged with emotion that it provoked a small riot. As an agent for the Western New York Antislavery Society, Brown also raised his voice against Northern racial discrimination, for the temperance cause, women's suffrage, and prison reform. Courier-Express Collection, courtesy Buffalo and Erie County Historical Society

There is not a blacker crime, nor a fouler offence, than slave dealing and slavery.

Buffalo Emporium, *Sept. 25, 1824*

Political abolition, therefore, seems to us all evil, and abating in nothing of our abhorrence of slavery, or of our earnest desire to see it circumscribed within its appointed bounds and finally, we hope, extinguished utterly— we would disclaim all fellowship with those whose fanatical zeal would overthrow the constitution itself, and hazard the safety of the whole social edifice in the attempt to eradicate a single defect.

Commerical Advertiser, *September 1, 1843*

Millard Fillmore

*Millard Fillmore Collection, courtesy
Buffalo and Erie County Historical Society*

Millard Fillmore was one of the Americans most important to the unfolding drama of the problem of slavery. The things that troubled him troubled many more. Early in his career Millard Fillmore showed some public sympathy to the antislavery cause. Later his reservations were more private. The question of Fillmore's attitude toward slavery is a complicated one. For example, Fillmore angered Southerners by pardoning two men convicted under provisions of the Fugitive Slave Law. Fillmore's cousin was a secretary in the Freedmen's Aid Society, and the president privately gave him money to support fugitive slaves.

But the implications of the slavery debate for the nation always stood at the forefront of Fillmore's thinking. He was most interested in the preservation of the union, and the avoidance of the kind of bloody civil war that eventually consumed six hundred thousand American lives. A conservative in a radical decade, Fillmore wrote to Daniel Webster: "God knows that I detest slavery, but it is an existing evil for which we are not responsible, and we must endure it, and give it such protection as is guaranteed by the constitution, till we can get rid of it without destroying the last hope of free government in the world."

In 1850, he signed the Fugitive Slave Law which mandated the return of that human "property" to its "owner." To Fillmore this was a legal matter. "I have sworn to support the Constitution," he said, "and I know no higher law that conflicts with it." But in Buffalo some believed there was a "higher law." Fellow parishioners, (especially women) with strong antislavery sentiments refused to attend the same church services as Fillmore.

The caring impulse was subject to particular strain over the question of slavery. Fillmore's ethics admitted individual acts of private charity or intercession on behalf of individuals, but he worried, as did other conservative Buffalonians before and afterward, about the social implications of an unregulated lower class. Like other members of the American Colonization Society he believed a free black population would be an anomaly in this country. Would free states "consent to be burdened with such a population?" he asked. Would they be willing to "fill their poor houses and penitentiaries with the unfortunate, the helpless and the vicious?" Fillmore accepted the vice-presidency of the American Colonization Society in 1851, and remained interested for twenty years.

America, North and South, did fight its Civil War. It proved to be bloodier than even the most fearful had imagined. If the rights of black Americans were not insured by the defeat of the Confederacy, or their position in American life guaranteed, at least the question of slavery was settled. With the most pressing of causes apparently settled, much of the steam leaked out of the radical reform movements. The character of reform, especially in the cities, once again became protective, conservative, and preoccupied with the changes that were overtaking American life. For the most prominent of the reformers in Buffalo, there was no real interruption in their idea of how to bring about a just society.

Temperance was one of the most important of the nineteenth-century reformers' campaigns. The cause seems quaint now, but it should be remembered that, as in all pioneering societies, Americans of the early nineteenth century were heroic drinkers. Alcohol abuse was common. This is a question quite separate from the strained relations of the reformers and the (potentially) reformed. Teetotalers were mostly native born Protestants, immigrants were often Roman Catholic. Drink was an essential social lubricant, especially in the ethnic voluntary organizations. Feeling ran so high that a German publication of 1898 could still describe the campaign (which began in 1850) in this sarcastic way. "A number of Christian women tried to shorten the Germans' joyful times and to convert the 'wicked' people to temperance." They picked St. Patrick's day to begin their campaign, angering the Irish too. The fight against temperance was mainly German though. Calling the campaigners "narrow minded hypocrites," and disparaging their version of Christianity, the Germans made anti-temperance a voting issue. Courtesy Buffalo and Erie County Historical Society

NIAGARA Temperance House,

FORMERLY

BENNET'S TEMPERANCE HOUSE,

Junction of Pearl, Terrace and Commercial Streets,

NEAR THE LIBERTY POLE,

Carriages in readiness to convey Patrons and their baggage to and from the House (Sabbaths excepted), *free of charge.*

☞ Passengers arriving in the Eastern Cars, will find our Sign at the Depot, where they will please place their baggage.

BOARD....$1,00 PER DAY.

JOHN H. BAYLEY, } Proprietors.
D. B. HULL,

BUFFALO, 1850.

Steam Press of Jewett Thomas & Co., Com. Adv. Buildings, Buffalo.

Together with "sixty of Buffalo's most courageous women" Harriet Townsend founded the Buffalo Women's Educational and Industrial Union in 1884. She was its president and driving force until 1905. She was an advocate of what historians have called "domestic feminism." So much has happened since to change women's roles that "domestic feminism" now seems to be a contradiction in terms. In this movement the caring "womanly" virtues were gathered to do good, to protect women in the workplace, to find them jobs, to train women in "some wage earning occupation," and to "Americanize" servants. Under Townsend's direction the organization fought for kindergartens for children, physical education for girls, and female matrons for jailed women. "There is no end to the necessities of a true woman's life," she said, "we cannot measure them or measure the power of her influence." Courtesy University Archives, State University of New York at Buffalo State Photographic Archives

In this unusual photograph, philanthropist Maria Love indulged some humor at her own expense. She appears dressed for a costume ball as Queen Elizabeth. From an elite Buffalo family, Love was a staunch Episcopalian, and a member of the Daughters of the American Revolution. Mabel Dodge, the rebel of Buffalo society, described her as "cold, regal, and self-assured." But Love was also one of the most prominent adherents to the "Social Gospel," a brand of late nineteenth-century Protestantism that was fervently humanitarian, and interested in the solution to urban problems, especially poverty. For Maria Love, as for many progressives, "Christian duty" and "democracy" were aspects of the same morality. Courtesy Buffalo and Erie County Historical Society

The demands of the costly war spurred industrial growth. Buffalo's first iron furnaces date from this era. This was an economy largely unregulated by government. It lurched wildly between excited boom and furious bust. In 1873 overbuilding in railroads caused the financial empires and railroad baronies to collapse like matchstick houses. The rest of the economy fell in the same crash. Workers, many of them newly immigrated, bore a particularly heavy burden. Discontent ended in revolt. In the depths of this depression a railroad strike grew to become the Great Upheaval of 1877. Workers disrupted national transportation and communication networks, or ran them themselves. Buffalo was the scene of pitched battles. Thoughtful people worried that the foundations of the republic might have been built on shifting sand.

Some fifty benevolent groups were active in the Buffalo area in the later nineteenth century. In the year of the great strike Buffalo's philanthropists bonded together in the Charity Organization Society to help alleviate the searing urban pauperism of that depression. In doing so they hoped to shore up a faltering polity. It was the first such organization in America.

The history of the Charity Organization Society—ambitious in its intentions, revealing in its limitations—is one of the best ways to examine the relationship between classes, or between immigrants and established groups. The Rev. S. Humphreys Gurteen was the architect of this "clearinghouse." He meant to bring efficiency and accountability to almsgiving. For Gurteen, pauperism posed a threat to "safety in life and property." If left unchecked, the result of pauperism would be class war. Like other humanitarian reformers of the gilded age he had no means of understanding "pauperism" save in personal

Rev. S. Humphreys Gurteen. Courtesy Buffalo and Erie County Historical Society

terms. By accident, illness or other calamity, good people might find themselves impoverished. All other poverty was unacceptable, since it was tied to some moral failing. The "undeserving poor" sometimes faced arrest for vagrancy or neglect on the report of a COS committee. Those who dispensed charity were committed to the idea that there was an iron law of almsgiving. If accepting charity corrupted, unlimited charity corrupted absolutely.

By Gurteen's calculations as much as half of all relief was wasted on the undeserving, "carried off by the imposter and the fraud." Among these were the large number of people who depended on labor that was intermittent or seasonal. This was a "crying evil" to Gurteen. But the evil lay not where we might think—in the built-in underemployment of grain shovelers and construction workers—but in their own bad habits, such as drinking, living in "vicious" neighborhoods, failing to make seasonal pay stretch through the year. Gurteen devised the "Buffalo Plan" to distinguish between the "honest poor" and the merely shiftless.

Humanitarian concerns were never far from sectarian considerations in the efforts of the Roman Catholic diocese to address the problem of urban poverty. During the 1870s Catholic authorities worried that the active recruiting by the "sending societies" (which raised agricultural labor for the American West) would leave boys in the care of Protestant farmers. Economic depressions, like the one which began in 1893 and lasted five years, only increased these tensions. Confronted with an army of ten thousand unemployed (many of them ethnic Poles, Irish, and Italians) the Catholic Church distributed relief supplies without consulting the mostly Protestant COS.

St Pauls Episcopal in 1884

We might expect the older, established, Delaware Avenue churches like St. Paul's Episcopal to be the most conservative. Instead, they were the carriers of the liberal Christian movement called the "Social Gospel." In the 1890s as other churches moved farther away from downtown, these churches came into closest contact with poor people. Prominent ministers, like the assistant rector of St. Paul's, Stephen Humphreys Gurteen, realized that as long as their churches were viewed as islands of wealth, unconcerned with the sea of poverty around them, their preaching could have little appeal to the working class. At the same time they stood solidly behind honest government and civic reform. Roy W. Nagle Collection, courtesy Buffalo and Erie County Historical Society

113

The most conservative of humanitarian reformers frowned upon "outdoor relief" such as was available at this soup kitchen. Courtesy Buffalo and Erie County Historical Society

One of the most remarkable stories in the history of Buffalo's charitable institutions belongs to Nelson H. Baker. Baker was ordained a Roman Catholic priest in 1876, but he began his career as a partner in one of Buffalo's successful feed and grain companies. Horrified by the poverty that attended the depression of 1873, Baker helped feed the destitute and "wayward" Catholic boys in the care of his friend the Rev. Thomas Hines. In 1888 Father Baker built Our Lady of Victory Home in Lackawanna where he hoped to "remove the sting of prison life" from the institutions which cared for poor and orphaned urban children.

Accustomed to the driver's seat, Baker is shown here front and right, ahead of the boys band. The merchant turned priest engineered a worldwide fund-raising campaign. The "Our Lady of Victory Association" gathered donations in nickels, dimes and quarters. His businessman's luck held so often in times of financial crisis that the most devout of his admirers have detected divine guidance, and hope for canonization. In 1891 he persuaded the bishop to invest in drilling for natural gas. The well yielded three thousand dollars of free heat per year. Operations in the Father Baker complex have since expanded to include a hospital, and a modern facility for the care of emotionally handicapped children. Consecrated in 1926, the Basilica that Baker built dominates the skyline of Lackawanna. Courtesy Baker Hall

Father Baker in the Driver's seat Basilica. Courtesy Baker Hall

Charity Organization Society volunteers—in the main, women of prominent families—monitored the habits of those registered in the police "poor books." In "friendly visits" they encouraged the formation of "provident habits," and "provident ideas." These were not indiscriminate ladies bountiful though: they did not hand out aid personally but acted as agents, disqualifying the lazy, the profligate, and the inebriate. Even the "deserving poor" were likely to be corrupted by charity if it was given carelessly. They accepted it at their peril. As Gurteen put it they ran the risk of "shooting the moral Niagara of Beggary, and disappearing into the ruin beyond."

We are likely to find the methods (and the assumptions) of the COS jarringly paternalist and old-fashioned. But the organization was also quite modern in one regard—however frequently it echoed the Social Gospel, this unsentimental organization was a secular bureaucracy. It forbade proselytizing because it found the queen of virtues too easily abused when compassionate missionaries scented a conversion. The group strictly avoided religious, political or national identity as a basis for dispensing aid. "There must be no sentiment in the matter," Gurteen said, "it must be treated as a business scheme if success is to attend its operations." This experiment in Buffalo was the beginning of professional social work.

Physicians were another caring group that became much more "professional" over the course of the nineteenth century. This was partly the result of a better understanding of the mechanisms of disease. Medical science got more scientific. But, to an astonishing degree, the history of medicine in the nineteenth century is not just the history of technological advance. The practice of medicine takes place upon individuals in society, and so, inevitably, it is intimately tied to the social questions and political disputes of the day. Buffalo is one of the best places to examine this process.

Healing physicians were by no means unanimous in their theories of the causes of disease. Was disease a measure of the vices of the patient? Was it linked to the intemperance of immigrants and foreigners? Did epidemic sickness arise from bad air? Was it contagious? Physicians could not agree. They were in even less agreement over appropriate treatment. The bitterest and most public disputes, however, took place over who had the right to call himself a doctor.

Buffalo's Social Service Buildings. Courtesy Buffalo and Erie County Historical Society

The Buffalo Board of Health. From the Collection, courtesy Buffalo and Erie County Historical Society

From the influential platform of the Buffalo Medical Journal, *Austin Flint educated generations of American doctors and helped to shape the "conservative" school of medical practice. During Flint's career, doctors became increasingly good at diagnosis, and much more familiar with anatomy. Surgical technique improved too. But physicians could do almost nothing for chronic and infectious diseases. Without a reliable theory of how sickness arose, or a consistent and workable stock of drugs, they were not good at cure. Flint's principal contribution in his earlier career may have been to restrain American doctors in their helplessness. He hoped to "conserve" the vital energies of the patient by avoiding the draining therapies of regular medicine. Preferred treatments like bloodletting and purging did so much to weaken people who were already sick. While his colleagues prescribed heroic doses of calomel for their unfortunate patients, or bled them to the point of unconsciousness, Flint treated tuberculosis with plenty of fresh air, and whiskey in quantity. If cure eluded them, at least they were tanned and giddy. Courtesy Medical Library, State University of New York at Buffalo*

Ebenezer Johnson, from the Collections, courtesy Buffalo and Erie County Historical Society

Regular doctors long held positions of importance in Buffalo. Two of the first five mayors were physicians. Drs. Ebenezer Johnson and Josiah Trowbridge were appointed to the post because of the natural respect due them. It is perhaps fortunate that they were. The largest challenge of Ebenezer Johnson's term as Buffalo's first mayor in 1832 was not political, it was the question of public health. It was in that year that a worldwide epidemic of cholera spread for the first time to the village of Buffalo and its neighborhood. Poorly drained areas like the flats, the area across Buffalo Creek, and the warehouse district were particularly hard hit. The disease recurred in 1834, though less fiercely. The tasks of caring for the sick and dying, burying the dead, and warning off ships and coaches taxed the meager resources of a town of ten thousand people. Trowbridge became the first president of the Buffalo Medical Society in 1845. Cholera again stalked the Niagara Frontier four years later.

Josiah Trowbridge, Roy W. Nagle Collection, courtesy Buffalo and Erie County Historical Society

117

The most dramatic of medical stories of the nineteenth century was the periodic scourge of the "asiatic" cholera which visited Western New York three times. Austin Flint was on hand for the epidemic of 1832, and played an important role when the disease raged again in 1849. By 1866, when cholera reappeared in force for the last time (though not so strongly in Buffalo) Flint had become one of the most famous physicians in the country. Later in the century he helped confirm European discovery of the bacterial origin of disease. At midcentury, as cholera stalked the world, there was no such confidence.

In the summer of 1848 physicians watched as the disease spread through revolution-torn Europe, and they awaited the outbreak in Buffalo. The first case was recorded in May of 1849. Five terrible months followed before frost inhibited the spread of the disease. Flint urged physicians to acknowledge their "utter ignorance of the essential nature" of cholera. When the epidemic had run its course, one case out of three had proved fatal. Twenty-five hundred cases were recognized, and in a city of under forty thousand, eight hundred and fifty people had died. Doctors could do little but tend the sick, manage the dying, and safely bury the dead. The authorities were so busy at the height of the epidemic that the board of health issued a special directive that burials wait twenty-four hours after death because of the danger of premature interment.

Even organizing a board of health was a difficult proposition because there was not just one undivided medical profession. Homeopaths competed with Thompsonians, who competed with eclectics, who competed with midwives, who competed with regular doctors.

When regular doctors came to think about what caused epidemic disease they inclined toward environmental factors. In this they best reflected the prevailing opinion of their times. Like other "gentlemen of property and standing" who were guided by the caring impulse, they tended to see causes where we see effects. They noticed that disease struck its heaviest blows near the canal, at the county poorhouse, and in those sections of the city that "abounded most in poverty and vice." It is now known that cholera spreads in crowded conditions where sanitation is poor. But during most of the nineteenth century doctors did not have the benefit of microbiology, or even a persuasive theory of contagion. They saw cholera as a social disease.

For those who had vaguely feared the "dangerous lower classes" the midcentury visitation seemed to provide a concrete basis for that fear. Weakened and depressed by the ocean crossing, anxious, impoverished, "ignorant and reckless," as one physician put it, immigrants seemed to be a prime target for disease. Another doctor said that the floating population of foreign laborers, combined with "the usual population of the laboring classes and the devotees of vice" made Buffalo particularly susceptible. The *Buffalo Medical Journal* editorialized that "the disease, for the most part, has been confined to those who, from insalubrity of situation, bad habits, and social position, are particularly exposed." The German laborers of "notoriously intemperate habits," and those who lived near Rock Street, Genesee and "the Hydraulics," were especially at risk.

Austin Flint, the preeminent theorist of the nineteenth century, was one of the founders of the University of Buffalo's Medical College. The second home of the school, at Main and Virginia streets was in use from 1849 to 1893. Courtesy University Archives, State University of New York at Buffalo

Homeopathic physicians, followers of the German physician Samuel Hahnemann, were denounced by regular physicians. Their methods had a countercultural feel even in the nineteenth century. They enjoyed a thriving practice in spite of the charges regular doctors leveled at them. During the cholera epidemic of 1849 thirty-two homeopaths ministered to the sick in Buffalo. They squabbled among themselves, however. Austin Flint, most prominent of regular doctors in Buffalo in the nineteenth century, reported that during the cholera epidemic, they fought "like Kilkenny cats." If the concoctions they administered did no good (because they were administered in such small doses) they also did little harm. Homeopaths resented the regular physicians. Regular doctors were wealthier and dominated the politically powerful Board of Health, but they had no better idea of how to cure epidemic disease.

Medical doctors had, by and large, abandoned the grosser tools of bloodletting, blistering, and scarring by 1860, but the homeopathic charge that one could be "doctored to death" found many sympathizers.

Their notions that "like cures like" and that medicines became more effective as the dosage decreased, were very medieval and

unscientific, of course. Nevertheless, their appeal was so widespread that the state of New York licensed them in 1857. The effect of these medicines administered in "infinitessimal" doses was mild, or even undetectable. To women who nursed small children, it was important to avoid the harsh purges and "pukes" administered by other medical sects. Homeopaths were still in practice in 1872 when their association opened a hospital at Washington Street and North Division. Buffalo's Homeopathic College appears here in a photograph taken in 1880. "Infinitessimals" photograph by Thomas Payne. Courtesy Buffalo and Erie County Historical Society

Over the next two decades theories of the origin of cholera multiplied. Most doctors believed that it was contageous in some way or other. But contagion was not thought to be sufficient to foster the disease. There were still predisposing causes. "The disease attacks, for the most part, only those who in some way provoke it," editorialized the *Buffalo Medical and Surgical Journal.* "The other portion of the community suffer it, if at all mainly from being found in bad company."

The doctors' recommendations for avoiding cholera were as much a program of moral uplift as they were a prescription for better health. As the "pestilence" again moved west in 1866 the *Buffalo Medical and Surgical Journal* outlined the precautions which citizens might take. In Buffalo, where there was one saloon for every fifteen adult residents, there was plenty of opportunity to be "imprudent" as the doctors put it. Prudent people could keep themselves and their property scrupulously clean and their houses well ventilated, they should clean their gutters and privies, they should avoid crowding, they should value temperance above all, and eat moderately, they should pursue a "regularity of life and habits," maintaining their equanimity and cheerfulness. Avoiding cholera seemed, in many respects, like avoiding sin.

The poverty of theory about the origin of cholera actually contributed to the cleaning up of the city. At the time of the last (and least severe) cholera epidemic in Buffalo in 1866, half the doctors in America still believed that poisoned air was the "exciting cause" of the cholera. The answer? Eliminate the source. Clean up the fermenting garbage and reeking sewage, and so do away with the miasma that arose from it, and cholera would be less likely to spread. By the 1890s there was a growing movement to turn over the care of the city to professionals engineers to pave the streets and construct sewer systems doctors to supervise public health. By the turn of the century medicine shaded into reform.

Buffalo Lithia Water

Even before the germ theory of disease was widely accepted, people had a notion that good water was curative. Buffalo Lithia Water purported to possess "Marvelous efficiency in Gout, Rheumatism and Gastro-Intestinal Dyspepsia." Marketers claimed the endorsement of the personal physician of the pope. From the Collections, Courtesy Buffalo and Erie County Historical Society

Aromatic Disinfector

The aromas of the nineteenth-century city
would assault modern senses. Standards of
cleanliness gradually rose, especially after
the germ theory of disease gained currency
in the 1870s. When bad smells couldn't be
eliminated, they might be masked. Courier
Express Collection, *courtesy Buffalo and
Erie County Historical Society*

In 1881 the president of the board of
managers of the Buffalo Insane Asylum
allowed that the plan of the Richardson
Building might be "unnecessarily elaborate
and expressive," but "in all the essential
requisites of a hospital for the insane, it has
no superior in any country." The institution was also a model of humane psychiatric
practice. Funded by the county and state,
officials made room for the indigent insane,
and arranged for a sliding scale of fees to be
assessed on the ability to pay. Construction
of the building proceeded alongside a
revolution in pyschiatric thought. The
Buffalo Medical and Surgical Journal
declared that "modern pathology has
transformed the Insane Asylum from a
prison for individual restraint to a hospital
for the scientific treatment of patients."
That particular medical revolution was not
to last beyond the turn of the century.
*Roy W. Nagle Collection, courtesy Buffalo
and Erie County Historical Society*

Old medical ideas survive in unexpected ways. The notion that bad smells caused disease could still be detected indirectly as late as 1890 when local philanthropists founded the "Fresh Air Mission." City children lived their lives mostly in the inadequately drained streets. Primitive sewage systems, hit-and-miss garbage collection, and the accumulated wastes of transport animals contributed to the foul and unhealthy atmosphere of nineteenth century Buffalo. Located at Cradle Beach near Angola, about thirty miles from Buffalo on Lake Erie, the Fresh Air Mission hosted four hundred children in the summer of 1891. Roy W. Nagle Collection, courtesy Buffalo and Erie County Historical Society

This retouched photo from the turn of the century speaks of reality and hope. City children in the Cradle Beach wagon are part of the real photograph. They squint into the sun. One has to be carried. At the bottom, four idyllic figures are drawn in. They illustrate a belief in the restorative power of the countryside. Charity organizations continued to be moved to action by the neglect and deprivation of city children. "The Children's Friend" from 1916

pictures a street scene that could easily describe conditions fifty years earlier.

Cradle Beach half photo/half painting. Roy W. Nagle Collection, courtesy Buffalo and Erie County Historical Society

THE CHILDREN'S FRIEND

Published Quarterly
by the
Children's Aid and Society for the Prevention of Cruelty to Children
of Erie County, New York

Vol. I · · · BUFFALO, AUGUST, 1916 · · · No. 4

SUMMER IN THE STREETS

Increase of Work—Rapid Growth of Society.

The summer months are again bringing an increased number of complaints involving child neglect. A reduction in the number of complaints is usually expected

family was brought into court. Both children were suffering from severe cases of rickets and statements from three physicians showed that under-nourishment and neglect had brought on this physical condition which unless relieved at once would leave the children crippled for life. The court committed both children to the care

The growth in the power of Democratic machine politics during the 1870s and 1880s gave immigrant groups in Buffalo easier access to the the benefits of the political system. In the absence of a real welfare system ward supervisors held out a small but important safety net—finding homes or jobs for immigrants, easing their way into a new country. All for a price of course, a percentage of wages, or the promise of a vote. By modern measures these useful arrangements were corrupt. And they alarmed the established citizenry with the specter of rising political power in groups that held no property.

During the 1890s, the heyday of reform in Buffalo, concerned men and women founded the Citizens Association, the Liberal Club, the Municipal Ownership League, and the Civil Service Reform Association. Their farsighted program envisioned government where jobs were dispersed by merit, not patronage, and a city where municipal services, such as trash collection and mass transit, would be administered evenly and efficiently as a public trust. It was the fervent hope of these reformers that government could be run in a businesslike way by experts rather than by political appointees.

One of these reformers, the prominent lawyer Frank Loomis, stated this principal most baldly. "Municipal government is business, not politics," he said. The result of reform would be a better run, more centralized, but less "democratic" government. These people were not outsiders, but they were not politicians either. They preferred to work for change from without, wielding influence. Theodore Roosevelt, who was schooled in the most difficult politics in the country, ridiculed these good government clubs, calling them "goo-goos" and "fool reformers" for their reluctance to engage in the "hurly-burly" of the democratic system.

History rarely divides easily into good or bad. In a city with a past as complex as Buffalo's, this is particularly true. In the 1880s and 1890s the effort to make government more efficient and less corrupt could not be separated from the prevailing unpleasant tendency toward "nativism"— the deep and systematic mistrust of foreigners. The substantial men of the community behind the reform movements (businessmen, lawyers, ministers) were mostly of old Yankee stock, and nearly all were Protestant. It is easy to appreciate why they felt overwhelmed by the new immigration. By 1900 nearly three of every four people living in Buffalo had been born in a foreign country. As old-line residents envisioned it, reform would come at the expense of the entrenched party machines, especially the Democratic machine that was dominated by immigrants.

Other countries with more restricted democratic traditions had little philosophical problem limiting access to power. Tradition and custom sanctioned priviledge. England, for example, maintained property qualifications for voting throughout the nineteenth century. But the United States was founded on egalitarian principles and universal (white) manhood suffrage. Because they had access to government, the foreign born represented a threat to establishment power. Reaction set in. Andrew D. White, a speaker at the Liberal Club in 1893, suggested that only property owners should be allowed to vote. The city ought to be run by "those who created it, who have a title to it, or a real substantial part in it." Otherwise "virtual control" might be seized by "a crowd of illiterate peasants, freshly raked in from Irish bogs, or Bohemian mines, or Italian robber nests." It is no coincidence that there was not even one civil service reformer with a Polish or Italian name.

However large was the problem that unassimilated immigrants posed for reformers, few of them thought that the situation was beyond remedy. If they held no hope for the "crowd of illiterate peasants" there was hope for the next generation. It was here that Buffalo made a significant contribution. In the words of one prominent progressive, Buffalo's effort to reform the public schools "made history" in the 1890s.

"Efficiency" and "uplift" became the watchwords of this drive. Activists pioneered a number of programs. They hoped that a vocational education, or manual training, would help produce an educated working class more independent of boss, *padrone* (and as was sometimes openly admitted) union control. Free textbooks, another innovation of that decade, made education more available to poor families. Reformers also fought truancy, high among the immigrant children. They helped to establish kindergartens in impoverished Irish and Italian neighborhoods. Night schools taught English to Italians and Poles and inculcated "American" values, of thrift, cleanliness, hard work and patriotism.

The most visible achievement of the reformers was the adoption of a new city charter in 1891. But high hopes for reform quickly were quashed in the practical business of operating a complicated city. The reformed city government of the 1890s was rocked by prosecutions for election fraud, charges of political control of the Police Department and the Department of Public Works, and scandals in letting out contracts for pumping and garbage collection. A student of this period, historian Brenda Shelton, concluded that despite the reforms, "municipal politics was still politics, not business."

The Children's Friend. From the Collections, courtesy Buffalo and Erie County Historical Society

Ansley Wilcox

Wealthy and powerful men like John Milburn, James Putnam, John Graves, and Ansley Wilcox founded the group called the Liberal Club in 1891. These reformers openly worried that democracy would be unable to withstand the influx of immigrant voters. Class tensions were brought to light by the effort to revise the Buffalo city charter in 1890. The Buffalo News of March 6, 1890, denounced the reformers as a "clique of social leaders who could not be elected, under manhood suffrage, to anything." Courtesy Buffalo and Erie County Historical Society

John Milburn

Mrs. John C. Lord.

Mrs. J. C. Lord and Smallweed

As a contemporary account had it, Mrs. Lord's "devotion to the dumb creation was strongly marked. Every act of cruelty in the streets made her heart sick." In this hustling commercial town where draft animals were often worked beyond their capacity, Mrs. Lord had plenty of *opportunity to show how much she cared. In the 1860s and 1870s she became the scourge of teamsters in the streets of Buffalo. As was the case for her husband, the Rev. J. C. Lord, the style of caring was direct and individual—"she knew no remedy except personal interference." She would herself block the way of a driver who had forced his horses to pull a load that was* *too heavy. In a cap strikingly out of date, and usually accompanied by her miniature collie Smallweed, Mrs. Lord was prepared to face down a swearing driver if it took hours for a fresh team to be brought, or for the load to be lightened. The photograph appears in a stained glass window at the Buffalo and Erie County Historical Society. Photograph by Thomas Payne*

Mrs. Lord's guerrilla tactics against animal abusers may strike us as romantic, quaint and, oh, so Victorian. But the hope that cruelty was preventable and undesirable indicated that an important psychological change had taken place. Compare this broadside from 1827. It advertised the earliest instance of a staged event that was to recur over the middle decades of the nineteenth century. Impresarios were given to exaggeration, and onlookers were almost certainly disappointed that there were no exotic animals aboard. The "vicious and worthless" curs that were sent over Niagara Falls in a burning, leaky boat were the butts of the ancient sense of humor that enjoyed bear baiting, cock fighting, and other comic ritual dismemberments. Occasionally familiar, the past can often be a foreign country. What once was funny is now horrifying. Courtesy Buffalo and Erie County Historical Society

ALMSHOUSE

Buffalo's original almshouse (built in 1828) stood at Porter and Fargo. The Buffalo Medical Journal condemned it as that "great lazar house." Abandoned children left there, those "little offsprings of misfortune and crime," had a life expectancy of only four weeks. A new building was constructed in 1851 and rebuilt in 1855 after a fire. That structure, pictured here, still stands on the Main Street Campus of the University of Buffalo. Criticisms about the conditions there did not abate. Underfeeding of the inmates was the most frequent charge. One critic said that it was "worse than anything which Dickens ever described." The board of supervisors refuted the criticism, but also acknowledged that "no one . . . would pretend that the diet of a poorhouse should be so inviting as to induce idlers and profligates to seek its hospitality at the public expense." Courtesy University Archives, State University at Buffalo

Located between Swan and Michigan Streets, the Fitch Institute was endowed in 1879 by philanthropist Benjamin Fitch. One of its most innovative services was the Fitch Creche, a day care center for working mothers. Courtesy Buffalo and Erie County Historical Society

William Pryor Letchworth shaped the role of the State Board of Charities and became one of the most vigilant watchdogs of the systems of poor relief. A practical man, Letchworth was more enthusiastic about private charity than public, because he believed that money was easier to raise for private institutions. These organizations needed watching. Placing children for adoption with families was much preferable to keeping them in at public expense in poorhouses, but there were still dangers. Children had been placed with neglectful parents, or with prostitutes. Letchworth launched an audit of adoptions. He noticed that most requests for children came from farms in outlying communities. In 1886 he wryly observed that "the applicant who asks for a child well matured, and examines his muscles as he would feel the legs of a horse he thought of purchasing, is not a desirable guardian for a child."

Growing up meant going to school. The cultural life of the Niagara Frontier is boosted by its colleges and universities. The University of Buffalo was a private institution until 1962. Until then it depended on the support of local philanthropic groups. Women were most active in the spectacularly successful development campaign that raised $5 million during the beginning of October 1920. Julian Park, the university's chronicler, said of the effort: "In ten days a comparatively unknown and poverty-stricken university acquired funds, friends by the thousands and international fame." Courtesy University Archives, State University of New York at Buffalo

127

Rural Holland had its tannery, cheese factory, planing mill, blacksmith and wagon shop, and furniture store. Fire took its toll of business and industry there. In 1896, the first volunteer fire company was chartered, and soon the fire hall shown was erected at a cost of three hundred dollars. For a while it was used as a meeting place for the town board. The downstairs is now rented by the Holland Historical Society for meetings and storing displays. Courtesy Holland Historical Society

Chapter Seven

Growing Up and Out

by Scott Eberle and Joseph Grande

Between the Civil War and World War I Western New York experienced a phenomenal boom. Railroads, iron and steel making, milling, metal working, machine manufacturing, lumbering, sugar making, dyemaking, ship building and hydropower generation were just a few of the industries that fueled an economic blast-off throughout the country and particularly in Buffalo. A ravenous need for strong backs, dexterous hands, and good minds attracted a population in Buffalo that leaped from eighty-one thousand in 1860 to half a million by 1920. Buffalo became the eleventh largest city in the country.

The burgeoning city and the outlying towns and villages needed to adapt or invent all the things we take for granted that make our lives organized and comfortable. Conveniently getting from here to there, buying fresh food, finding livable houses, providing police and fire protection, encouraging greater safety in industry and commerce, all this required great changes, most of which derived from late nineteenth-century revolutions in transportation, food distribution, and city planning.

The boom was also social, cultural and political. By World War I Buffalo was profoundly changed; in many ways it had grown up. City government had experienced significant reform. An educational system responded to the enormous demand placed on it by foreign immigration. Throughout the country social services and hospital care became more sophisticated. Medical innovation and public health measures allowed people to depend on a more normal life span. Women emerged as consumers and campaigned for voting rights. Universities, colleges and museums elevated the cultural life of the city. One of the great international fairs, the Pan-American Exposition, announced to the world that Buffalo was no longer only a rough-and-tumble canal town. The city had arrived.

Early twentieth-century mail service in Holland was by horse and buggy. Shown about 1910 is mailman George Allen, who lived on Olean Road near the northeast end of the village. Courtesy Holland Historical Society

The newly incorporated city of Tonawanda, shown in 1910 on Niagara Street along the Erie Canal, was a thriving lumber town. Not only were millions of feet of sawed lumber shipped eastward on the Erie Canal, but millions of white pine shingles of all shapes and sizes, as well as pieces of wood lath, were manufactured for export. Other industries had also been attracted to the booming little city. There were a pipe works, a pump works, several brickyards, a machine shop, a brewery, a cider-vinegar and yeast works, and several boat builders. One of the best known boatyards was the one operated by Ira M. Rose, where mule-drawn lumber carriers were built until 1905, when it was sold to William Follette, who built steam-powered canal boats until 1912. Some canal boats made Tonawanda their home port, among them the William Hengerer, *a name eventually familiar to Western New Yorkers as a major Buffalo department store until it was sold in the 1980s. Courtesy Tonawanda-Kenmore Historical Society*

The first big manufacturing business in Alden was Moffat's Tannery, started in 1882, where both local and foreign hides were processed. The oak bark used in the process was obtained locally or shipped in by freight. It was stored on the lot next to the tannery and piled to look like a building. A steam whistle blew at six o'clock in the morning to awaken the workers, most of whom came to work by horse and wagon. It sounded again at seven to start work, at noon for lunch, and at five-thirty to end the workday. Courtesy Norma M. Sweet, Alden Town Historian

130

Rumors abounded in 1895 that the state legislature would divide Erie County in two, creating a county of Buffalo including the city and several northern towns. The remainder of the county would then need a new county seat. The town fathers of Lancaster, boasting that their town had the largest grist mill and brickyard in the county and the only high school outside of Buffalo, authorized this new town hall with its tower rising 110 feet into the sky. The division of Erie County never materialized, and the hall was much larger than needed for government purposes. While government offices occupied the first floor, the upper floors became a theater and meeting hall serving area citizens. The first play performance there was on June 7, 1895, when a comedy, The Old District School, was staged. Because there was no electricity in the building, the performance was lit by a string of lights hooked to the trolley lines outside. After years of disrepair, the Lancaster Opera House theater was restored in the 1970s and was reopened with a regular schedule of entertainment. Courtesy Dr. Harley E. Scott, Lancaster Town Historian

Life in the village of Lancaster was typical of small-town life around the county. Children and adults enjoyed the advantages of a quiet existence, working or attending school and enjoying social events in the pleasant surroundings of their community. This 1908 photograph shows the town hall in the background and young women standing on the dam of Mook's Mill, which was washed out by ice two years later. The women in the photograph are, left to right, Ella Follett, Louise Huber-Hennessy, and Ida Stukie-Huber. Anna Mook, whose family owned the mill, later became a teacher in Lancaster. Courtesy Dr. Harley E. Scott, Lancaster Town Historian

A Boom in Learning

As Erie County's population passed the half-million mark with a larger and larger percentage residing in the Buffalo urban core, education expanded to meet growing community needs. The state imposed compulsory-attendance laws, and in the countryside other legislation replaced school oversight by district commissioners with a system of district superintendents to run the schools. Rural schoolhouses expanded from one or two rooms to double the size. There already existed by 1870 a number of educational institutions such as the Springville Academy, the Lancaster Academy, the Aurora Academy, the Williamsville Classical Institute and the East Hamburg Friends Institute. As state laws encouraged district consolidation, some of these originally private schools became public to serve as the core of the new Union Free school districts.

Expansion and reorganization were the key trends in education in Buffalo as well as the rest of the county. In the city, an elected superintendent and a committee of the city council ran the school system, composed of elementary schools and one central high school, serving three-quarters of the city children. An evening school opened to meet the needs of older pupils working during the day. German language teachers were hired, and courses in art and music added. From 1893 to 1918, Superintendent Henry P. Emerson reformed the system to make it better able to serve the practical needs of the pupils of all social classes. He promoted Yankee values, citizenship, and job training. Courses were introduced in typing, manual training, sewing, mechanical arts and domestic science. Cooperating with the Chamber of Commerce and the trade unions, vocational high schools were established with Seneca High School in 1909 and three others in 1910. Meanwhile, Emerson labored to raise the quality of the teachers and improve the system of teacher supervision.

There were several small rural schools in the town of Tonawanda during the nineteenth century. At the corner of Brighton and Delaware roads stood School No. 4, where Ida Zimmerman taught the class shown in the photograph taken about 1890. Also shown is Kenmore's first school, the wooden Union School, located in the village triangle. Because of overcrowding, a new brick school was built across the street and opened in 1911. The old building was then sold to the village of Kenmore for ninety-five hundred dollars to be used as the village hall. It was torn down in 1936 to make way for the new municipal building which serves as a town-village hall. Courtesy Tonawanda-Kenmore Historical Society

Henry Pendexter Emerson, the superintendent of Buffalo schools from 1893 to 1916, was a flinty New Englander, and a canny politician. Educated at the University of Rochester, he was committed to "child-centered" education and was therefore a darling of local Progressives. Free textbooks, free medical care, a free-meal program, and the free lending library were among his innovations that made life easier for the three out of four pupils who were immigrants, or immigrants' children. Progressive social programs always had an element of control, however, and Emerson was also behind the "Americanization" programs in area schools which sought to detach immigrant children from their foreign roots. The hope for Americanization rarely extended to mixing immigrant schoolchildren with the native-born though. During Emerson's tenure school district lines were gerrymandered to conform to ethnic settlement. Courtesy Buffalo and Erie County Historical Society

Emerson joined the faculty of the Buffalo Central School and became its principal nine years later, by which time it was called Central High School. Shown is the 1891 senior class of that school during his principalship. The school tripled in size under his capable leadership, and in 1893, he was first elected superintendent of Schools by the people of Buffalo. During his long tenure, the schools expanded under his guidance to better serve the new industrial system of providing vocational, extension, and adult study. Roy W. Nagle Collection, courtesy Buffalo and Erie County Historical Society

Private education also experienced growth and change. The children of the well-to-do attended the Buffalo Female Academy, which in 1889 became the Buffalo Seminary. Soon came the Elmwood-Franklin School, the Nichols School, the Park School, and, under Episcopal sponsorship, St. Margaret's School. Catholics were served by an expanding system of parish elementary schools, where they were urged to send their children. Parochial schools in ethnic parishes instructed the children in the immigrant tongue. Consequently, a special English studies syllabus was prepared, aiming to make English the general language of instruction. A diocesan-wide course of studies was developed, as were standardized tests.

This system of parish schools was complemented by a number of private secondary institutions. By the dawn of the new century, these included such schools for girls as Holy Angels, Mt. St. Joseph, Nardin and Sacred Heart academies. For the boys, there were such schools as Canisius High School and St. Joseph's Collegiate Institute. The Catholic system was rounded out by such special institutions as St. Mary's School for the Deaf, which pioneered in vocational education as early as 1876 by introducing courses in shoemaking and printing.

Pioneering efforts in higher education were made with the establishment of the Buffalo Normal School to prepare elementary school teachers for the area. Buffalo School Superintendent J. S. Fosdick had convinced the city council to petition New York State for a normal school in 1866; and one year later, the state legislature responded favorably. With the help of businessman Jesse Ketchum, land was obtained on Buffalo's West Side, where the school was built and opened in 1871 with a student body of eighty-six. Twenty years later, over seven hundred students attended the institution. Just before the Buffalo Normal School

opened, German Jesuits, fleeing persecution in Germany, established the first Catholic college in Erie County, Canisius College.

The oldest institution of higher education in the county, the University of Buffalo, expanded from the medical school founded in 1846 to include schools of pharmacy, law, and dentistry. In 1905, University Chancellor Charles Norton led efforts to establish a liberal arts college supported by city funds. He joined community leaders and educators to petition the city council for $75,000, but despite broad popular support, opposition arose. When councilmen insisted on majority control of the new college's council, Norton turned to private benefactors. Department-store magnate Seymour Knox, Sr., came forward and generously donated $250,000 for the establishment of a new college of arts and sciences.

Prior to the opening of the College of Arts and Sciences, another college opened its doors on Buffalo's West Side. There the Grey Nuns of the Cross, originally brought from Ottawa, Canada, in 1857 by Bishop Timon, already operated Holy Angels Academy. Early in 1908, Bishop Charles Colton, outstanding for his interest in education, made known his desire that a college for women be added to the academy. He then applied to the New York Legislature for a college charter, and appropriate legislation was passed and signed by Governor Charles Evans Hughes on April 4, 1908. Nearly six months later, D'Youville College, named for the foundress of the Grey Nuns in eighteenth-century Montreal, held its first classes for nine young women. D'Youville became the first college for women in Western New York and the second oldest Catholic college in New York State. It originally concentrated its efforts on preparing secondary school teachers, later adding programs in business and social work.

Among the growing number of Catholic schools were specialized institutions to meet special needs. One such institution was established by the St. Mary's Benevolent Society for the Deaf and Dumb in 1857. The St. Mary's School for the Deaf was housed in the building shown, built in 1862, at Elmwood Avenue and Edward Street until the end of the century, when it moved to its present location at 2253 Main Street in Buffalo. It was the first school in Buffalo to offer trade classes, starting in 1876 by teaching shoemaking and printing. Classes produced the local Catholic newspaper for ten years. Both Catholic children and children of other denominations attended the school, where speech was *the center of the curriculum until the fifth grade. The old school building still stands, recently redeveloped as the St. Mary's* *Square condominium complex. Roy W. Nagle Collection, courtesy Buffalo and Erie County Historical Society*

The German Jesuits opened the doors of Canisius College for the first time on September 5, 1870. By the end of the first year, there were thirty-four students, mostly of German origin. Canisius High School and the college were one institution, then located in the same campus complex shown on Buffalo's Washington Street next to the Jesuit-staffed St. Michael's Church. The first A. B. degrees were not granted until 1883, and four years later, the college awarded its first master's degree. In 1912, the college moved to separate quarters on a new campus at Main and Jefferson, and Canisius High School left the old location in 1948 for a prestigious mansion on Delaware Avenue. The old campus no longer stands though St. Michael's Church remains, rebuilt after a disastrous fire in 1962. Roy W. Nagle Collection, courtesy Buffalo and Erie County Historical Society

In 1866 the New York State Legislature authorized four new normal schools, or elementary teacher-training schools, to be opened around the state. Educators pressured the Buffalo Common Council to act quickly to acquire one for the area. Public benefactor Jesse Ketchum proposed to donate a block of city land for the erection of suitable buildings for the Normal School and the payment of three hundred dollars annually for the purchase of prizes to be awarded to outstanding pupils in the public schools. Both Buffalo and Erie County authorized equal amounts of forty-five thousand dollars for the school, and on September 13, 1871, upon completion of the building shown here, the first students arrived for classes. Located at Jersey, Normal and Fourteenth streets, the Normal School rapidly outgrew its facilities, and the building was replaced by a new structure, now Grover Cleveland High School. After the Normal School became a four-year college—now the State University College at Buffalo—it moved in 1931 to a new campus on Elmwood Avenue next to Delaware Park. Roy W. Nagle Collection, courtesy Buffalo and Erie County Historical Society

Seymour H. Knox, Sr., was a five-and-dime store pioneer who opened one of his early stores in Buffalo and in 1890 moved his office there. The S. H. Knox chain had over a hundred stores when Knox merged it with other chains to form the F. W. Woolworth Company. The first store on Main Street was destroyed by fire in 1893, whereupon he opened at a nearby location four days later. He prospered greatly in his enterprises to achieve a preeminent status in the Buffalo business community. He became a public benefactor when he donated $250,000 toward the establishment of the University of Buffalo's College of Arts and Sciences. Knox family philanthropy was later extended to other enterprises, among which was the Albright Art Gallery, now renamed the Albright-Knox Art Gallery. Courtesy Buffalo and Erie County Historical Society

Though plowed fields stood between Main Street and the University of Buffalo in 1921, the school had come a long way. Founded in 1846 as a medical school, the University of Buffalo established a number of other divisions for professional training, a law school in 1891, a dental school in 1892, a teachers' college in 1895, and the College of Liberal Arts, sixty-seven years after its founding, in 1913. The largest building in this photograph, Foster Hall, was dedicated in 1922. Orin Foster, a member of the University Council, donated the half-million dollars needed to build the "hall of chemistry." Courtesy University Archives, State University of New York at Buffalo

136

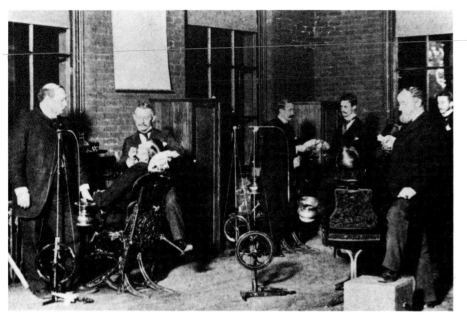

In the nineteenth century dentistry fought for a position within the regular medical field. Physicians generally thought of these practitioners more as technicians than as doctors. Obliged to lead a separate professional life, and trained in separate professional schools, American dentistry rapidly progressed, eventually becoming the world's envy. Because a toothache, however, excruciating, is not life-threatening, seeing a dentist can be postponed. A dentist's livelihood depended on being able to alleviate pain, and to cause as little as possible while doing so. It is for this reason that dentists pioneered the use of anesthetics in the 1840s when even surgeons strenuously resisted the practice on moral and theoretical grounds. The expectation that we can lead more comfortable lives is one of the profoundest modern developments. The view here is of a teaching infirmary at the University of Buffalo's dental school in 1893. Torturingly slow drills were operated by foot pedals. Courtesy University Archives, State University of New York at Buffalo

In 1872, the Grey Nuns of the Cross purchased land on Porter Avenue to erect a building to house their Holy Angels Academy. That mansard-roofed red brick building was damaged by fire in 1879 and rebuilt with additions being expanded in 1887. Shown here as it looked in 1890, it has new wings added, and in 1907, it became the home of the new D'Youville College, which took over the entire building when the grade school and high school were moved to new quarters in 1923 and 1930 respectively. It is now the center of a large complex of connected wings which extend along Porter Avenue from Fargo to Prospect avenues, surrounded by an urban campus on both sides of Porter Avenue. Roy W. Nagle Collection, courtesy Buffalo and Erie County Historical Society

A Toadstool Millionaire

Though education enjoyed a boom in the city, scientific knowledge lagged behind. The fabulous success of local medical nostrums, in fact, depended upon the poverty of regular medicine. In the later nineteenth century Buffalo was famous for the manufacture and distribution of patent medicine. The story has as much to do with business, culture, and politics as it has to do with ministering to the sick. The most famous of the patent-medicine wizards was Dr. Ray Vaughn Pierce, who operated the World's Dispensary. The medicines that Pierce concocted— *Smart Weed,* the *Favorite Prescription* and *Dr. Pierce's Pleasant Pellets*—made him one of the most successful examples of the class that Oliver Wendell Holmes called the "toadstool millionaires."

Dr. Pierce was a champion of free enterprise. As president of a proprietary association of mail-order medicine sellers, Pierce made sure that government would keep its hands off the regulatory tools. On behalf of his colleagues, Pierce vehemently responded to the doctors who questioned the effectiveness of the nostrums, cure-alls and tonics advertised in newspapers and sold through the mail. The association also protested the encroachments of pharmacists into mail-order territory. In the thirteen years between 1867 and 1880 his ventures took in almost half a million dollars per year. With the possible exception of William G. Fargo (of Wells Fargo fame) he was probably the city's most renowned person. Nearly one million bottles of Dr. Pierce's Smart Weed and other preparations left Buffalo annually.

Did the potions work? Surely in some cases they did. Not because of any ingredient, but because hope, expectation, and the effort to get well are factors in cure. People believed in Pierce; they wrote him their testimony. One woman, who had given birth to her eighteenth child (a ten-pounder) boasted of the "happy benefits" of Pierce's Favorite Prescription. An older couple attributed the birth of their son "solely" to the treatment they received at his hospital. Pierce capitalized a popular hostility to regular medicine and its heroic practices. The rough tools of the regular physician, such as bloodletting and purging, were rarely practiced after the Civil War. But the memory of these therapies was still alive, and it transferred to other practices. Because surgery was the only really sophisticated medical tool at the end of the nineteenth century, the temptation to operate was strong. Some of Pierce's most ardent admirers were those who had been treated repeatedly and unsuccessfully for chronic conditions.

Dr. Ray Vaughn Pierce. Courtesy Buffalo and Erie County Historical Society

Dr. Pierce's Smart-Weed and other patent medicines. Photograph by Thomas Payne, from the Collections, courtesy Buffalo and Erie County Historical Society

The Palace Hotel located on what is now the D'Youville College campus facing Prospect Park. Courtesy Buffalo and Erie County Historical Society

Pierce's claims were actually less ambitious than most of his colleagues in the patent medicine field. His appeal dwelt less on the horrific, and relied less upon frightening customers with the details of dread diseases which might develop if they failed to swallow this preparation or that one. The message was more positive.

In marketing the concoction Golden Medical Discovery, he really sold good feelings and a promise of cure. Pierce wrote one of Buffalo's biggest best sellers, *The People's Common Sense Medical Adviser in Plain English* to accompany the preparation. The book ran to a hundred editions in the sixty years that it remained in print. The *Adviser* was in large part advertisements for himself, of course. (Personal success always seems to be an element in American faith healing.) And the volume talked a good deal of silliness, especially on sexual topics. But there was much common sense too. In the volume from 1909 Pierce advised a good diet, moderate but sustained exercise, and (a particularly revealing piece of advice) regular bathing. "Such neglect," of bathing the *entire body,* he wrote, "should never exceed one week."

With the profits from his nostrums Pierce erected the lavish Palace Hotel in Buffalo, a spa for the "nervous and careworn." Though he preached against the soft life, the hotel had the first elevator in the city, and offered a sumptuous fare. He referred to it as the "grand national resort for invalids." Fire destroyed the hotel in February of 1881. A more modest Invalids Hotel replaced it and stood on Main Street in Buffalo until 1941.

Spread by national advertising, bolstered by the testimonials of ordinary individuals, Pierce's appeal was "populist." The Golden Medical Cure capitalized resentment against expertise, and against the remote power of the establishment. Pierce's entry into politics was a natural progression. Pierce ran for the state senate on the Republican ticket as a friend of the working man. Despite his fabulous wealth, he won. Pierce again was successful in 1878, winning a seat in the U.S. Congress after a particularly hard-fought campaign. The Democratic *Courier* accused him of abusing and underpaying his workers, of obscenity and lewdness for his medical pamphlets, and of being a "lying, bragging, deadbeat" who had "swindled thousands." But it was not accusations of fraud that ended his political career; Gilded Age political ethics were far more flexible than today's. Ironically, the medicine man resigned his Congressional seat in 1880 because of ill health.

How do we evaluate Pierce? The charge of fraud is too facile. It dismisses the patent-medicine phenomena too easily, and misses the opportunity to discover something important about the philosophy of self-help and success in the Gilded Age. Pierce's career was not so much about medicine as it was about free enterprise and success, the twin articles of faith for that era. As late as 1908 he could still be described proudly as one of Buffalo's "representative men." A *Buffalo Evening News* history noted that he was "known throughout the land as an eminent physician and here at home as one of our most public-spirited physicians."

There is no reason to believe that the Golden Medical Discovery had any value. That does not amount to fraud though. Pierce himself appeared to believe sincerely in his product. Cynics point out that as the money rolled in, it became easier to be convinced. But Pierce seems to have been both a genius at marketing and a credulous man himself. He also believed other dreamers. Pierce lost a fortune in a grandiose plan to tunnel for gold and coal in California.

A phenomenal rail boom in the post-Civil War decades boosted Buffalo's role in national commerce. Growing up and out also meant that the area could not be insulated from national problems. When successive wage cuts at the low point of the depression of the 1870s provoked a rail strike in West Virginia, it quickly spread along the lines to Pittsburgh, Buffalo, Toledo and Chicago, then to points west and into Canada. Here the strike became general, spreading to canal workers, tanneries, and stockyards. Mills, factories and coal depots also closed. Who was to maintain order? A fledgling police force, not yet ten years old, numbered under two hundred officers. Local militias were reluctant to use their specially issued truncheons on neighbors and friends. When a crowd seized the Erie Roundhouse in July, there was little that police could do to keep the trains running. Photograph by Thomas Payne, from the Collections, courtesy Buffalo and Erie County Historical Society

The Springville Royal Templars blended whimsy, morality, and practicality. The revival fires of the 1830s still smoldered in rural Erie County in 1879 when the organization was founded. Celebrating the virtues of Charity, Benevolence, and Equity the Royal Templars also preached temperance. Rural people everywhere banded together for mutual security. The Royal Templars maintained a life insurance group and benefit association. Courtesy Eden Historical Society

Shopping Becomes Fashionable

Although the American economy of the later nineteenth century yoyoed between boom and bust, each plateau of prosperity tended to be higher than the last. Buffalo's economic miracle was part of this jerky upward growth in the American economy. One consequence of greater wealth was a larger and more leisured middle class. More people had more money to spend, and they had more time to spend it in. Middle-class women were especially affected.

The department store, which capitalized these trends, was an invention of the post-Civil War decade. Stores such as Macy's in New York, Marshall Field's in Chicago, and Wanamaker's in Philadelphia became the showcases of new technology and fashion. In 1876 Buffalo's Adam and Meldrum formed their durable partnership. (The firm became Adam Meldrum and Anderson in 1892). Other Buffalo department stores, Flint and Kent, Hengerer, and the Sweeney Company were particularly successful in the 1880s and 1890s. These new retail ventures offered women an impressive array of goods and services. They offered cooking classes, restaurants, and beauty parlors. The department stores introduced and demonstrated labor-saving devices: washing and sewing machines, vacuum cleaners, and iceboxes.

Adam Meldrum and Anderson, for long a Main Street fixture, was one of several department stores to emerge and expand in post-Civil War Buffalo. One of its founders was Robert Borthwick Adam, a clever Scottish dry-goods merchant who capitalized and helped shape the needs of a new middle class. Roy W. Nagle Collection, courtesy Buffalo and Erie County Historical Society

The Flint and Kent Department Store. Courtesy Buffalo and Erie County Historical Society

If the department stores became a kind of social center for middle-class women, they also helped women move out into the wider world in another way. In these stores it was largely women who marketed goods to women. For the working-class woman the department store was a pleasant alternative to the factory. For the middle-class woman it permitted a time away from home between girlhood and motherhood. Although we are likely to notice that women were usually the clerks and never the managers, department-store work was sometimes cheered by nineteenth-century feminists who saw employment there as a stroke for women's equality and self-sufficiency.

Direct and quizzical in her gaze, this woman from the 1880s was nonetheless hampered by her dress. Though it would not be proper to conclude that "clothes make the woman," fashion can still tell us a great deal about the women of the time. Corseted down to the wasp-waist characteristic of the 1870s and 1880s, women were elaborately draped and trimmed in closely fitting dresses which amplified the bustline. Bustles, which wiggled while they walked, completed the exaggeration of the female form. Shoes also became more extreme, the toes pointier, the heels higher. High heels had the effect of emphasizing feminine curves as well. As some women imitated the "true women" of the ladies' magazines, they became more reticent and coquettish. Fashions encouraged this. In public, fans and hats concealed women's faces, and thereby accented the atmospherics of flirtation and separateness. Courtesy Buffalo and Erie County Historical Society

Parks for Buffalo

While nineteenth-century feminists sought to improve conditions for women, the quality of life in Buffalo became a matter of concern to civic leaders as the population explosion threatened more and more congestion. The Buffalo Park System was the end result of that concern. In 1868 civic leaders like Pascal Pratt, Dexter Rumsey, William Dorsheimer and Sherman S. Jewett met at Jewett's home to discuss their concern. Renowned landscape architect Frederick Law Olmsted was invited to Buffalo where he surveyed the terrain and met with a group of civic-minded citizens and city officials to explain the advantages of developing a rural park in a large city. A board of parks was established. Olmsted was retained to draw up a long-term park plan for the city. That plan began with a 350-acre park with meadow, picnic groves and lakes several miles north from the center of town. Known first as the Park, and later as Delaware Park, it was surrounded and protected against congested building by the several hundred acres of Forest Lawn Cemetery on the south, and by a privately developed rural-like community, Parkside on the east and the north. To Parkside came the affluent fleeing the busy hub of the city in favor of a parklike setting with curvilinear streets, tree-lined boulevards and spacious homes.

The greenbelt near Delaware Park was completed by the grounds of the Buffalo State Hospital to the west. Dr. James P. White had convinced the state to establish a state mental hospital in western New York about the time Olmsted's plans were getting underway. Because of its population, labor supply and medical school, a 250-acre tract in Buffalo just west of the park was selected as the site. The architect chosen was Henry Hobson Richardson, who asked his friend Olmsted to design the grounds.

The growing population of Erie County needed more recreational facilities, especially as the advent of the commuter train, the electric trolley, and the automobile afforded greater mobility. One such facility was the Buffalo Athletic Field at Main, East Delevan and Jefferson in Buffalo, a popular rendezvous for cyclers during the 1890s. Courtesy Tonawanda-Kenmore Historical Society

In West Seneca, Leins Park, with its arched entrance, was a popular amusement park operated from 1896 to 1926 on the south bank of Cazenovia Creek at Union Road. The present site of the West Seneca campus of Houghton College, it included a merry-go-round, bowling alley, dance hall, bear pit and other animal attractions. Courtesy James J. Ciesla, West Seneca Town Historian

New England-born Frederick Law Olmsted spent much of his life in the open spaces of the countryside. After several careers, among them farming and writing, he turned to pioneering in landscape architecture because he was concerned about the quality of life in the nation's growingly congested urban centers. His success with Central Park in New York City earned him a national reputation which took him to Boston, California, Chicago, Washington, and Buffalo. Inspired by the carefully designed parks of England, many of them the preserve of the aristocracy, he wished to create a system of open spaces in urban centers where people of all classes could intermingle to enjoy trees, lakes, and meadows. For three decades, he and his associates spent time on plans to develop a park and parkway system for the booming Buffalo community. Additionally he planned the Parkside community just off Delaware Park, which became possible with the extension of the Belt Line Railroad to Amherst Street in 1883. Courtesy Buffalo and Erie County Historical Society

Some recreational resorts could only be reached by water. Grand Island, where many of Buffalo's affluent families had summer homes, was the location of the Bedell House, shown here, which opened in 1887 and long was one of the area's popular resorts. Some affluent families established summer homes across the border in nearby Canada, where smart investors opened the Crystal Beach resort with its fine beach and amusement park. Located on the northern shore of Lake Erie, it was a short boat ride from the urban core at Buffalo. In the days of shoebox lunches, long skirts, and parasols, a forty-five minute ride on the Canadiana to Crystal Beach was a thrill for thousands of pleasure-seekers. Looking forward to an enjoyable day's outing, the crowd is anxiously waiting to board the Canadiana on July 4, 1912, at the foot of Buffalo's commercial Street. Roy W. Nagle Collection, courtesy Buffalo and Erie County Historical Society

Alden became a popular destination for Buffalonians and people from the Northeast in general after 1891 when, while drilling for gas, some of the finest black mineral water in the nation, high in carbon and sulphur content, was discovered at a depth of over nine hundred feet. Bath houses sprang up, providing over five hundred baths a day during the peak summer season. These baths were described as the "fountain of youth" or "nature's cure for rheumatism," beneficial for the treatment of neutritis, nervousness, skin diseases, and high and low blood pressure. Some Western New Yorkers came to enjoy the baths for a day while others came for the full three-week treatment, which included balanced homemade meals, baths in mineral water at 100 to 110 degrees Fahrenheit, and massages. The Alden

Black Water Bath House was the first to open near the site of the original well. Shown here is another popular bathhouse, the frame Alden Bath House and Sanitarium. Courtesy Norma M. Sweet, Alden Town Historian

The Buffalo Women's Wheel and Athletic Club organized in 1888. When they disbanded eleven years later, one wheelwoman claimed that it was no longer necessary to have a club—nearly everyone could accept a woman on a bicycle. At the beginning, however, women needed to band together. Medical theorists in America and Europe warned that the bicycle would cause "voluptuous sensations" and "lubricious overcitement" and "excesses of sensual madness." One social pundit claimed "with the bicycle the last appearance of feminine modesty disappeared." The Buffalo Women's Wheel and Athletic Club adopted a club costume as much for mutual support as for team spirit. As a group they could more easily cope with being (as one wheelwoman put it) "sneered at by conservative people" or "openly hooted by hoodlums." By the time this photograph was taken on July 4, 1901, attitudes had changed thoroughly; and "looking sweet on a bicycle built for two" was celebrated in a popular song. The two rode a tandem for fun. Roy W. Nagle Collection, courtesy Buffalo and Erie County Historical Society

Shown is Dexter P. Rumsey, who with William Dorsheimer and Sherman S. Jewett, fellow civic leaders and reformers, were among those leading the campaign to give Buffalo a first-rate park system. Influential businessmen and bankers, they met in Jewett's home on August 5, 1868, to plan strategy for their efforts to convince the city government to develop a park design. Out of this meeting eventually came the Board of Buffalo Parks Commissioners. The already renowned Frederick Law Olmsted was invited to Buffalo to survey the scene and begin planning a park network which he later described as one of the best in the nation. Roy W. Nagle Collection, courtesy Buffalo and Erie County Historical Society

The center of Olmsted's park system was the Park, now called Delaware Park. Originally hundreds of acres had been plowed to level the land and unwanted trees removed to create farmland. Out of the undeveloped north section of the city grew a beautiful greenspace with a lake, meadows, and thousands of trees and shrubs of every practicable variety. When Delaware Avenue was extended north until it reached Tonawanda, it gracefully wound through the park. People moved safely over the parkway on the stone bridge shown here. In what came to be called Delaware Park Lake, a casino and boathouse rose to afford visitors the pleasures of canoeing in pleasant summer days. In winter the thick ice on the lake was cleared to be used by those seeking the thrills of ice skating in brisk winter air in a veritable wonderland. Roy W. Nagle Collection, courtesy Buffalo and Erie County Historical Society

147

The vast greenbelt from the hospital to Parkside composed only part of the Olmsted plan. Closer to the city center overlooking Lake Erie and the Niagara River was to be the fifty-acre Front with its bandstand, gardens, and promenades. Across town was to be the fifty-six acre Parade, later Humboldt, and then Martin Luther King Park, mostly level lawn for games and military displays. Scattered across the city were to be more acres of squares and parks like Cazenovia Park in the south and Riverside Park at the city's northwest extremity. On the southwest extremity, Olmsted proposed a beautiful park sweeping down to the beaches of Lake Erie and connecting to the rest of the city by canals. The expense involved and the desire of steel interests to use the lakefront resulted in a substitute plan for a 155-acre South Park with lakes and a botanical garden. To interconnect the park lands, Olmsted designed a system of wide, tree-lined, landscaped parkways. Thus the local citizenry came to enjoy among them, McKinley, Red Jacket, Humboldt, Chapin, and Bidwell parkways as well as Porter and Richmond avenues.

By the dawn of the twentieth century, Buffalo enjoyed one of the best park systems in the world. The activities of the Society for the Beautifying of Buffalo promoted urban splendor by encouraging landscaping, obelisks and monuments in central places like Niagara Square, for which new designs were submitted by the Olmsted-Richardson partnership.

Additionally, by 1900 Erie County and Buffalo had cooperated in building an impressive Victorian Gothic city-county hall through the efforts of project commissioners like John Nice of Tonawanda, Allen Potter of Hamburg and Jasper Youngs of Williamsville.

Other Olmsted parks included Front Park on the West Side along the Niagara River and South Park on the city's southern border with what is now the city of Lackawanna. This scene shows the Front in 1906 with people sitting on the cannons and enjoying the formal gardens of the park, where an athletic field and bandstand were also located. Roy W. Nagle Collection, courtesy Buffalo and Erie County Historical Society

This scene of South Park shows the Botanical Gardens, with the park in the foreground looking toward the Father Baker institutions at South Park Avenue and Ridge Road. The Botanical Gardens in South Park, recently renovated by Erie County, are complemented by a lake and many varieties of trees and shrubs. Roy W. Nagle Collection, courtesy Buffalo and Erie County Historical Society

These children are enjoying their dip, clothes and all, in the wading pool of Humboldt Park, originally the Parade.

The Olmsted plan for Buffalo called for a network of landscaped, treed parkways to connect the parks he developed. One such parkway was Richmond Avenue, which on the north connected with Delaware Park eastward over Forest Avenue, which ran along the grounds of the Buffalo State Hospital. Richmond Avenue went south to a circle, now Symphony Circle, from which Porter Avenue ran west to the Front and Lake Erie. Richmond Avenue became a parkway with substantial architecturally varied homes fronted by elm trees, which eventually grew to cover the street with what looked like a high, arched cathedral ceiling. On Richmond Avenue, the citizenry enjoyed winter sleigh races during carnivals like the one shown on Washington's Birthday in 1896. Courtesy Buffalo and Erie County Historical Society

The Pan-American Exposition

The completion of Buffalo's park system created a superb setting for the 1901 Pan-American Exposition, which is the most familiar landmark in the historical imagination of Western New Yorkers. Sometimes we look back to the fair, a little ruefully, and with longing, as the best representative feat of strength of the era when money and power had settled upon Buffalo. In the summer of 1901 eight million visitors came to see what one enthusiast called the "spiritual synthesis of the far future." Electricity was the keynote of the fair. Hydropower had arrived five years before from Niagara Falls. No city had an electric trolley system more extensive than Buffalo's. A four-hundred-foot Electric Tower dominated the skyline looking north from the city.

Roy W. Nagle Collection, courtesy Buffalo and Erie County Historical Society

By day, the city of Light became the Rainbow City. Building designers had chosen a bold color scheme which began with the "savage salmon" and proceeded upward to a "civilized blue." The long climb up the biological and social ladders was also illustrated by the inclusion of ethnographic exhibits of peoples recently brought into the Western orb by colonization and conquest. On the popular Midway, "Darkest Africa," and the "Evolution of Man" reinforced pseudoscientific notions of European racial superiority.

When the Spanish-American War postponed the Exposition for two years, a much grander fair was planned for Buffalo. Astonishingly, it took only a year and a half for a small army of workers and craftsmen to fill the 350-acre grounds on Delaware Lake with the fabulous, eclectic, and overwrought Spanish Renaissance architecture that honored Latin American participants. The director general of the fair, a former ambassador to Argentina, thought that the Exposition was the "first available opportunity we have had to justify, by means of the most available object lessons we can produce, the acquisition of new territory." This was a benevolent vision of a Latin America steered and dominated by American democracy and technology.

President William McKinley was one of the most

Courtesy Buffalo and Erie County Historical Society

Architecture can occasionally tell us a great deal about the society that sponsors it. Most of the Exposition buildings were built in an elaborate baroque style to honor the contributions of Latin American culture. The New York State building recalls the simplicity and power of Greek classical architecture. The Greeks were admired for being both democratic and imperialist. Like sixth-century Athens, the United States was both a democracy at home and an aspiring imperialist power abroad. When he visited the fair, William McKinley was saluted by a pyrotechnic display that proclaimed him "President of our Nation and Empire." The only major structure to have survived the Exposition intact, the New York State building was designated a national landmark. Situated on a natural incline above Mirror Lake, it now houses the Buffalo and Erie County Historical Society. Courtesy Buffalo and Erie County Historical Society

enthusiastic of fairgoers. In 1897 he drove the ceremonial stake at Cayuga Island, a site originally proposed for the Exposition. When the fair was finally held in Buffalo, McKinley's visit to it proved fateful. On September 6, 1901, while shaking hands with well wishers at the Temple of Music, a half-crazed, self-proclaimed anarchist shot the president with a handgun he had concealed in a bandage. The country kept watch as the president's life ebbed away. McKinley was dead of the wounds within two weeks. Leon Czolgosz, the assassin, died a month later in the electric chair. Vice-president Teddy Roosevelt, much better prepared than McKinley to pilot the American ship of state in world politics, took his oath of office in Buffalo.

The Pan-American Exposition was here and gone in a brief, shining moment. The buildings, meant only to last the summer, were already crumbling when the fair closed in November. If the ruins of the Exposition were a demoralizing sight, people had only to look to the south, where Bethlehem Steel at Lackawanna embodied the hope that sustained the area's economy until the 1970s.

The creation of Bethlehem Steel was an indirect result of the search for an Exposition site. The Lackawanna Iron and Steel Company in Scranton, Pennsylvania, wanted to move its operations to a location closer to the sources of iron ore. They contacted John Milburn, president of the Exposition, who got in touch with his associate John Albright, who had a minor interest in steelmaking. The two concluded a land deal for the site south of Buffalo. It was assumed that Milburn was scouting a site for the Exposition, so the owners of the land let the options go for a reasonable sum.

Originally foreseen as a permanent building for the Pan-American Exposition, the Albright Gallery was not completed until 1905. The brash young city demonstrated its "culture" by evoking the past. Designed by Buffalo architect E. B. Green, the structure explicitly recalls the Erectheum on the Athenian acropolis. The dedication of the upper class to civic improvement by becoming the patrons of museums, libraries and outdoor monuments was self-conscious and purposeful. After the bruising political battles of the 1890s, upper-class reformers like steel magnate John J. Albright increasingly channeled their efforts at social reform into philanthropy. At the ceremony dedicating the gallery, Harvard University President Charles W. Eliot commended "the high example of private beneficence, which will promote, in a wise and sound way, democratic happiness." In the words of University of Buffalo Chancellor Samuel P. Capen, Albright had "dignified Buffalo in the eyes of the world." The Albright Gallery is shown here in an early photograph that lacks two important details—the sculptured caryatids which now decorate the flanks, and the new wing donated by Seymour Knox, which opened in 1962. The Albright-Knox boasts one of the finest collections of contemporary art in the world. Courtesy Buffalo and Erie County Historical Society

James F. Parker is a forgotten hero. It was "Big Jim" who swung his great fist into the face of Leon Czolgosz, wrestled him to the ground, and prevented him from shooting William McKinley a third time. Midway impresarios hoped to put Parker on display as one of the "living heroes." He declined. History loses track of him afterward. Courtesy Buffalo and Erie County Historical Society

As Buffalo's population skyrocketed, a trolley network developed to serve the public need to move outside the neighborhood vicinity. The first trolleys were horse-drawn vehicles like the Buffalo East Ride Railway trolley, shown here at Michigan and Genesee Streets about 1889. It was not long before the horse-drawn trolleys were replaced by the much faster electric trolleys. Trolley lines now sprang up not only around the city but also in the towns around Buffalo, tying them to the urban core. Shown is an electric trolley of the Buffalo Southern line around 1900, one at Hamburg. Courtesy Buffalo and Erie County Historical Society

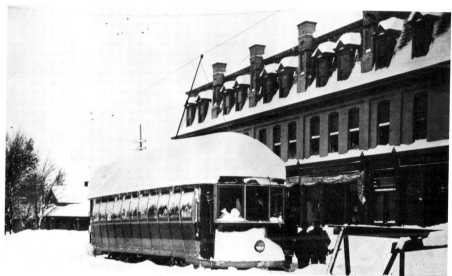

A group of men from Buffalo and Williamsville joined to form the Buffalo and Williamsville Electric Railway, which operated the "Toonerville" electric trolley into Buffalo. The greater mobility afforded by these trolleys helped to diminish the isolation of Erie County's communities from each other and made it possible for people to live a longer distance from their jobs. Courtesy Old Amherst Colony Museum

Around the turn of the century, citizens
outside the city who needed to travel by
trolley sometimes came to a trolley stop by
wagon or buggy. There they patiently
awaited the arrival of their transportation
into the city. One such stop is the trolley
stand shown around 1900 in the town of
West Seneca at the corner of Indian
Church and Union roads. The trolley
stand provided the commuter with a
waiting room where candy and ice cream
were sold. Courtesy James J. Ciesla, West
Seneca Town Historian

A large cemetery was established in 1901
on Delaware Avenue in the town of Tonawanda at what is now Brighton Road,
formerly Schell Road. Here the old Schell
farm made way for Elmlawn Cemetery,
where an original homestead, used later as
a roadhouse and a summer home, served as
the first office building. Because of the
distance from Buffalo, the cemetery was
served by the appropriately fitted-out
electric trolley car, the Elmlawn Funeral
Car, which could carry both the coffin and
mourners to the burial site outside the city.
When Elmlawn Cemetery opened, its
neighbor across Delaware Avenue for a
brief time was Palace Park, a popular
amusement resort with bicycle races,
confections, booths, tables for picnics, a
carousel, a saloon, and a dance hall. Town
officials soon closed down the park because
it had degenerated out of control. In 1912,
the Roman Catholic Diocese of Buffalo
established Mt. Olivet Cemetery on the site,
converting the saloon building into the
superintendent's offices. Roy W. Nagle
Collection, courtesy Buffalo and Erie
County Historical Society

Commuter travel to Buffalo from the towns
was also available by train to those
communities lucky enough to be crossed by
rail lines. One very lucky settlement was
what came to be known as the village of
Blasdell in the town of Hamburg, where
several railroads had tracks. Herman
Blasdell came to the area from North
Collins in 1885 to develop a real estate
project at the crossing of the Erie and
Nickel Plate railroads. The development
included a store, a hotel, several cottages,
and the depot shown. When residents of the
area were considering a name for their new
community, incorporated May 23, 1898,
the names of old families going back to the
earlier nineteenth century were suggested.
However, the story goes that a brazen Mr.
Blasdell boldly hung a sign bearing his
name on the depot. Thus the village of
Blasdell it became and remained. Courtesy
Nina M. Brown, Blasdell Village Historian

One form of recreation in the late nineteenth century was tinkering with what many considered a toy, the automobile. This horseless carriage was at first seen very infrequently around Erie County, but gradually, it became more and more familiar. Henry Seedorf, one of the first trustees of the new village of Blasdell, incorporated in 1898, is shown seated with his family around him in an early automobile in front of his Pearl Avenue home. Courtesy Nina M. Brown, Blasdell Village Historian

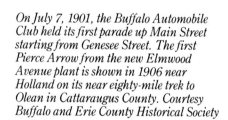

On July 7, 1901, the Buffalo Automobile Club held its first parade up Main Street starting from Genesee Street. The first Pierce Arrow from the new Elmwood Avenue plant is shown in 1906 near Holland on its near eighty-mile trek to Olean in Cattaraugus County. Courtesy Buffalo and Erie County Historical Society

Even before the time of the Pan-American Exposition in 1901, the ability to move around the city and out into the county had been greatly increased with the advent of the electric trolley and commuter trains, which broke down neighborhood parochialism by allowing fast movement to downtown and other neighborhoods. People could also conveniently live farther away from their jobs. Thus the city's affluent flocked to Parkside and smart entrepreneurs opened trolley lines to Hamburg, Orchard Park, Williamsville, and Tonawanda. Trolley tracks began to weave the city and its neighbors together.

Louis P. A. Eberhardt was one of the most fascinating entrepreneurs of the time. A real estate developer, he began his career in 1882 at the age of twenty-two by subdividing a forty-acre farm inside the city at its northern fringe. By 1888, he began purchasing land just outside the city limits in the town of Tonawanda. On Delaware Avenue, he erected his first suburban home. When it burned, he had even more pretentious homes designed and built for himself and his brother Fred by noted local architect Cyrus Porter. A horse-drawn omnibus enabled people to travel to his new home from the New York Central Belt Line Railroad, one mile south of the city line. Near the "twin mansions" he constructed, Eberhardt envisaged a village of large stone and brick homes with carriage houses and spacious lawns. While his suburban village, Kenmore, never quite reached that scale, it did become a community of comfortable, mostly frame homes for people fleeing the hustle-bustle of urban life for the small-town atmosphere. By 1890 there were nearly three hundred inhabitants in Kenmore, fifty of whom used the omnibus daily to commute into the city. Nine years later, the citizens of Kenmore formally incorporated into a village, Buffalo's pioneer planned suburb.

When the Belt Line railroad was extended to Amherst Street in 1883, development of the open lands to the northern city limits and beyond became a real possibility. An entrepreneur who quickly took advantage of this fact was young Louis Phillip Adolph Eberhardt, who had recently subdivided a farm just south of the city line in Buffalo. Land was purchased north of the city line in the town of Tonawanda from two farm families, the Ackermans and the Mangs. It was located on Delaware Avenue running north toward the village of Tonawanda at the northern end of the town. Courtesy Tonawanda-Kenmore Historical Society

Louis P. A. Eberhardt hoped to develop a new community just north of the Buffalo city line. There he hoped to lure people who wished to escape the congestion, noise, and fast pace of urban life and to reside in a pleasant community with a small-town atmosphere. There he constructed the substantial home shown, with a large carriage house for himself and his family on the east side of Delaware Avenue in 1888 to 1889. When this home burned six years later, he had the carriage house moved to the west side of Delaware Avenue, where he began construction of two pretentious red Medina sandstone Romanesque mansions, as shown, one for himself and one for his brother Fred. These "twin sentinels" signaling arrival in Kenmore were familiar landmarks for generations of travelers along Delaware Avenue. The Fred Eberhardt home still stands today as a business, but the other mansion was torn down in 1977 after serving many years as a YWCA building. Courtesy Tonawanda-Kenmore Historical Society

Transportation to the Eberhardt community, which incorporated as the village of Kenmore in 1899, was first provided by a horse-drawn omnibus, which carried passengers free of charge from the village to the Belt Line Railroad one mile south of the city line. By 1894, Kenmore had electric trolley access to Buffalo's Main Street through a line which came south along Delaware Avenue and turned west at the city line to continue on to Military Road, where it turned south into the city. Shown in the photograph is a winter scene with a trolley coming south near the completed Eberhardt homes, where it turned west toward Military Road. Courtesy Tonawanda-Kenmore Historical Society

What Louis Eberhardt first envisioned was a village of substantial homes like his own, inhabited by affluent businessmen and professionals. Eberhardt spent many years dividing up and developing the land of Kenmore into a community of people of more modest means than those he had originally sought. Street upon street of comfortable, mostly frame houses were built to accommodate the growing demand for homes in Buffalo's pioneer suburb. Frame houses on West Hazeltine near the southern end of the village are shown in a turn-of-the-century photograph which features children running on plank board sidewalks along a dirt road. Courtesy Tonawanda-Kenmore Historical Society

Streetcar Strike!

The transportation on which the new suburbanites depended was plagued with special problems. Streetcars bore their heaviest loads at the beginning and end of the day, and at the noontime rush hour when many returned home to lunch. Six of every ten men hired by the International Railway Company (IRC), which held the monopoly of street rail traffic in Buffalo, were hired to work the peak periods. These permanent "extras," started at low pay (twenty-three cents an hour) and advanced very slowly. Only one in ten took home as much as eighteen dollars a week, and these men worked seven days out of seven.

Long-brewing discontent bubbled over in 1913. Local socialist organizers worked to turn unfocused unhappiness to action in March of 1913. The IRC got wind of the activity and fired a hundred men. This attracted the attention of the American Federation of Labor, a powerful national union. From this point a strike was inevitable; seventeen hundred walked off the job.

The company hired twenty-five hundred tough strikebreakers from other cities. One east coast labor organizer described the people the company recruited in Philadelphia as a collection of "every thug, tenderloin lounger, wharf-rat and ex-convict that can be located." Though this source could not claim to be objective, hiring strikebreakers did cost the IRC public support in a town that already had 110 labor unions. Mobs numbering in the thousands met the strikebreakers who attempted to run the trolleys. The addition of several hundred city policemen failed to get the trains running, and a judge ordered that the militia be called up. After more than a million dollars in lost retail revenues, a hundred arrests, numerous injuries and property damage, the company accepted a "fair plan of arbitration" under the gavel of Buffalo's popular mayor Louis Fuhrmann. In the end, motormen accepted a settlement that granted them a raise in pay of one cent per hour.

Two conductors on train. Courtesy Buffalo and Erie County Historical Society

Roy W. Nagle Collection, courtesy Buffalo and Erie County Historical Society

EXTRA! BUFFALO SOCIALIST EXTRA!

SOCIALIST PARTY — WORKERS OF THE WORLD UNITE

Vol. 1—No. 45 BUFFALO, N. Y., APRIL 8, 1913 Price Two Cents

IMPORTED THUGS COME TO CLUB BUFFALO STRIKERS BACK TO SLAVERY

Capitalist Papers Full of Slippery, Baseless Tales

Workers, With Solid Front, Fold Arms and Defy Professional Strike-Breakers to Run Cars; Only Violence is Due to International Spies Who Try to Stir Up The Crowds to Make Trouble; Public Enthusiastic For Strikers' Victory.

Driven desperate by the show of spirit on the part of the hitherto docile workers, the international Railway Company, aided by its servile lackeys of courts and city officials, is riding rough-shod over the city in its effort to drive the workers back to their ancient slavery. The policemen, workers themselves, are trying to treat the men fairly, in spite of the International's orders to club and shoot.

No stone is being left unturned by the masters; but the men with folded arms, secure in the loyalty of the working class, can well afford to laugh at the transparent schemes that are being framed up to shackle them again to the starvation wages and slavish conditions under which they have hitherto been forced to work.

Never before in the history of Buffalo has a strike been met with such enthusiastic approval on the part of the whole working class as has this one. The few workers who are forced to ride on the half dozen cars which continue running, manned by imported thugs, do not hesitate to hoot and jeer and show the familiar "scab sign" to the hired bullies, making life miserable for them.

The strike is a peaceful one, outside of the ruffianly tactics of the spies of the International, who have tried to urge the men to do violence, without success.

At least one murder is already scored to the credit of one of the inexperienced "motormen," together with one automobile wreck. The murder occurred on the Niagara street line Monday afternoon, when a scab "motorman," ignorant of how to run his car, ran down a child. The fact was carefully covered up by the capitalist papers, who were too busy dreaming out fake stories about spook policemen alleged to have been attacked by mysterious "mobs." In the majority of cases, people living in the neighborhood where these "mobs" are alleged to be congregating, do not know of any such occurrences, and it is believed that most of the fanciful tales originate in the heads of the capitalist newspaper lackeys. The auto was wrecked at Main and Utica streets, Monday morning. This was also covered up by the capitalist papers.

All of the capitalist newspapers are lined up with the masters, together with the courts, the city and county officials, while the soldiers of the overlords are shining up their bayonets with a view to jabbing them into the tender flesh of the workingmen of Buffalo who dare to refuse to slave for the International on starvation wages.

The Employers' Association, Chamber of Commerce, and other organizations of slave-drivers are rallying to the support of the International, while on the other hand, the organizations of workers are also rallying to the support of their own class—the working class. Branch 3, Socialist Party, had voted to donate almost all of the cash in its treasury within 12 hours after the strike was called; at the same time, Branch 4 voted to give a benefit dance in its quarters, Colonial Parlors, the proceeds to go to the strike fund. Branch 4 also voted to purchase 2,000 copies of The Buffalo Socialist to distribute free in the 22d Ward, giving the people of that territory, the facts of the case which is being so sadly garbled by the capitalist papers in their effort to crush the revolt. A special meeting of the Executive Committee of Local Buffalo has been called to render aid, and other Branches are expected to take quick action.

The labor unions of the city are also arranging to help their brothers in the fight in which they realize that "an injury to one is the concern of all workingmen."

The International officials, together with their lackeys of the press, bench and bar, are frothing at the mouth in their rage, but so long as the men stand firm with folded arms, and refuse to knuckle under, their victory is regarded as practically certain.

A herd of about 100 reckless thugs, the most ruffianly body of men ever allowed to congregate in Buffalo in one gang, have arrived, armed to the teeth, and prepared to stop at nothing in carrying out the orders of the International, regardless of the lives of workers, whether they be strikers or not.

So far the strikers have resisted all of the attempts of the spies of the International to tempt them into one violent act giving the capitalist politicians an excuse for calling out the soldiers.

The old party politicians who were "friends of the workers" during the last campaign, have forgotten their "friendship," and the toilers are speedily learning that if they are to gain the right to live, they must unite at the ballot-box as well as at the factories and car-barns, and elect their own fellow-workers to office, subject to their orders instead of the bosses' orders.

The Buffalo Socialist will issue a daily edition so long as the situation requires it. One look at the capitalist papers is enough to show any workingmen what kind of treatment to expect from them.

KEPT PRESS LIE

It is necessary for us to nail a capitalist lie down at once. The Express published a statement to the effect that the Socialist Party did not want the striking street car men to meet in their hall. The truth of the matter is that the applications came in so rapidly that the officials of the Amalgamated Association of Street and Electric Railway men had to engage four halls. The Socialist Party stands ready at all times to help this organization or any other working class organization with their moral and financial support, and they are welcome to the use of our hall any time, day or night. No official of the Socialist Party in Buffalo ever made the statement referred to, but we do not and never have expected anything different from The Express.

INTERNATIONAL SPIES HELPLESS TO PREVENT ORGANIZATION OF MEN

The International never thought the men would ever organize. The officers of the company thought they had a spy system that not only equalled any Russian police system, but was superior.

The big brains of the company made a mistake this time and the result will be a big addition to the union forces of this city.

A meeting was called for the purpose of completing the organization of a Street Car Men's Union, which took place last Saturday night at 52 W. Eagle Street. The company, of course, knew of it and an army of trained spies and spotters were in attendance. These spies and spotters had the gall of the devil himself, going right into the room where the meeting was to be held, and had it not been that the men were not a law-abiding set, it would have gone hard with them.

All along Eagle Street barn bosses and inspectors lay in wait for any employee that might attempt to attend the meeting, and congregated in groups expressing their opinions of what unions were, and some of the language used was of the worst order.

A more determined set of fellows never was got together than these sane street car employees, who have always been looked down on by the people and treated like dogs by the company.

Down the street they came and up the stairs to the hall, passing the time of company spotters. The meeting was held and when a vote was taken every man was eager for the strike. It was not necessary to call for volunteers to picket the balance of the men on the cars, for all were eager to get on the job and all that was necessary was the call to come out. The response was general and by early morning the company discovered that it had a surprise of the first magnitude on its hands.

All day Sunday the men continued to drop into the ranks of the union until not a car was to be seen running anywhere. The company were not the wise guys they thought they were, and it is up to the strikers to give them a lesson never to be forgotten.

In line with the policy of President Connette of the company, he stated that only 100 men were out on Sunday night—the utter untruthfulness of the statement was proved by the statement that Main Street cars would not run after 8 o'clock that night. All other lines had previously ceased operation. The system is completely tied up.

STRIKERS' DEMANDS

"We are now demanding from the International Street Railway company that the rights of organization, which are ours, be not interfered with.

"Secondly—That all men dismissed for expressing their sentiments for organization be reinstated in their former position.

"Thirdly—That an agreement be entered into between the company and the association, covering the wages and working conditions of the men as stated in the following:

First—Seventy-five per cent of all runs on the schedules to be known as earlies and lates, and to be complete dwithin eleven consecutive hours.

Second—Swing runs to be completed within thirteen consecutive hours.

Third—All runs working less than nine hours to pay nine hours time.

Fourth—Time and one-half for all time worked over the daily schedule.

Fifth—A flat rate of wages of thirty-two cents per hour.

Sixth—The right to have the men's grievances presented to the company by a committee of their organization.

These demands are perfectly reasonable, and have been complied with in many neighboring cities. There is no reason whatever why the International Street Railway Company should not immediately meet the demands. If the traveling public are inconvenienced in any way, the blame rests with the company and not with the men.

A DAILY

From now on, the Buffalo Socialist will be issued as a Daily Paper, until further notice.

STRIKE MEETINGS

The meetings of the newly roganized Union are being held daily in the following halls. Street Car Employes are urgently requested to attend each meeting.

The Broadway and Walden men meet in the Columbia Turn Verein Hall at the corner of Genesee and Kehr Streets.

The Cold Spring and Forest Avenue men meet in Arnold's Hall at the corner of Main and Ferry Streets.

The men from the Hertel barn meet in the hall at the corner of Austin and Kail Streets.

The Seneca men meet in Elks Hall at the corner of Elk and Seneca. The arrangements have not yet been completed for the great Mass Meeting in the Elmwood Music Hall. This will be announced in our next issue.

Four enthusiastic meetings were held yesterday and were addressed by Wm. B. Fitzgerald, J. J. Thorpe of the Amalgamated, Tom Flynn of the American Federation of Labor, and Sam Atkinson of the Buffalo Socialist.

Representatives were elected from each barn for the Central Committee, which will present the demands of the men to the company.

Mr. Connette whines about the men having made no requests for improved conditions. Anybody with brains knows that the moment a man applies for his badge. The men are powerless without organization. They have now got it and are sure to win.

CATTELL SLUGGED BY COMPANY DETECTIVE

Another example of the International's methods took place at the corner of Utica and Jefferson streets last Saturday night. William F. Cattell stood on the corner waiting for Frank Olson, who was distributing circulars to some street car men. Cattell noticed the approach of the famous spy of the company named Morris Bouris and another questionable character of the secret service of the International.

Bouris, who, it is claimed, is sworn in by the city as a special officer for the company, ordered a policeman to arrest Cattell and Olson. While in the hands of the policeman Bouris struck Cattell a cowardly blow in the face, taking advantage of the position of Cattell at the time.

Both men were taken to No. 6 station on Bouris' complaint for distributing circulars without a license, even though they had licenses in their possession.

After a talk with the captain, Inspector Mulligan had the first charge scratched out and the charge of interfering with people on the sidewalks not amounting to assault, was made. Again the charge was changed to suit the complainant.

Cattell and Olson have six witnesses to prove that their acts were within the law.

This man named Bouris has made the declaration that the street car company would "get him," meaning Cattell.

Cattell's place of residence is under the tender care of three private detectives at all times. One set of three leave, another three appear.

KEEPING 'EM CONTENTED

Men are required to serve thirteen days breaking in. Then a week's pay is held back, so it is upwards of a month before they draw any money. Many are discharged shortly after breaking in and the pay held back goes to pay for their clothes at Saperston's. All clothes must be bought at Saperston's and the International's rake-off there is purported to be large.

The company keeps standing advertisements for men in papers throughout the United States and Canada. This is owing to the transitory nature of their working force, and no other company has ever been obliged to adopt such a policy.

STREET RAILWAY COMPANY RECEIVES BIG SURPRISE

Everybody walks,—including father. Yes, the employees of the International Railway are on strike.

The men have proved to the public of Buffalo that when it comes to doing the trick, they are the people who run the International Railway. They have always done the work, but lawyers and capitalists have been receiving all the benefits.

It has been said that a job on the street railway lines is the last resort, and that the men could not be organized, but the surprise sprung on the pessimists of Buffalo is the greatest thing that ever happened.

These men have joined a union and intend that they shall receive pay for their labor that will enable them to live like human beings.

They have risen up spontaneously and called a strike, the likes of which has not been known to this city before.

The capitalist press sneered at the meeting held by the men on Saturday night and said that "foreign agitators" were the instigators and that it would amount to nothing. The foreign agitators were J. J. Thorpe of Pittsburgh and William B. Fitzgerald of Philadelphia, both foreign countries.

To prove their patriotism and their hatred of foreigners, the International tried to induce two carloads of Polish men to go to the Cold Spring barns to be used as strike-breakers.

For years the International has imposed upon its employees in every conceivable manner, and now that it has been hit it squeals like a stuck pig. The company and its officers has hogged it so long and so much that it claimed the privilege as a natural right.

Now that the men have turned, the company cringes like a crying bully and **demands** protection from the authorities at the expense of the city and county, and sleeping Mike has been aroused from his slumbers and orders men hither and thither at the dictation of the officers of the International.

We ask Mayor Fuhrmann if he is the lackey of the International or does he intend to represent that great majority, the working class, in this struggle!

Why was it that the police were ordered to allow the company's scab-herders in the form of barn bosses and inspectors to hang around the union hall on Eagle Street while everyone else was compelled to move on? This was no mistake. Anyone could see that the police as individuals were not to blame and knew the injustice of it, but like other men working for a living had to obey orders in order to keep their jobs.

We will not attempt to criticize the police as individuals in this case, but the man higher up, the mayor, is the responsible party. Private property is not more valuable than human life, and these men are absolutely fighting for a chance to live, and the mayor of this city, elected by the working people, turns on his constituents and obeys the orders of the International in preference.

IN THE SLAVE PEN

In no place on the north American continent have the working conditions of street car employees been as rotten as in Buffalo.

The men are on the job seven days a week and they are rarely able to get a day off. When they do it's after having had an application in for probably two weeks, and then on a so-called day off they are obliged to make a trip or two morning and evening. The day thus broken up is of little use to them. No man is allowed off at all from May till October.

Sixty per cent. of the men are extras and they sometimes make as little as \$6 or \$7 a week, with a maximum of \$12. About ten per cent. reach \$18 a week and this princely stipend is held out as a bait for recruits.

Extra men show up for work three times a day and this takes up eighteen hours of their time. The maximum wage is only reached after nine years' service.

The officers of the company are overbearing to a degree and the men receive scant courtesy at their hands. In complaints against employees there is no justice for them. The complainant invariably gets the benefit of the doubt.

HAMMOND INTERPRETS LAW TO SUIT INTERNATIONAL

One Law For Workers, Another For Capitalists — Must Please International Railway Company or Get Off the Job — Hammond's Letter Shows How Law Acts Against Workers.

The Corporation Counsel keeps two kinds of interpretation on tap, when it comes to instruction for the police and the subordinates of the legal department of the city. If the perfumed Bull Moosettes want to infest the streets o fthe city to harass, annoy and browbeat everybody into giving up money for their political party, the corporation counsel gives what he calls a liberal interpretation to the ordinances. They get a free hand. But if workingmen go about in an orderly way to give to their fellow workingmen, folded circular letters inclosed in envelopes, asking them to join a union of their craft, the corporation counsel at once resorts to the doctrine of strict construction.

The police are turned loose, these workingmen are arrested, locked up and presented under a far fetched ordinance that is strained to the cracking point, and a sentence is demanded of a hundred dollars five or a hundred days in the penitentiary.

On October 9th, 1912, the Bull Moosettes had their lawyer write to the corporation counsel asking if they could under the ordinances sell tags to get money for their particular political cult. The letter of the corporation counsel in reply is in the words and figures following:

"October 10, 1912.

"Frank H. Callan, Esq.,
Attorney and Counsellor at Law,
907 D. S. Morgan Bldg., Buffalo, N. Y.

"Dear Sir:

"Your letter asking for an opinion whether or not the selling of badges and buttons on October 26th and 27th, the latter being Colonel Roosevelt's birthday and to be called Founder's Day, the same to be celebrated all over the United States by the women of the Progressive party, would be a violation of the Ordinances of the City was duly received.

"In reply thereto, would say that Section 1, of Chapter XVII of the City Ordinances provides in part, viz.:

"Sec. 1. No person shall sell, peddle, hawk or vend upon the streets, or public places of the City, by going from house to house soliciting purchases or otherwise, unless a license or permit so to do has been previously obtained by him or her from the Mayor, which license must be shown. * * *

"While this ordinance would seem to be designed to regulate peddlers, hawkers and junk dealers and license them under a yearly license system for the purpose of carrying on their business within this city, nevertheless, it would seem, under a strict construction of section 1, that it is necessary to secure a permit from the Mayor for any person or persons desiring to sell badges, buttons and the like, upon one or two days, the proceeds to be devoted to some particular cause.

"I have that the foregoing would be a correct statement of the law, under a strict interpretation. However, I would place upon the section quoted a more liberal construction, if asked to pass officially upon the same, and would incline, to the opinion that the same does not apply to the particular occasions mentioned by you.

"Very truly yours,
CLARK H. HAMMOND,
Corporation Counsel."

William F. Cattell was arrested on March the 20th, and is now being prosecuted with all the vigor and venom at the command of the Corporation Counsel, assisted by the attorneys for the International Railway Company. Mr. Cattell's crime was that he handed out, to motormen and conductors, folded circular letters, inclosed in envelopes, inviting the men to join a union of their craft. The protectors of law and order claim that Mr. Cattell violated section one of chapter 28, of the city ordinances. This sacred section in its business end reads:

"No person shall engage in and carry on the business of bill-posting or bill distributing, or sign-advertising in the City of Buffalo without previously having obtained a lisense so to do under the provisions of this chapter."

The remainder of the section and chapter leave it to the Mayor to grant a license or to refuse it, and to charge \$50.00 for it and to require a \$2,000.00 bond, and fixes the rates that the bill poster may charge his customers.

How is this for an interpretation of an ordinance?

The International Railway Company was not interested in the opinion for the Bull Moosettes. It is interested, however, in the prosecution of Mr. Cattell.

Whole International System Is Tied Up

When this edition of the Buffalo Socialist gets eon the street the entire International system will probably be tied up. All interurban lines are out of commision, no cars are running in Lockport and all the Niagara Falls men were expected to go out last night.

INJUNCTION SERVED ON UNION OFFICIALS

Notwithstanding the intimidation of the men by the International for some months, or years, in regard to organizing a union, the company officials act like a lot of mongrel pups, and as soon as a strike occurs, run to the courts for that good old weapon of the capitalist class invented to subject the workers—the **Injunction**.

Justice Charles A. Pooley lost no time in complying with the request of his fellow capitalist politicians, and the **injunction** which all workingmen know prevents a man from almost thinking, was issued on Sunday. Injunction, or no injunction, the union is a fact, and that the men are not running the cars is another fact, and so long as this condition exists the International can have its injunction.

Of course, all the legal talent will rush to the service of that eminent jurist, Thomas Penney, and every dirty trick known to the law craft and courts will be turned against the men, yet the fact that the men have tied up the system tight as a drum proves their strength, and, if necessary, the union men of this town could teach the pettyfogging law courts and capitalists the lesson of their lives right now by laying down their tools.

Yes, intimidation, that is what the injunction says. The company is granted an injunction on affidavits alleging intimidation!

Well, fellow workers, what do you think of it? The company has discharged men right and left for even daring to mention the word "union," and now it gets out an injunction on the plea that the union is trying to intimidate themselves.

The judge that grants an injunction on these grounds, knowing as everyone in this city knows, how these men have been treated, deserves a medal from the Society for the Prevention of Cruelty to corporations, and a room in the department of brainstorms.

DEPUTIES TO PREVENT ALL MEETINGS.

Sheriff Becker, this morning, acting on the advice of County Attorney, Sullivan, assigned ten deputies to attend the halls where the carious meetings of the strikers are scheduled to be held.

The officers carried copies of the the injunction secured yesterday, preventing the men from meeting and were instructed to see that no demonstrations were held.

But there was no interference with meetings yesterday and none is anticipated.

Buffalo Socialist Newspaper. *From the Collections, courtesy Buffalo and Erie County Historical Society*

The Kellogg family had a long-standing interest in vegetable oil extraction and marketing. Spencer Kellogg erected a mill at Buffalo in 1879, and ten years later the business survived intense competition from the National Linseed Oil Trust. Buffalo was an ideal location. Flaxseed grown in the upper midwest could be processed here and the oil sent down the Erie Canal. Kellogg, a self-taught chemist, discovered ways of treating linseed oil to make it dry faster when exposed to air. This made it an ideal paint medium. America had been an exporter of flaxseed since colonial times, but demand became so great that seed had to be imported. Kellogg's interests became worldwide. A thoughtful but eccentric man, Kellogg believed in, among other things, the mystical significance of numbers, and in particular, cube roots. Roy W. Nagle Collection, courtesy Buffalo and Erie County Historical Society

A company picnic at John D. Larkin's summer home in Ontario. Direct marketing was not the only bold stroke of the Larkin Company. The firm is also remembered for its pioneering reform of personnel management policies. Labor activism during World War I had shattered management complacency. In response, a number of firms initiated reforms that historians have called "welfare capitalism." At Larkin a social committee organized an orchestra, a drama club, several sports teams, a Bible Study Committee, instruction in French, a "citizenship" class for immigrant workers, a physical committee that did a five-minute warmup before work, and a health maintenance organization. Recently reimported as "Japanese management," this style is often likely to strike us as paternalistic and jarringly naive. For instance, a company publication congratulated the War Relief Committee this way: "Stick out your chests Larkin Girls! You have a right to be proud!" Courtesy Buffalo and Erie County Historical Society

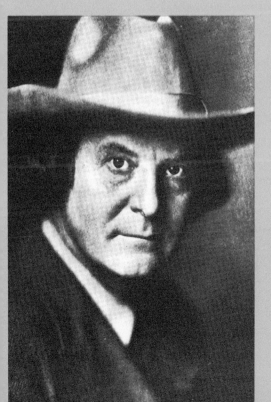

In 1878 soap manufacturer John D. Larkin entered a partnership with marketing genius Elbert Hubbard. Hubbard pioneered the idea of mail-order merchandising. The idea was hugely successful. By offering premiums and bonuses to the "Groups of Ten" in return for sales, the company was able to dispense with a sales force. By 1910 the company was receiving nearly ten thousand letters of request per day, and could hardly keep pace with orders. His fortune made, Hubbard retired in 1893 to East Aurora, where he styled himself as Fra Elbertus, sage of the Roycrofters. His inspirational tract A Message to Garcia sold millions of copies to managers and would-be managers throughout the world. Roy W. Nagle Collection, courtesy Buffalo and Erie County Historical Society

163

Designed for Larkin Company executive Darwin D. Martin by Frank Lloyd Wright, this national landmark is one of the finest of his prairie-style houses. Wright was as original and imperious as his mentor Louis Sullivan. He detested the eclectic borrowings of other architects and hoped to find a particularly American expression for his buildings. The design of the Martin House suggests freedom from traditional architectural constraints: to onlookers at the time, even the law of gravity seemed not to apply. Roomy inside (in fact, virtually roomless) the Jewett Parkway structure is divided mostly by internal columns and ceiling detail. Wright also designed furniture to match the house, and to Mrs. Martin's chagrin, dictated its arrangement even after they moved in. Wealthy enough at the turn of the century to build this innovative and expensive home without asking how much it cost, the Martin family was bankrupt by the 1930s. The house fell into disrepair and was nearly demolished. Saved by a real estate developer who separated the house into apartments, it is now owned by the University of Buffalo. Efforts are under way to restore it. Courtesy Buffalo and Erie County Historical Society

Labor-saving technology is the hallmark of the latest phase of the industrial revolution. Its direct result, technological unemployment, has become one of our greatest local quandaries. At the turn of the century, though, innovation offered only bright promises. In 1908 one journalist wrote admiringly of the Buffalo and Susquehanna Iron Company:

> The particular claim of this institution to distinction lies in the ingenuity of the machinery employed to handle, without muscular effort, the thousands of tons of material which are daily handled at such a plant. Steam and electricity are the forces used, controlled by skilled men, who pull levers and touch buttons, so that from the time the iron ore leaves the mines of Minnesota and Michigan, the coke the ovens of Pennsylvania, and the limestone the near-by quarries, until the iron itself is unloaded in the distant customer's yard, the hand of man is not required to lift a pound of material.

From A History of the City of Buffalo, 1908.

The Dun Building, at Pearl and Swan
streets (now also called the flatiron
building) still contributes its distinctive
shape to the downtown skyline. It originally
housed R. G. Dun and Company, a pioneer
in the business of rating the credit of
prospective borrowers. Founded in 1841 by
the abolitionist Lewis Tappan to serve the
New York City area, R. G. Dun and
Company also played a vital role on the
Niagara Frontier in greasing the bearings
of the economic locomotive. In the boom
times, lending and borrowing were mostly
transactions between strangers. R. G. Dun
and Company recruited reliable local
reporters to assess the solvency of the
peddlers, grocers, and other traders who
wished to borrow money. This essential tool
sometimes worked to the disadvantage of
ethnic groups. Tightly knit Buffalo
communities like the Irish or the Jews
would sometimes refuse to talk to Dun and
Company agents. And the agents themselves carried prejudice into their work. By
the early twentieth century the company
had a hundred thousand credit reporters.
The Buffalo office was one of the most
active. Courtesy Buffalo and Erie County
Historical Society

Asphalt paving of Buffalo's streets began as
early as 1882. By 1908 there were 335
miles of pavement in the city. One publication claimed that this made Buffalo the
"finest paved city in the world." Advocates
of paving argued that reduced transportation costs and the additional taxes paid by
the new businesses attracted to the city
would more than offset the added municipal expenditures. Roy W. Nagle Collection,
courtesy Buffalo and Erie County Historical Society

The nineteenth-century revolution in productivity was not all industrial; it was also agricultural. Machines manufactured in Buffalo helped make it possible to cultivate the empty plains of four continents. J. A. and H. A. Pitts began their manufacturing operation in 1837. Over the next decades they made traction engines, stackers, baggers, pumps and other farm machines. The heyday of Buffalo Pitts came after the American Civil War, when the vast bonanza farms appeared. Buffalo Pitts served the need for large steam-driven gang plows on the North American plains, on the steppes of Russia, on the pampas of Argentina, even in Australia and Turkey. A vigorous company in the nineteenth century, Buffalo Pitts could not adapt to the new technology of the twentieth. Competition with gasoline tractors drove them from the market after World War I. From Buffalo Evening News, History of the City of Buffalo, *1908.*

Pictured here dressed for winter, Samuel Clemens was brought to Buffalo by a love interest. He wished to marry an Elmira heiress named Olivia Langdon. Already well known and successful under the pen name Mark Twain, Clemens needed to convince his future father-in-law, the formidable Jervis Langdon, that the itinerant reporter, wandering lecturer, and sometime riverboat captain was also a solid citizen. Twain considered buying an interest in the New York Tribune, *the* Cleveland Herald, *and the* Toledo Blade. *When in 1868 a share of the* Buffalo Express *became available, Langdon lent him half the money he needed to buy in. In his initial column for the paper Twain made a promise that is now famous. "I shall always confine myself to the truth," he wrote, "except when it is attended with inconvenience." Had his book* Innocents Abroad *(which appeared three weeks after his arrival here) done only moderately well, Twain might have spent a lifetime delighting and tweaking readers of the* Express. *Instead, the comical travelogue became a phenomenal success. Twain retired from editing in 1871, leaving Buffalo to devote all his time to writing. He wrote the larger part of* Roughing It *while still at the* Express, *and before he left also began to plan* Tom Sawyer. *Courtesy Buffalo and Erie County Historical Society*

Buffalo's first citizen to serve as president of
the United States was Millard Fillmore,
who occupied the White House from 1850
to 1853. Two years after Fillmore retired
from the presidency, a small-town boy from
central New York, Stephen Grover Cleveland, arrived in Buffalo enroute to an Ohio
town which bore his family's name.
Cleveland stopped in Buffalo to pay respects
to his uncle, Lewis F. Allen, who now
resided at the old Porter mansion at Black
Rock, recently annexed to Buffalo. Allen
convinced his ambitious nephew to stay in
Buffalo to pursue a career in law. Thus
Cleveland became well connected to the
Buffalo business and social establishment,
whose views he reflected. Politics was closely
akin to law, and there he began to apply his
energies. While many of his friends were
Republicans, he chose to be a Democrat.
However, Republican or Democrat, he and
his friends had no tolerance for corrupt,
boss-ridden politics as practiced in Buffalo
and around the nation after the Civil War.
Cleveland embarked on a career in public
service which stamped him as a reformer,
and led to his election as sheriff of Erie
County, mayor of Buffalo, governor of New
York, and in 1884 President of the United
States. Roy W. Nagle Collection, courtesy
Buffalo and Erie County Historical Society

Grover Cleveland was the first Democrat to
be elected president since before the Civil
War. Like his last Democratic predecessor,
James Buchanan, he was a bachelor at the
time of his election to the presidency. His
more than casual involvement with a Buffalo widow, Maria Halpin, had become an
issue in the 1884 campaign when it was revealed that he provided financial support for
her child, though he was only one of several
men with whom she had been involved. A
more acceptable image was projected when
the new president announced he would
marry a twenty-two-year-old beauty from
Buffalo, Frances Folsom, shown here.
Many years Cleveland's junior, the young
bride was the daughter of Oscar Folsom, a
good friend and former law partner. The
excitement of a White House wedding, set
for the Blue Room on June 2, 1886,
brought close press coverage of the event, to
the annoyance of the president, who
disliked newspaper publicity of what he
considered personal matters. Roy W. Nagle
Collection, courtesy Buffalo and Erie
County Historical Society

James Noble Adam was born in Peebles, Scotland, in 1842, the son of a Presbyterian minister. He began a business career in Scotland where he remained until about 1872, when his brother Robert, owner of a Buffalo department store now the Adam, Meldrum and Anderson Company (AM&A's), lured him to western New York. J. N. Adam then worked briefly in New Haven, Connecticut, until he returned to Buffalo to found J. N. Adam and Company, an economy dry-goods store which for many years was located on the east side of Main Street where AM&A's, then located across the street, now stands. A success at this new enterprise, Adam entered politics when the Progressive Movement was rising, led by honest civic leaders who worked for popular control of political parties and honest government. It is to these ideals that he devoted his administration as mayor of Buffalo from 1906 to 1910. To him, government was a business which should be run on a business-like basis, honestly and economically. Roy W. Nagle Collection, courtesy Buffalo and Erie County Historical Society

Prominent Buffalo lawyer Ansley Wilcox was a good example of the civic reformers in Buffalo. Involved in charitable endeavors since his days as a young law student, this advocate of civil-service reform became a friend to such national leaders as Theodore Roosevelt, who was governor of New York and then vice president before assuming the presidency when William McKinley was assassinated in Buffalo. Roosevelt took the oath of office in the library of Wilcox's home, now called the Theodore Roosevelt Inaugural Site. In the photograph shown, Wilcox stands at the center and behind another U.S. president who stayed at his home, William Howard Taft. Taft visited Buffalo on April 30, 1910, to speak at a banquet in the Elmwood Music Hall to memorialize the merging of the Buffalo Chamber of Commerce and the Manufacturer's Club. Roy W. Nagle Collection, courtesy Buffalo and Erie County Historical Society

By 1914, reformers were anxious to change the form of Buffalo city government, which dispersed power so widely that it made accountability for detrimental actions difficult to determine. Two events which gave impetus to the reform campaign were the collapse of the roof of the new Ward Pumping Station in 1911 while under construction and the violent streetcar strike of 1913. The Ward Pumping Station on Lake Erie at the foot of Porter Avenue was just about complete when the roof mysteriously collapsed in June. Shown are two photographs of the station, one as it neared completion in February 1911, and the other after the roof collapsed in June killing eight workmen and causing a loss estimated at three hundred thousand dollars. The public was scandalized when an investigation revealed a sordid picture of government incompetence. Roy W. Nagle Collection, courtesy Buffalo and Erie County Historical Society

When World War I broke out in Europe, tensions along the Mexican-American border already were a matter of concern. Mexico was then experiencing a revolutionary period, and several revolutionary leaders like Pancho Villa challenged the government in Mexico City. When Villa's forces raided Columbus, New Mexico, in March 1916, this violation of American territory could not go unanswered. President Woodrow Wilson sent troops to pursue Villa into Mexico but with little success. A clash between American soldiers in Mexico and the Mexican army in June 1916 led to the summoning of units of the National Guard to the Mexican border as the two nations came to the verge of war. One of the units federalized was Troop 1 of the first New York Cavalry from Buffalo, which served on the border from July 1, 1916, to March 13, 1917, by which time international mediation had calmed the crisis. Two photographs picturing Troop 1 are shown. In the first, the men of Troop 1 are parading prior to departure for the border. In the other, they are shown in their border camp near tents pitched along dirt streets. Their lives were far from glamorous in the heat and dirt of the arid summer. Courtesy Buffalo and Erie County Historical Society

Chapter Eight

War, Boom and Depression

by Joseph A. Grande

The triumph of the Progressive Reform Movement in Buffalo mirrored similar successes in other cities and states, and in Washington, D. C., where the inauguration of Woodrow Wilson in 1913 signaled the beginning of his New Freedom program. The winds of reform brought a sense of optimism about perfecting the capitalist and democratic system in the United States, and indeed, in the rest of the world. But as the winds of reform were reaching their greatest force, conditions, little noticed in America, were developing which were to spawn the winds of war and lead to World War I.

The outbreak of war so far away was of little concern to most Americans. Some were troubled by the German invasion of little Belgium, whose neutrality had been guaranteed by international treaty, but in Buffalo most attention was focused on the city-charter reform campaign in an atmosphere where industry thrived and jobs were plentiful. President Woodrow Wilson's plea to the American people to be neutral "in thought as well as in action" was accepted as a natural position consistent with traditional American policy against "entangling alliances." The president could not be neutral, however, when Mexican revolutionaries raided across the border into American towns, killing American citizens. He concentrated substantial forces on the border, including large elements of the National Guard, some of them from Erie County.

Consciousness of the serious implications of World War I grew gradually. Local citizens of German descent received letters with news about the war. British requests for the assistance of Canadian troops made the press. The shortage of American regulars to deal with the Mexican situation and the deterioration of German-American relations over the use of submarines against unarmed passenger liners gave rise to a concern about the lack of American preparedness. The sinking of the British liner *Lusitania* along the Irish coast on May 7, 1915, with the loss of 128 American lives among the over 1,000 casualties, caused the thrill of horror to seize the land. Erie County's own Elbert Hubbard of Roycroft fame perished in that tragic event. When a patient President Wilson accepted German assurances that the practice of unrestricted submarine warfare would be ended, the crisis in German-American relations subsided.

The *Lusitania* affair fed the movement to promote American preparedness. A local branch of the National Security League, with the assistance of Mayor Louis Fuhrmann and other prominent leaders, promoted recruitment for the local units of the National Guard. The use of the National Guard against the strikers in the recent streetcar strike made the task a hard one. Nevertheless, league members went into factories, theaters, stores, and churches to whip up enthusiasm for their preparedness campaign. In February 1916, Governor Charles S. Whitman spoke in support of the campaign at the Broadway Auditorium in Buffalo. The campaign culminated on June 24, 1916, with the Preparedness Parade, which took three hours to pass the reviewing stand at Buffalo's Lafayette Square. By the dawn of 1917 the fear of war with Germany led government officials and the Chamber of Commerce to agree on posting sentries at grain elevators, water and power plants, munitions plants and factories to guard against sabotage. It would appear that the heavy concentration of German-Americans in Buffalo and Erie County caused anxiety about the security of these vital facilities as rumors spread that President Wilson would soon mobilize the regular army and the National Guard.

On January 31, 1917, Germany announced the resumption of unrestricted submarine warfare, and four days later, the United States severed diplomatic relations. American civilians and American ships alleged to be carrying war materials to Germany's enemies again felt the fury of submarine attacks. President Wilson reluctantly recommended a declaration of war on April 2, before a special session of Congress, and within five days, both the House of Representatives and the Senate obliged. While Congress was still considering the declaration, a mass meeting in support of war against Germany was held at the Elmwood Music Hall. The formal outbreak of war led to the quick mobilization of the local contingents of the naval militia of the National Guard.

In the nineteenth century the women's movement was often associated with radical causes like abolition, temperance, pacifism, and dress reform. These women hoped to transform American society fundamentally and radically to change the relation between the sexes. As the movement drew closer to its goal, it became more conservative, and more nearly approximated the politics of the time. Even the Daughters of the American Revolution felt comfortable in attending a woman's suffrage convention held in Buffalo in 1908. Local women agitated for the vote partly on the basis that women's traditional sensitivity in caring for children would translate to uplifting society. The Lackawanna women pictured here, for instance, promised to vote for school appropriations. New York State defeated a female suffrage bill in 1915, but in 1917, during World War I, the measure passed. The victory was owed largely to the recognition of women's contribution to the war effort. Three years later, women's right to vote was formally incorporated into the U.S. Constitution as the Nineteenth Amendment. Roy W. Nagle Collection, courtesy Buffalo and Erie County Historical Society

These ten motorcycle policemen who posed in 1916 in Niagara Square patrolled a modern city with the latest equipment. They were part of an organized police force, that, surprisingly, was only forty-five years old. Though Buffalo's population stood at 120,000 in 1871, it was not until then that the city had a regular police force. Before that, deputies and regional police kept the peace. Courtesy Buffalo and Erie County Historical Society

From 1914 to 1917, President Woodrow Wilson tried to follow a policy of neutrality between the warring coalitions in World War I. Differences of opinion existed with both sides, though American condemnation of unrestricted submarine warfare involving the losses of innocent civilian lives caused more and more people to feel that war against Germany would eventually come. Concerned about the poor state of American preparedness, a preparedness campaign was launched across the nation.

Public meetings were held in Buffalo as elsewhere and on June 24, 1916, as National Guardsmen were about to depart for the Mexican border because of a shortage of regular troops, a massive Preparedness Day Parade marched up Main Street. In the picture shown, the parade is passing the reviewing stand at Main Street and LaFayette Square. Roy W. Nagle Collection, courtesy Buffalo and Erie County Historical Society

Patriotism became the order of the day. Citizens were called to unite in the war effort from pulpits, in classrooms, and at flag-raising ceremonies around the county as well as in factories like the Pratt & Letchworth and Pierce Arrow plants and on the steps of public schools, where pupils sang the national anthem. A concerted effort to promote patriotism was managed by a coalition of businessmen, newspaper editors, and advertising men. Erie County boys filled up the National Guard units rather than wait to be drafted. In August 1917, a crowd of fifty thousand gathered at the Delaware Park meadow to bid farewell to newly mobilized National Guard units. Three thousand troops paraded at this "Festival of Lights and Song." A month later the Seventh Regiment held its last review at Kenilworth Field in the town of Tonawanda, and on September 29, as National Guard units marched to the train station, over three hundred thousand citizens lined the streets to cheer them on and wish them well as they went off to war. Infantry and artillery units of the National Guard were joined by the Guard's Aero Company, trained at the area's first airport, Curtiss Field, in the town of Tonawanda.

When Congress enacted the draft, twenty local draft boards staffed by civilians were established, sixteen in Buffalo and four in the rest of the county. The execution of their responsibilities resulted in the induction of 19,000 units out of 171,000 registrants, of whom 3,000 came from the county outside Buffalo.

Mobilization for the war effort continued unabated on the home front as men went off to war. Fort Porter served as an officers' training camp and a base for hospital units.

In November 1917 it became a military hospital staffed by units of the Army Nurses Corps and by 1918, it had received over a thousand patients.

On the civilian front, the need to conserve precious resources led to meatless Sundays, heatless Mondays, and coal-less Tuesdays. The severe winter of 1917-1918 saw a coal shortage which was especially hard on the villages and rural areas of the county, where distribution was more difficult. Despite hardships, the people of Erie County responded well to the dislocations of war. Women collected garbage and ashes, and farmers' wives and daughters took over tasks normally performed by their husbands and brothers. Volunteers joined the Red Cross to staff its many activities, helping to raise money to finance them. The Red Cross opened a canteen for servicemen, organized a motor corps to collect clothes, and established an ambulance service. New chapters were set up across Erie county, where its Civilian Relief Committee worked to assist in hardship cases. Its salvage committee ran drives to collect paper, rubber and shoes.

The most ambitious and carefully organized drives were the five Liberty Loan drives conducted during the war. Special committees for public relations, schools, factories, and businesses organized volunteers from the "grass roots" using such vehicles as a Mothers' Parade. Local police canvassed fifty thousand homes to obtain pledges in support of Liberty Loans. The millions of dollars raised in the county were ample testimony to the success of these efforts.

Mayor Fuhrmann, though of German ancestry,

In World War I Buffalo's black citizens were recruited to "fight for democracy" in segregated regiments. Buffalo's black community was historically small, only 1 percent of the population in 1905. The war years saw the first surge of black migration to serve labor-scarce industry. One-half million moved north in the decade after 1910. In the year 1916 the black population of Buffalo doubled as nearly nineteen hundred arrived in the city. Sociologist Niles Carpenter observed that to poor Southern blacks, as to other immigrants, Buffalo looked like "an occupational El Dorado." Even so, they occupied the lowest rungs of the occupational ladder. Formally and informally, one out of three unions excluded blacks. Carpenter called it a "racial-economic caste system." Courtesy Buffalo and Erie County Historical Society

VOL. 1   JUNE 15, 1918   NO. 4

Wanted : Women

Women Must Fill Places Vacated by Factory Men who Have Gone to War. War Work Production Depends Upon Them.

Unless the women of America express their patriotism in a practical manner by taking their places at the benches left vacant by factory men who have gone to war, industry will be so crippled that war work cannot progress.

This is the message that every Pierce-Arrow worker should preach to his or her acquaintances. The work that women are performing and must perform in increasing measure is vital to the country's war preparation. It is not stretching the truth to state that some factories would be compelled to close their doors altogether were it not for the women who have donned overalls.

More Must Respond

In the Pierce-Arrow factory there now are about 700 women at work. A great many more must be added to the list to replace the 1400 men who have been drafted or enlisted.

In normal times the Pierce-Arrow factory did not deem it advisable to employ women in the shop. So long as male labor was plentiful, there seemed to be no reason why women should be employed. The advent of the war changed conditions. As men began to leave to serve their country, it became difficult to maintain production. Something had to be done. The solution of the problem was the employment of women.

The Pierce-Arrow company began to employ women last December. At first, there was no difficulty in obtaining applicants. Patriotic women, whose husbands or brothers had enlisted, pleaded that they should be allowed to do their share. The Pierce-Arrow company gladly afforded them this opportunity.

With the government urging maximum production, however, it is essential that more women be acquainted with the fact that they are needed.

Desirable Work

Factory work is not undesirable work for women, despite notions to the contrary. Women have been used in some factories in the country for many years. In some capacities, women are more rapid and better workers than men. In top-making, upholstering, light bench work, or small machine work, they proved excellent workers.

The women employed in the Pierce-Arrow plant have proved no exceptions. Under ideal factory conditions they can be found at work in many important departments.

The class of women employed by the Pierce-Arrow factory is exceptionally high. Business is attended to strictly during working hours. The men treat them with courtesy.

The women of the Pierce-Arrow plant are highly patriotic. This was proved by their loyal response of the Liberty Loan campaigns and the Red Cross drives.

It should need but little effort to attract an added number of women to Pierce-Arrow employment. The working conditions are pleasant, the renumeration liberal and the government's need constitutes a powerful appeal.

Mayor Louis Fuhrmann patriotically led his fellow Buffalonians in supporting the war effort during World War I. He was a leading meatpacker in the large German-American community in the city. He had been instrumental in ending the streetcar strike of 1913 and had fostered better public health services. When the United States entered the war against Germany, it must have been difficult for him and fellow German-Americans because of family and cultural ties. Nevertheless, he plunged into the war effort, mobilizing leaders of all ethnic communities to rally. Here he is shown bidding artillerymen goodbye as they depart for service on the war fronts across the Atlantic Ocean in France. Roy W. Nagle Collection, courtesy Buffalo and Erie County Historical Society

Until 1917, the war in Europe was indecisive. Germany decided to resume unrestricted submarine warfare because Russia was collapsing into revolution, and German leaders did not believe American entry into the war to aid the British and French armies would come in time to avert defeat. They were badly mistaken, as the United States quickly entered the war and rushed into full mobilization of its natural and human resources. By the fall of 1918, after several unsuccessful assaults on Allied lines, German military leaders informed the emperor that the war was lost. The abdication of the emperor led to a new government which agreed to an armistice in which the Germans surrendered their weapons of war. News of the armistice on November 11, 1918, drew crowds by the thousands into the streets of Buffalo, as shown, and other American cities, where there was universal rejoicing at the end of the "war to end all wars." Roy W. Nagle Collection, courtesy Buffalo and Erie County Historical Society

jumped patriotically on the bandwagon, cooperating fully with the war effort. He appointed an Americanization Committee of fifty leading citizens of Buffalo's ethnic communities to facilitate their full cooperation. It is only natural that some resentment surfaced in the large German-American community because its patriotism seemed suspect, its press was carefully watched, and German language classes in the schools were dropped. Some even found it advisable to Anglicize their names.

The depth of German-American concern based on ties of family and culture may be discerned in the mayoral election of 1917, when the majority ignored the two major party candidates, Louis Fuhrmann and George Buck, both of German ancestry, to vote for Socialist Franklin Bliss, who called for an immediate end to the war and justice for Germany.

To the relief of all citizens, World War I came to an end on November 11, 1918. Feverish efforts began in Erie County to give the troops a fitting homecoming. An immense arch rose at Lafayette Square as countless people focused their efforts on preparing an appropriate celebration to welcome local sons home from "the war to end all wars." A throng of five hundred thousand people lined the parade route on April 1, 1919, as units of the old 74th and 65th regiments, now renamed the 108th Infantry and 106th Artillery, marched up Main Street with their wounded confreres carried in automobiles. Their welcome and cheers signaled not only joy at the war's end but also a yearning to return to their personal pursuits in a peaceful world, a world of "normalcy" as President Warren G. Harding later expressed it.

The black veterans who returned from the battlefields of Europe during World War I encountered economic discrimination in Western New York. We might conclude that all immigrant groups faced hardships, and that these newest "immigrants" from the rural South were simply repeating the process. But the situation is special in some ways. There was a black community of long standing here. The figures seem to indicate that after World War I blacks were less well off than the community had been in the mid-nineteenth century. In the middle 1920s six out of ten blacks were unskilled laborers. Half of all black families took in boarders. Many worked in domestic service. Though there was a small corps of professionals (doctors, dentists, preachers, a lawyer) blacks were the poorest paid of all groups. Courtesy Buffalo and Erie County Historical Society

By February 1919, Buffalo men began to arrive home from the trenches of Europe, changed forever by their wartime experiences. Appreciative of their sacrifices, the city planned a massive reception to welcome them home. Despite cold, damp weather on April 1, they gathered by the hundreds of thousands along Main Street to cheer the returning veterans from across the sea. The parade of troops marched proudly up Main Street, passed the reviewing stand at LaFayette Square and moved onward to Main and Genessee streets, where they went by the magnificently domed Buffalo Savings Bank building. The bank building was an imperial example of the neoclassical style, built in 1900 to 1901, and symbolized the vitality of a thriving city which looked optimistically to the future in a peaceful world. Roy W. Nagle Collection, courtesy Buffalo and Erie County Historical Society

The decade following World War I, sometimes called the Age of Normalcy, evidenced continued industrial and commercial growth. The population of Erie County, which stood at 630,000 in 1920, grew 140,000 over the following ten years, while the population of Buffalo rose from 507,000 to 573,000. This heavy population dominance by the city was not reflected in county government, where the rural towns dominated. That government was composed of a board of fifty-four supervisors, half of them from outside Buffalo, where only 20 percent of the people resided.

The Board of Supervisors in the 1920s began to consider its responsibilities to provide parks and recreation outside the city, and its Erie County Parks Commission acquired seventeen hundred acres to develop four parks: Chestnut Ridge, Emery, Como Lake and Ellicott Creek. Expanded county parks were accompanied by a decline in farming acreage between 1920 and 1930 from 538,052 to 433,712. Declines also occurred in the number of dairy cows and the acreage devoted to oats, corn, and potatoes while bean, grape, and berry production grew. The stark reality in agriculture during the 1920s, however, was economic hardship brought on by overproduction and consequent price declines. Private endeavors to meet the problem proved inadequate, and government assistance failed to materialize. Fortunately, the Erie County farm community had access to the vast urban market in Buffalo.

The area commercial-industrial complex in contrast was healthy, and optimism for the future seemed justified. A diversified economy based on steel, grain, lumber, and rubber served by a splendid rail network moved in positive directions. The prosperity of the railroads was signaled by the building of new stations by the Lackawanna (1917), Lehigh Valley (1919) and the New York Central (1929). The New York Central Terminal on Buffalo's East Side was a magnificent fifteen-story structure which could accommodate two hundred passenger trains a day. By 1930, Buffalo's daily grain-milling capacity outstripped Minneapolis for the first time. The steel industry, centered along the lake south of Buffalo in Lackawanna, flourished with the advantage of one of the single largest and most modern steel plants in the world, which in 1922 was absorbed by the Bethlehem Steel empire.

North of the city line in the town of Tonawanda,

The ice houses of East Buffalo below Broadway stored blocks sawed from the lake in the winter. In summer the ice cooled milk in Joseph Schmidbauer's wagon. Schmidbauer's dairy in Sloan served the east side from the mid 1890s until 1920.

Farm discontent after World War I grew out of overproduction and falling prices as farm costs continued to rise. Demands for effective government assistance went largely unanswered as greater competition on the world markets caused the further decline of prices. Demonstrations by farm groups were aimed at putting pressure on government officials by focusing publicity on the problem. In 1920, the farm stewards of the New York Grange sent a "prairie schooner" from Albany to Washington to highlight the fight for help in the form of lowered taxes. In the photo shown, the prairie schooner is parked in Buffalo's Niagara Square. Roy W. Nagle Collection, courtesy Buffalo and Erie County Historical Society

Wickwire-Spencer Steel had opened a plant on the Niagara River during World War I. Nearby, the Buffalo General Electric Company had built a generating power plant where a new station was opened in 1923, thus making the area attractive to industry. The British Dunlop Rubber and Tire Company built its first American plant there in the early 1920s. A short distance away, Dupont Chemicals began production of rayon and manufactured the first cellophane in the nation. Just to the north, an oil refinery and oil storage tanks began to rise. Tonawanda also became a leading center of airplane development. Glenn Curtiss built a factory in the southwestern part of the town near the Buffalo City line. At the eastern end of the town Curtiss Field opened to serve as the main airport in the area until 1926 and the opening of the Buffalo Airport in Cheektowaga. Consolidated Aircraft operated another airfield in Tonawanda, where flying exhibitions were frequently held. Kenmore resident Leslie L. Irvin, developer of the modern parachute, used these fields to fly.

Courtesy Tonawanda-Kenmore Historical Society

The waterfront industrial belt north of Buffalo in the town of Tonawanda expanded considerably during the 1920s. Easy access to the water and the nearby electric generating plant, now the Huntley plant of the Niagara Mohawk Power Corporation, lured major industries to the area. Other factors, such as a plentiful labor supply and ample transportation facilities, also played a role. Thus in 1919, the English Dunlop Tire and Rubber Company selected Tonawanda as the site for its first American operation. The plant,

shown here under construction, opened in 1923 to become one of the ten largest tire plants in the United States. A short distance away, the DuPont Company bought an abandoned rubber-reclaiming plant and opened operations in a facility, shown here in 1926, where it began production of "fibersilk," or rayon, in 1921, and where the first cellophane in the United States was made a few years later. Such new employers as these provided thousands of jobs for the citizens of Erie County.

Roy W. Nagle Collection, courtesy Buffalo and Erie County Historical Society

The town of Tonawanda was a center of aviation pioneering in the 1920s. Aviation pioneer Glenn H. Curtiss came from Hammondsport to Tonawanda to establish an airstrip from which he flew on a regular basis in the 1920s. Curtiss Field, the first airport in the Buffalo area, is shown here on October 19, 1924, as cars line Niagara Falls Boulevard and Eggert Road and jammed the parking area line to watch planes take off and land. One of the other pilots who flew from Curtiss Field was Kenmore resident Leslie Irvin, inventor of the modern free-fall ripcord-activated parachute. In 1922 he was appointed, as shown, aerial policeman of the village of Kenmore, the first such appointment in the nation. Curtiss Field was run by the Curtiss Company until 1925, when field manager Edwin M. Ronne, a test pilot of renown, took it over for passenger flying and instruction. It was soon replaced as the area's major airport by the Buffalo Airport, which opened in 1926 in the town of Cheektowaga. Courtesy Tonawanda-Kenmore Historical Society

Shortly after the new Buffalo Airport opened, it captured the limelight with the visit of young aviator Charles Lindbergh. Lindbergh's spectacular feat in flying non-stop from New York to Paris in a single-engine airplane gave new impetus to the growing aviation industry. Arriving at the Buffalo Airport on July 29, five weeks after the completion of his famous flight, he was greeted with enthusiastic public adulation. People who never visited the airport arrived in droves, as shown in the photograph, to catch a glimpse of the flier and his silver Ryan monoplane, the Spirit of St. Louis. A parade in his honor attracted an esti-mated one hundred to three hundred thou-sand spectators, and thousands gathered to see him in the Delaware Park meadow. He predicted, at a civic banquet which followed, that there would be regular air traffic across the Atlantic Ocean, and he commended the people for their support in creating and maintaining an airport. Courtesy Niagara Frontier Transportation Authority. Buffalo Airports 1926-1976.

If planes and flying were somewhat exotic in the 1920s, the automobile became commonplace as mass production techniques brought costs down to the affordable range of more and more people. The area already enjoyed the presence of several Ford operations and the prestige of being the home of the Pierce-Arrow Company. The automotive industry expanded here when General Motors selected Buffalo as the site to build an assembly and body plant in 1922. Added to this was the opening of the Dunlop plant in Tonawanda in 1923 and the origin and expansion of the Trico Products Corporation. The latter enterprise began in 1917, when John R. Oishei saw the need for automobile windshield wipers. After first developing a simple improvisation, he perfected an automatic wiper which became the basis for expanding the corporation and eventually provided over five thousand jobs for local residents.

The appearance of more and more automobiles on city streets and county roads had an inevitable impact. Auto owners organized the Buffalo Automobile Club, which by 1920, had over three thousand members. Demands for higher speed limits, the construction of new roads and the widening and extension of old roads arose with wide support in the community press.

Courtesy Buffalo and Erie County Historical Society

In 1916, a man named John Roffo Oishei met with an accident while driving his car in a rainstorm along Delaware Avenue at Utica Street. His car struck a bicycler, who fortunately escaped serious injury. This frightening event convinced Oishei that a way had to be found to enable drivers to maintain vision while driving in the rain. He first went into business making the hand-operated "Rain Rubber." Eventually he developed automatic windshield wipers, founding what is now the multi-million dollar Trico Products Corporation. For many years, this Buffalo-based enterprise operated three plants employing thousands of Western New Yorkers. Shown are the headquarters of the Trico manufacturing facilities at Washington and Goodell streets and a photograph of Trico's founder in 1967 when he received an honorary degree from D'Youville College. In the group photograph are right to left, Sister Francis Xavier Lynch, president of D'Youville College; Alexander B. Trowbridge, U.S. secretary of commerce; John Roffo Oishei; and Buffalo businesswoman Amelia M. Moran. Courtesy D'Youville College Archives

184

The village of Kenmore, Buffalo's pioneer suburb, boomed in the 1920s as the advent of the automobile made living there very convenient. The decade of the 1920s was Kenmore's golden years as the population rose from about three thousand to nearly seventeen thousand residents by 1930. Realtors and builders were kept very busy as advertisements in the Buffalo press attracted customers seeking the advantages of a small-town atmosphere within easy reach of the assets of a large city. The largely bedroom community is shown in two photographs, one a 1924 aerial view looking northeast, over partially vacant land in north Buffalo, across Kenmore Avenue into the more densely built-up village. The other photograph shows a stretch of the village's main street, Delaware Avenue, with businesses decorated for summer festivities the same year. Courtesy Tonawanda-Kenmore Historical Society

Louis Eberhardt worked out of this real estate office as his pioneer suburb of Kenmore slowly grew over many years. While most houses in the development were of frame construction, some were built of brick, like those shown on East Girard Boulevard at the northern end of the village. Courtesy Tonawanda-Kenmore Historical Society

Local press had been undergoing changes as more and more newspapers disappeared, eventually leaving the *Courier-Express* and the *Buffalo Evening News* to serve Buffalo and its expanding suburbs. The number of legitimate theaters declined, though the number of little theaters grew when Jane Keeler of the Buffalo Players established a studio school. Service organizations such as the Lions, Kiwanis, Rotary, Quota, and Zonta Clubs expanded as new chapters were founded in Buffalo and around the county. A new campus, adjacent to the Buffalo State Hospital, opened for the Buffalo Normal School, now renamed the Buffalo State Teachers' College, with a four-year curriculum. A new Buffalo city hall in Niagara Square was proposed by the City Planning Association, which drew up a master plan for the city.

Michael Shea, born in 1859, had close ties with the famous First Ward. After jobs as a dock worker, iron worker, and saloonkeeper, he began to move into the downtown area as a restaurateur, hotel owner, and music hall operator. He opened his first theater in the Brisbane Arcade in 1892. In 1898, he bought a skating rink on Pearl Street which he remodeled as the Garden Theater, and seven years later he opened Shea's Court Street Theater at the corner of Pearl. He was well on his way to becoming the area's major vaudeville producer with a string of theaters like the one shown. His vaudeville stages attracted such performers as Eddie Cantor, W. C. Fields, Marie Dressler, and Mae West, to the joy of countless Buffalonians. It was he who encouraged Eddie Cantor, at first a juggler's assistant, to speak his first lines. It was Shea who also urged humorist Will Rogers to tell jokes about his rope tricks. His Garden Theater, it is claimed, is where the strip-tease was invented by a trapeze artist named Charmion who finished her act by throwing her jacket and a garter to the audience. Shea was veritably Western New York's greatest showman by the 1920s, presiding over a theater empire which successfully converted to movie houses when the advent of motion pictures dealt a fatal blow to vaudeville. Roy W. Nagle Collection, courtesy Buffalo and Erie County Historical Society

The construction of a bridge between Buffalo and Fort Erie was one of the most exciting events of the 1920s. Ferry service across the border dated back over a century, and rail access opened in the 1870s with the International Bridge. The coming of the automobile promoted the desire for a more convenient way to allow Americans to cross to the Canadian shore. Thus, through international cooperation, an impressive structure rose over the Niagara River rapids just off Lake Erie. On August 7, 1927, the bridge opened to direct automobile traffic as millions of people listened to radio broadcasts of the opening ceremonies. Fort Porter was demolished to make way for the bridge and a fitting name was selected, the International Peace Bridge, as a tribute to the close relations between two peace-loving nations.

The opening of the Peace Bridge complicated the task of law-enforcement officials in enforcing the Eighteenth Amendment—Prohibition—adopted at the end of World War I. Sympathy for the "noble experiment" existed around the county but it had little support in heavily ethnic Buffalo, where Prohibition devastated the brewery industry and seriously injured local taverns which served as neighborhood social centers. The illegal liquor trade fell into the hands of gangsters, who quarreled and killed over its profits. Speakeasies and "bath tub" gin became plentiful, and saloons flourished under the guise of soft-drink emporiums. Old breweries made "near beer" at first and then dropped pretenses by producing regular beer. A profitable liquor trade sprang up along the Niagara River as Canadian farms shifted to grain crops to provide the necessary raw materials. The United States Coast Guard had a difficult, if not impossible, job and Canadian authorities were slow in responding to American demands for action to prevent the trade. Immigration authorities at the International Peace Bridge had to deal constantly with ingenious attempts to smuggle liquor across the border.

Numerous organized efforts had failed since 1851 to construct a bridge between Buffalo and Fort Erie, Ontario. Livestock businessman and banker Alonzo C. Mather labored unsuccessfully for many years beginning in the 1890s to bring the project to fruition. Influential businessmen on both sides of the border embraced the Mather dream, and enthusiasm for the project grew. Delayed by World War I, the cause was again taken up after the Armistice when an international company, the Buffalo and Fort Erie Public Bridge Company, was established to construct the span with private funds. On August 17, 1925, ground was broken and construction commenced. The bridge was to be called the International Peace Bridge, and it required the demolition of old Fort Porter, from which the last troops were evacuated on June 28, 1926 (photograph). By October 14, 1926, the last steel girders were being raised into place, as shown here, as construction approached an end. Roy W. Nagle Collection, courtesy Buffalo and Erie County Historical Society

188

Dedication ceremonies for the International Peace Bridge were held on August 7, 1927, attended by a galaxy of internationally renowned personages. Representing Canada and the British Commonwealth were Prince Edward of Wales, heir to the British throne; his younger brother, Prince George, duke of York; British Prime Minister Stanley Baldwin; and Canadian Prime Minister W. L. MacKenzie King. When the hoped-for appearance of President Calvin Coolidge failed to materialize, Vice-President Charles Dawes represented the United States, accompanied by Secretary of State Frank Kellogg and New York Governor Alfred E. Smith. Shown are four photographs of the ceremonies. The first is of the Fort Erie Plaza as the Prince of Wales arrives for the dedication. The second is of the ceremonies at the center of the bridge, where delegations for both nations gather to celebrate the event. The third photograph shows the handsome and popular Prince of Wales, on the right, and his shy brother, Prince George, during the ceremonies at the center of the bridge. Both eventually became Kings of Great Britain. The last is an aerial view of the completed span.

The prohibition movement was closely related to the women's rights crusade, both aiming to raise the level of public morality. It is no coincidence that the Eighteenth Amendment to the United States Constitution, establishing Prohibition, and the Nineteenth Amendment, giving women the right to vote, were adopted about the same time. The Women's Christian Temperance Union along with both Protestant and Roman Catholic churchmen labored to make the "noble experiment" work. Buffalo, however, was never a center of the crusade against alcohol. The economic interests and cultural patterns of many, including the city's ethnic communities, opposed the idea, and the local press, while warring on gambling and vice, feared Prohibition would increase the appeal of alcoholic beverages. Enforcing Prohibition was an almost impossible task, especially along the international border with Canada, where alcohol was legal. Smuggling across the Niagara River and Lake Erie was commonplace in boats like the one shown and even in canoes. Enforcement efforts by the Coast Guard led to highly publicized incidents like the one in May 1928, when the pleasure yacht Ticker carrying a prominent Buffalo lawyer was fired on off Sturgeon Point. Courtesy Buffalo and Erie County Historical Society

Mayor Frank X. Schwab provided the "plain people" of Buffalo with exciting leadership during the 1920s. His roots were in the German community and he was educated in area parochial schools. After a brief career as a cabinetmaker, he hired on as a salesman for the Iroquois Brewing Company, then founded the Schwab Liquor Company, and eventually joined the management of the Buffalo Brewing Company. He was very active in religious and business groups, organizing, among other things, toy drives for orphans. His election as mayor in 1921 was viewed by some as a defiant protest by people in Buffalo against Prohibition. While he felt obligated to enforce the law, he did urge the legalization of light wines and beer to undercut the vast bootleg trade. Mayor Schwab was good press copy, with a flair for attracting attention at public events like the one shown as he marches in a parade with fur coat, cane, and carnation. Courtesy Buffalo and Erie County Historical Society

Federal agents were shocked at the widespread evasion of Prohibition in Buffalo. Their difficult task was assisted by concerted though unsuccessful efforts of the Anti-Saloon League and the Buffalo Women's Clubs to dry up the city. This was a hopeless effort in a community where the police, politicians, government officials and the public generally opposed Prohibition.

One such politician was brewer Frank X. Schwab, a colorful and energetic Catholic businessman who unseated the Protestant Yale-educated Mayor George Sturges by a close vote in 1921. Schwab promised to be an accessible mayor of "the plain people." He opened his own mail, directly answered telephone calls, and dominated the City Commission by the force of his personality. As a member of that commission, he directed the city's police, fire, and health departments. He opposed Prohibition and urged that the sale of light wines and beer be legalized. Prohibition was a failure, he believed, and the only beneficiaries were the bootleggers who reaped the profits of their illegal trade. However, he promised to enforce the law, and he ordered a careful watch on the so-called soft-drink emporiums and social clubs around the city where vice and gambling were suspected. Extra police patrols were also sent into the city's "tenderloin" districts. He personally led the clean-up campaign, making night raids and closing a number of places.

Yet despite his efforts, city reformers accused him of allowing a wide-open city and the Council of Churches blamed the Catholic mayor for tolerating vice. An investigator was hired by the Anti-Saloon League and the Council of Churches to expose vice, and a group of Methodist ministers demanded Schwab's removal from office. When the mayor asked for specific information on legal violations, his critics made no response. With a poorly paid police department, violations probably did exist with the connivance of some elements who gave advance warnings when raids were planned. Schwab tried to remedy the problem by reorganizing the police department, placing more responsibility on the shoulders of precinct captains. He successfully engineered a salary increase in 1924, and he cooperated with a grand jury in uncovering a tip-off system in the police department. In 1925 he appointed a new police chief, James W. Higgins, who tightened discipline in the ranks, with a resulting decrease in crime, vice, and scandal.

Schwab fought other battles as well. He cracked down on the sale of salacious literature and cooperated with federal authorities in anti-drug efforts. He led gambling raids and sought to padlock disorderly houses and prosecute the property owners who rented them. He warred against the Ku Klux Klan by promoting the publication of membership lists. Klan funds were used to finance opposition to the mayor, and threats against his life led to an assassination attempt while he was enroute to the J. N. Adam Hospital in Perrysburg. A public outcry against the Klan led to investigations, legal proceedings and the sensational revelation of Klan ties by several prominent local Protestant ministers.

William "Wild Bill" Donovan became director of the OSS (the forerunner of the CIA) during World War II. But he began his career in Buffalo. Born in South Buffalo, Donovan compiled a distinguished record in World War I, returned as Colonel Donovan, and married into the prominent Rumsey family. Already regarded as an outsider, Donovan alienated Buffalo society when, as U.S. attorney in Western New York, he staged raids on the exclusive Saturn Club and the Country Club of Buffalo to look for violations of the Volsted Act. As a member of these clubs Donovan was certain he would find liquor. One-inch banner headlines reported the raid. A locker-room attendant blocked the way at the Country Club allowing time for the evidence to be destroyed, but the Saturn Club was not so lucky. The bartender was arrested. Names of members who held contraband liquor were published in the newspaper. If Donovan left this group feeling betrayed, there was also little enthusiasm for Prohibition at home in the Irish First Ward. When Donovan ran for governor of New York in 1939 on the Republican ticket he lost heavily in this area. From the Buffalo Star, *courtesy Buffalo and Erie County Historical Society*

Sensationalism touched the public contest between Schwab and the International Railway Company (IAC), which enjoyed monopoly control of area trolley service. Complaints of poor service and low wages led to public boycotts and a violent strike in 1922. Schwab urged arbitration and issued over five thousand jitney permits to minimize the effects of the strike. An IRC challenge in the courts failed, and the mayor retaliated by demanding an investigation by the state Public Service Commission. He also called for the introduction of a city-owned bus system and a city takeover of the trolley network. The mayor's tenacity and adverse findings by the Public Service Commission led to an improvement in IRC services by 1927.

Construction of public facilities met with Schwab's enthusiastic support. He pressured for the rapid construction of the Peace Bridge and was instrumental in the development of the Buffalo International Airport, which opened for business in 1926. During his administration, Buffalo got the impressive Museum of Science building in Humboldt Park and a new filtration and incinerator plant. Plans were finalized for a magnificent 32-story city hall, which was constructed between 1929 and 1931. School construction had a high priority because of overcrowded conditions, which forced classes to be held in basements, rental stores, and houses. A combative mayor blamed the Board of Education for these conditions, and because he had little control over its members, he used public pressure and financial leverage to push through a program resulting

Wages did not keep up with inflation during World War I and bitterness remained from the 1913 streetcar strike. When the International Railway Company announced a cut in wages in 1922, the union immediately called another strike, which lasted through the summer. A fare hike and wage cuts were meant to improve the company's financial condition though the result aggravated its problems. Violence flared as bombs and bricks were thrown and police gunfire killed one person and wounded three others. In the town of Tonawanda, the Niagara Falls-Buffalo trolley shown here was derailed as the tracks were dynamited by strikers. Trolleys were armed and troops called in by the end of July. Strikers were fired and strikebreakers brought in to further fuel an already explosive situation. In the long run, public sympathy for the strikers declined because of violence, and the IRC permanently lost patrons as complaints of poor service continued to be heard. Courtesy Tonawanda-Kenmore Historical Society

in thirteen new school buildings and nineteen additions to older ones. New homes were opened for Bennett, East and Riverside High Schools as well as Seneca and Burgard vocational schools. A crippled children's school whicn he proposed to be attached to Children's Hospital was eventually funded on the condition it be built on City Hospital land.

Schwab's two terms as mayor were years in which more and more sentiment developed for a restructuring of the city government. The supposedly nonpartisan city commission system had evolved into a highly political system, with each of the commissioners supported by his own political machine. Schwab's aggressive personality had resulted in frequent clashes among the commissioners. In

1926, the mayor appointed highly respected Judge Daniel J. Kenefick to head a commission to study city government. A popular referendum endorsed a new city charter, which provided for a strong mayor with veto and appointive powers, a single-house, fifteen-member council, and an independently elected comptroller to monitor city funds. The new charter went into effect in 1928 and the first mayoral election was scheduled for 1929. In that year, Schwab, though insisting he was nonpartisan, accepted the Democratic Party's nomination. Charles Roesch, an old friend alienated because of political disagreements, accepted the Republican nomination to challenge Schwab, who ran on his record. A Republican sweep unseated the colorful mayor and brought the end of an exciting political era,

The need for a new city hall was evident by the 1920s. The facilities of the 1876 city-county hall on Franklin Street had long been inadequate, and plans had to be drawn up for a new building. The site selected was on the west side of Niagara Square, the same site once occupied by the gallows used in the 1825 Thayer hangings, and later by the home of Judge Samuel Wilkeson, who had contributed so much to making Buffalo a great urban center. Plans for the building required that Court Street be closed off on the west side of Niagara Square, the first major alteration of Joseph Ellicott's original street plan. architects Charles J. Dietel and James J. Wade produced designs for a structure which would reflect the power of a great industrial and commercial community. Built between 1929 and 1931, the City Hall was a massive 32-story art deco building which dominated the Buffalo skyline. At its main entrance were giant columns and bronze doors. At its corners were bronze statues of Buffalo's two presidents, Millard Fillmore and Grover Cleveland. Inside were marble floors, ceiling mosaics, and colorful murals. At the top, 330 feet up, was an observation deck affording an unforgettable view of the city and its environs. Courtesy Buffalo and Erie County Historical Society

The predecessor of the new city hall was the elaborate High Victorian Romanesque City-County Hall completed on March 13, 1876. For many years the building served as a fitting symbol of a thriving community. Now the Erie County Court House, it had been built at Franklin Square, the site of Buffalo's first burial ground, where in 1813 Colonel Cyrenius Chapin surrendered Buffalo to the British. It was the first public building to cost in excess of $1 million. Roy W. Nagle Collection, courtesy Buffalo and Erie County Historical Society

The Buffalo Society of Natural Sciences
was founded in 1862 and soon developed
an outstanding herbarium as it also began
to gather collections of fossils, mineral rock,
shells, birds and mammals. Its educational
program, dating back to 1869, included
programs for schoolchildren, public lectures, adult education classes, and publications. By 1887, the society's collections were
housed in the new Buffalo Public Library
at LaFayette Square. In 1920, the society
moved into its own building on Elmwood
Avenue just south of the Albright Art
Gallery. The need for better facilities led to
the construction of a new home, matching
those of the historical society and art
gallery. Located at the opposite end of
Humboldt Parkway from Delaware Park,
surrounded by Humboldt Park, the new
Museum of Science shown opened in 1929
with eleven exhibition halls, an auditorium
and an observatory. Roy W. Nagle Collection, courtesy Buffalo and Erie County
Historical Society, Goldome

This aerial view of Buffalo about 1930
looks across downtown toward the harbor.
The tall building on the right center is the
new city hall, and in the upper left is the
new Ford plant jutting out into the harbor.
That harbor reached its peak after World
War I with an impressive panorama of
facilities including dozens of grain elevators, coal and ore docks, bulk-freight docks
and merchandise wharves. Federal and
municipal funds were used to maintain the
harbor, which topped many world ports in
sailings and tonnage. Courtesy Buffalo and
Erie County Historical Society

replete with controversy and accomplishment.

Schwab's reign as mayor paralleled an age of general
prosperity and optimism, the "Roaring Twenties," which
came to an end with the Stock Market Crash of 1929. The
Wall Street collapse did not result in immediate panic in
Erie County, where public reaction was reported to be one
of detachment. The stock market was not a good indicator
of the condition of the nation's economy, according to the
Courier-Express. Leaders of the banking community issued
a statement noting the soundness of the area's business.
Trade volume was on the increase and labor turnover was
small. The First National Bank of Kenmore reported
record earnings and Ford Motor Company advertisements
in the press expressed optimism. This situation, however,
soon began to change as the backlog of orders was filled
and new orders began to drop. Construction contracts

declined and unemployment rose to near 10 percent.

To combat unemployment, Mayor Roesch's administration developed an ambitious public works program, and
with the assistance of state money, over two thousand jobs
improving parks, cleaning streets and raking leaves were
given to the unemployed. The job situation improved temporarily in the spring of 1930, and the number of building
permits issued rose. Then the trend reversed and unemployment doubled to the point where public works projects
and the city treasury could not handle the crisis. Mayor
Roesch urged New York State to stimulate local employment by rushing plans to build a bridge connecting Tonawanda and Grand Island, a project which went out to bid
in 1931. During the snowy winter of 1930-1931, he won
national attention by organizing a "man a block" campaign
to create a thousand jobs. Thirty families per block were

asked to contributed fifty to seventy-five cents to pay one man fifteen dollars a week to clear snow and do other odd jobs. Despite such worthy efforts, unemployment worsened in 1931 as factory employment dropped over 18 percent and wages declined over 27 percent. By the following year, only 44 percent of the male population had full-time jobs, and local government found it impossible to deal with a situation of such magnitude.

In the countryside, the financial panic which set off an industrial depression worsened the long-standing agricultural recession. Milk, wheat, corn and pork prices tumbled well below pre-World War I levels. Income dropped well below production costs, and indebtedness soared as the specter of mortgage foreclosure reared its head. The prosperous Erie County farm community, with its easy access to the huge Buffalo market, did not suffer the worst effects of the Depression. Farmers ran wholesale produce markets in the city, selling directly to the consumer, and they coop-

erated with the Farm Bureau in attacking the problems facing them.

One of the worst problems needing immediate attention during the Great Depression was relief for the desperate and needy. Volunteer endeavors to held the needy included collections of money, food and clothing by local policemen, firemen, scouts and Sunday school children. Ex-mayor Schwab donated a hundred bushels of apples to jobless veterans and helped thirty-four men get jobs. Organized private charities like the Salvation Army and Catholic Charities established bread lines, soup kitchens and milk stations to assist the desperate. However, private voluntary efforts could not deal adequately with such a serious need. City, county, and state moneys were contributed to the efforts to provide relief, and both Buffalo and Erie County set up emergency food centers and temporary shelters. There were complaints that Gov. Franklin D. Roosevelt concentrated too many of his efforts on New

Many Buffalonians suffered severe hardships during the Great Depression, losing their jobs and frequently their homes. The humiliation of standing in bread lines or being forced to accept public assistance was something never to be forgotten. Such experiences left an inevitable psychological impact on individuals, families, and the entire community. A feeling of despondency caused one old couple to commit sui-

cide by gas inhalation and one man to kill himself by crashing his own plane. Even those fortunate enough to keep their jobs, even on a part-time basis, did not escape the scars of these insecure times. The somber tone of the time is shown in the accompanying 1936 photograph taken during a March snow storm as commuters awaited IRC trolleys at Shelton Square. Courtesy Buffalo and Erie County Historical Society

York City, and President Herbert Hoover's administration refused to provide assistance except for providing funds for the construction of the federal courthouse and the expansion of the Coast Guard station. During the holiday season in the winter of 1931, over twenty thousand people ate Christmas dinner in the soup kitchens of Erie County.

Economic depression tumbled into economic disaster by 1932. While Ford opened a new plant in Hamburg, railroad business, steel production and lake shipping continued to decline. In 1931, two hundred small businesses, mostly retailers and small factories, closed with a loss of income estimated at twenty-five thousand dollars. Christmas receipts were way down as consumers used their money for such essentials as food and shelter. One hundred and fifty businesses, mostly large, closed in 1932 when private construction came to a standstill. In that year, Buffalo doled out $6 million in welfare benefits to more than a hundred thousand people. It also celebrated its centennial as a city by building Centennial Park, a downtown park overlooking the waterfront, with a stadium, midway, airplane exhibits, exposition buildings and firework shows.

The fanfare of the Buffalo Centennial did little to relieve popular frustration over the Depression and the lack of federal action. The elections of 1932 produced a Democratic landslide catapulting Gov. Franklin D. Roosevelt into the White House on his promise to give the American people a New Deal. Roosevelt's priorities were to provide federal emergency relief funds for the needy and generate jobs for the unemployed. Federal funds for relief now came to the rescue of many near-bankrupt local governments. Additionally, such New Deal agencies as the Public Works Administration and the Works Progress Administration made money available for a vast assortment of local projects designed to take citizens off the unemployment roles.

Both Buffalo and Erie County were ready with project plans when federal public-works funds became available. The city requested money for a new sewage-disposal system, a convention hall, a recreation center, a new police headquarters, and a new high school. Erie County had plans for a new jail, a county office building, and additions to the County Home and Infirmary in Alden as well as road improvements and new highway bridges. The PWA extended $7 million plus low-interest loans to undertake construction of a new sewage facility to be administered by the new Buffalo Sewer Authority. An urban redevelopment project attracting national attention was the building of a convention hall, to be called Memorial Auditorium, for which the PWA provided $2 million. WPA funds made possible the construction of a major sports arena, Civic Stadium, surrounded by playgrounds, tennis courts, and a swimming pool. Federal moneys assisted in the building of the acoustically perfect Kleinhans Music Hall, which became the home of the Buffalo Philharmonic Orchestra, whose existence on a permanent basis was promoted by WPA funds.

The city of Buffalo observed the centennial of its city charter in 1932 at the depths of the Great Depression. Despite troubled times, a suitable program of events was planned by civic groups and city government. Mayor Charles E. Roesch formally opened the Buffalo Centennial at the ceremonies shown here in the Elmwood Music Hall on Sunday afternoon, June 26, 1932. Many events took place at Centennial Park downtown overlooking the lake. Others, like the pageant in the photograph, took place around town. The pageant was staged by the Republican Women's Club on the steps of the Buffalo Historical Society building looking toward the lake in Delaware Park. Roy W. Nagle Collection, courtesy Buffalo and Erie County Historical Society

In an attempt to get the American economy moving again, Franklin Roosevelt's New Deal program appropriated billions of dollars to stimulate jobs which would put people to work again. Public works projects to build needed municipal buildings, parks, roads, and schools were funded in communities across the land by the Public Works Administration. The Works Progress Administration not only funded public works but it also found part-time jobs for needy high school and college students and provided employment for white-collar workers such as actors, writers, musicians and painters. One such major project in Buffalo was the 15,000-seat Memorial Auditorium at the historic terrace on lower Main Street, built between 1938 and 1940. Roy W. Nagle Collection, courtesy Buffalo and Erie County Historical Society

Other New Deal projects included modernization of the Buffalo Zoo, a new municipal building for Kenmore and the town of Tonawanda, and a county office building including a jail and welfare offices. The Alden County Infirmary used federal funds to double the size of the complex and add a new cafeteria area. The over three hundred PWA and WPA projects led to new housing projects as well as road and river improvements. By 1937, the federal government had spent over $45 million in permanent projects providing seventy-five thousand jobs. If these New Deal projects did not end unemployment, they did much to alleviate conditions spawned by the worst depression in American history. Even scandals in the use of federal funds involving Mayor George Zimmerman and nine city councilmen did not dim the positive side of the New Deal programs, designed as temporary expedients to stimulate economic recovery. A sign of that recovery appeared in 1937 when Chevrolet announced plans for a new $12.5 mil-

lion plant complex along the Niagara River just north of the city line in the town of Tonawanda industrial sector. Erie County surrendered lands designed for park development to accommodate a project expected to create three to four thousand jobs.

By the late 1930s, the worst effects of the Great Depression had passed as an active federal administration showed its determination to bring a return to prosperity. The shock and insecurity created by the Depression was replaced by a more optimistic outlook about the future, although such optimism had to be tempered by the ominous clouds of war gathering in Asia and Europe. Ironically new business generated by the coming war helped to create booming prosperity to end the Great Depression. Unfortunately, those who yearned for a more secure and stable world were to be disappointed by the advent of international anarchy and the outbreak of World War II.

The Convertible Coupe-Roadster
WITH RUMBLE SEAT

As a maker of luxury automobiles Pierce-Arrow always pitched its advertising high. At the turn of the century one slogan insisted that "the man who owns a Pierce-Arrow envies no one." Much later the campaign copy read, "there is something indescribably reassuring about the staunchness and stability of the 1936 Pierce-Arrow." In the end the company

became a victim of this strategy. Fine craftsmanship and technical excellence counted for less and less as fewer and fewer people were able to afford a Pierce-Arrow. In 1936 Pierce-Arrow sold only a third as many automobiles as it had sold in 1933. In 1937 a recession within the Depression spelled the end of the Pierce-Arrow Company. With an army of restless unem-

ployed, ostentatious wealth was no longer tasteful, or, perhaps, even safe. This 1937 Convertible Coupe was one of the last automobiles built by Pierce-Arrow. The company was sold at auction in 1938. Roy W. Nagle Collection, courtesy Buffalo and Erie County Historical Society

1917 Given to Buffalo Airport in 1931

The two accompanying photographs high-light the use of motor vehicles for purposes other than pleasure during the 1930s. The first is an old ambulance given to the Buffalo Airport in 1931 for use in emergencies. The second is a school bus in the Holland Central School district. In 1932, that district was the first to be centralized in Western New York. Shown with driver Plin Geiger is the first school bus used by the district. Holland Central district school buses were first privately owned by Ross E. Brown, a Ford dealer and town supervisor from 1933 to 1947. Courtesy Holland Historical Society

Btry. F will be equipped with eight 37mm. guns like this.

One of the 15 searchlights that will be part of the 209th equipment.

50 cal. Machine Guns with which Btry. E of the regiment is armed.

Searchlight and sound locators like these are part of the basic equipment of Btry. A. Skilled electricians are required.

Buffalo will have two complete four gun Btries. of these 3-inch guns forming equipment of Btries. B & C.

Units of the gun Bn. firing at night at targets illuminated by searchlight btry.

Buffalo's New 209th
OFFERS YOU ENLISTMENT

1. In a new rapidly expanding arm of the service.
2. Opportunity to choose work for which you are best suited; electricians, auto mechanics, chauffeurs, telephone men, engineers (civil), cooks, buglers, and clerks are needed.
3. Wide opportunity for training in many different weapons with which the regiment is armed.
4. Service in a mounted truck-drawn organization; fine new modern equipment.
5. Chance for rapid advancement.
6. Association with a fine group of Buffalo men already enlisted.

Buffalo can accept only 350 men at present from whom key men will be chosen for later expansion upon induction into federal service.

Enlist now while vacancies still exist and choose your arm of service, which may later be impossible if you are conscripted.

Enlistment Days MONDAY and THURSDAY At the 106th Armory
29 MASTEN STREET

From the collections, Buffalo and Erie County Historical Society

International Railway Company Collection, courtesy Buffalo and Erie County Historical Society

Chapter Nine

The Creation of Greater Buffalo: Problems and Prospects

by Scott Eberle

We have become accustomed to speaking of Erie County and its environs as the "Niagara Frontier," or the "Greater Buffalo" area. When asked where we hail from by outsiders, the likely answer is, "Buffalo." As a figure of speech the idea is firmly set: the students enroll at the University of Buffalo but many study at its largest campus in Amherst, the Buffalo Bills play in Orchard Park, planes fly to the Buffalo Airport but they land in Cheektowaga.

If the process of creating a truly metropolitan area in Erie County were merely a manner of speaking, the job would have been accomplished long ago. In reality the task has been difficult, halting and incomplete. Suburbs of Buffalo have grown dramatically, often on their own merits, but sometimes because of the city's problems, and sometimes at the city's expense.

World War II

Though Americans were shocked by the attack on Pearl Harbor in December 1941, few were surprised that war had come. Local National Guard units had been activated more than a year before in anticipation of the conflict.

This second world war was to be a total war. The lines between civilian and soldier began to blur.

Total war required the full mobilization of the home front, and unswerving patriotic enthusiasm. Americans justifiably believed that their democracy was superior to the vicious totalitarianisms which started the war. But moral superiority had little to do with the outcome. It was the astounding productive capacity of American industry, and the efficient application of its innovative technology, which finally turned the tide. No other area in New York State was awarded more war-related contracts than the Buffalo region. Placing the government-designated Buffalo Industrial Area on a war footing required unprecedented regulation of industry—rationing of essential resources, oversight of transportation, protection and direction of labor, even special provisions for working women and their children. A government role in the economy had become familiar from the New Deal, but these were interventions on a scale not even imagined during the Depression.

Improved weaponry and changed tactics accounted for the huge numbers of casualties in the war, estimated as high as 58 million for all the nations which fought. Three Buffalo men won the Congressional Medal of Honor in

Wartime necessities combined to produce a transportation crisis in the Buffalo area. The demand for fighting machines precluded production of many automobiles during the war. To conserve needed gasoline and rubber, car owners had to curtail their driving. At the same time more people needed to travel to war-related jobs. The number of bus passengers doubled, from 100 million riders in the Depression economy of 1939 to well over 200 million in each of the war years. More bus drivers were needed, but the war required soldiers in enormous numbers, twelve million of them in fact. The labor shortage became critical. The solution? Hire women. But this increased the need for bus transportation even more, since in the 1940s women were less likely than men to be licensed drivers. The result was that by 1943 one out of five IRC drivers was a woman. International Railway Company Collection, courtesy Buffalo and Erie County Historical Society

World War II; thousands of others fought bravely and mostly unsung. Despite the staggering human costs, very few people, then or now, would dispute the necessity of fighting this war. Americans welcomed veterans home as heroes.

The Suburbs

The roots of suburban development established a firm hold in Erie County in the 1920s and 1930s. Over the course of the 1920s just as many towns in Erie County lost population as gained it. But a few made dramatic strides that pointed toward future growth. Cheektowaga and West Seneca grew by more than half. In the 1930s Amherst's population doubled. Tonawanda's increased three and one-half times.

The really explosive growth came a generation later. Forces which created Greater Buffalo were driven by the powerful twin engines of postwar change: a surge of population growth, and the economic boom which lasted, with only minor interruptions, until the early 1970s. This dramatic shift was to affect the way people lived in the city and the county as profoundly as had the construction of the Erie Canal, the European immigration, or the arrival of Big Steel.

The picture of a prosperous and expanding Erie County ought, on the face of it, to have been nothing but good news. After all, isn't it true that a rising tide floats all the boats? In fact, suburban development was a wrenching experience. City partisans and county boosters were rarely generous with each other. Part of the reason was money, of course. Tax bases and expenditures dwindled or grew with the fortunes of specific areas, and this was always a source of friction. But there are deeper intellectual and emotional reasons for the clash. The growth of suburbs turned upon sharply conflicting visions of the future.

During and after World War II Buffalo was a vital city. It was also a city bursting its seams. Population was well over half a million in the 1940s and 1950s, and peaked (officially) at 618,000 in 1960. In fact, for cities of this size, Milwaukee was the only one which could compare in population density. When the area for streets, parks and business is subtracted from the available living space, people were packed in at the astonishing rate of 23,000 for each of Buffalo's forty-three square miles. That is about 10 families to the acre.

The crowding strained both the resources of the city and the patience of its residents. The problems were rarely isolated, and sometimes they added to each other in ways that made solutions more difficult. What happened to transportation is a good example. Getting from here to there became harder. Between 1947 and 1957 ridership on city buses dropped by 60 percent. Fewer riders meant increased costs. Remaining riders complained of raised fares, and deteriorating service. So people took to their cars, many of them first-time owners. In winter this exacerbated the traffic problem on roads already often piled with snow. Parking on streets slowed the buses down further. All of this made buses less attractive.

Labor-short World War II industry employed American women in unprecedented numbers. By the war's end, almost nine in ten women in their twenties were working. As a rule they were paid well, they were represented by unions, and they contributed vitally to the war effort. Locally women worked at Bell Aircraft, Dunlop Tire, Trico Products, and many other plants. In the photo women are assembling hydraulic parts for the Houde Engineering Division of the Houdaille Corporation. The Buffalo War Council recognized that the thousands of married women had thousands more children who needed day care if they were to work. Various agencies cooperated in a pioneering program. By 1943, centers operated on twelve-hour days to look after the children of working women in the Buffalo area. Courtesy Buffalo and Erie County Historical Society

The basic principle of any migration, whether it is across the Atlantic, or across Erie County, is that something encourages people to leave, and something draws them to their destination. Togetherness has its charms, particularly in recreation, as these Delaware Park skaters believed. But togetherness wears thin when there is an alternative. The hope for a roomier life was one factor that squeezed people out into the more spacious suburbs. According to accepted formulas in the 1950s the city had only one-quarter of the park area it needed. Because no provision was made for them early in the boom years, city parks tend to be near the city limits in Buffalo. Roy W. Nagle Collection, courtesy Buffalo and Erie County Historical Society

Were there too many automobiles which, by competing with traction systems and for space on the roads caused bus transportation to deteriorate? Or were there too many bad buses, which encouraged people to drive themselves? Either way, the practical result was the same. Mass transportation suffered in the 1950s. International Railroad Company Collection, courtesy Buffalo and Erie County Historical Society

203

During World War II there were very few private passenger cars produced. After the war, however, automobile production accelerated. In Erie County in the decade after 1946 population rose by 20 percent. Automobile registration increased by nearly four times that figure. That translates to 155,000 new vehicles for Erie County roads—almost one new automobile for every new person. In the 1950s the stylists of Detroit designed cars that became the marvel of the world for their length, width and weight. On an average day sixty thousand of them piled onto city streets that had been laid out with the horse and buggy in mind. A 1957 editorial in the Courier-Express bemoaned the "metropolitan-sized traffic headache" that resulted. The writer noted ruefully that the situation showed no prospect of improvement, and "during the next decade, a whole new generation of Erie County children will reach driving age." Affordable automobiles had already allowed teenagers more freedom and independence.

This car lot on Delaware Avenue helped supply the need. International Railroad Company Collection, courtesy Buffalo and Erie County Historical Society

Coping with the burgeoning teen-age population posed special challenges to adults in the 1950s. The Hi-Teen Club was one response. Emceed by the personable Bob Wells, the weekly dances held at the Dellwood Ballroom on Main Street in Buffalo avoided rhythm and blues and rock 'n roll. Fast, danceable, and sexy, rock n'roll music did most to give youth the sense that they belonged to a separate culture. Hi-Teen hoped to anchor teenagers closer to the mainstream. The club picked a "teen of the month" to reward the most wholesome. Hi-Teen meant more Pat Boone and less Elvis. Perry Como reached out to this Dellwood audience. Courtesy Bob Wells

The idea that's transforming high-school kids across the nation

Buffalo's Magic Mirror

These youngsters took stock of themselves, and voted for a clothing revolution. As a result, they've made their teachers, their parents and themselves feel a whole lot better

By JHAN and JUNE ROBBINS

BUFFALO, N. Y.

Students in a high school here have installed a full-length, plate-glass mirror at one end of a heavily traveled corridor. Over it hangs a sign: "Look! This is you. Are you satisfied?"

The answer these days is mostly "Yes." Boys and girls who attend the public schools in Buffalo have adopted "dress right" regulations which, teachers say, have cut classroom horseplay 30 per cent, produced an astonishing change for the better in student attitudes, and made the kids pleased with themselves.

They really are proud of how nice they look. To see how appearance-conscious the students actually are, THIS WEEK set up a two-way mirror, provided by Libbey-Owens Ford Glass Company, in one high school, stationed a photographer behind it to record what passed by. Students not only stopped to look at their reflections in the glass, they stopped to "spruce up."

It wasn't always this way. Buffalo's school-age youngsters once delighted in dressing with calculated slovenliness. Sweat shirts, sneakers or boots, and soiled, ragged jeans made up the usual boys' costume. Girls hobbled themselves in tightly-fitted, pencil-slim skirts or, in warm weather, appeared in Bermuda shorts. Sweaters that seemed to have shrunk alarmingly were the usual toppers. Three years ago, Superintendent of Schools Joseph Manch stood up in a high-school auditorium and surveyed the assembled student body with a feeling of profound shock.

School or Clambake?

"As far as I could see there wasn't a single tie, buttoned collar or ironed shirt in the school," he told us. "Some of the girls looked as though they were auditioning for a night-club chorus — others looked like female stable hands. Parents and teachers alike were complaining of poor discipline in the classroom, uproar on school buses, disrespect for teachers and disinterest in learning.

"What occurred to me was this: If we let our students show up for class dressed for a hayride or a clambake, can we really blame them if they act as if they're on one?"

Buffalo's 14 high schools have a city-wide Inter-High School Student Council. Dr. Manch handed the problem to this group. The time had come, he said firmly, to do something about the way students dress. To his surprise, the council agreed. They decided to draw up a voluntary "dress right" code and went to work on it.

Dr. Manch observed, "It was almost as if they were relieved to have someone take a strong stand. They were ready to clean up but nobody wanted to do it alone."

Within the month, the code was completed. The new rules were read at assemblies, posted on bulletin boards, sent home in mimeographed leaflets to parents. It took about half a term to get general compliance.

The program took hold in a good-natured atmosphere. In one high school, boys who appear in the morning without neckties are sent to the "Breakfast Club" (the principal's office) to rent ties, the biggest and gaudiest imaginable, for two cents a day. In another school, a history teacher keeps a supply of ties on hand for offenders and puts them on the kids himself, making sure they are tied as peculiarly as possible.

Clothes Influence Behavior

At the start, some parents had to go out and buy their children proper school clothes. Authorities expected some protests on this score but received very few. One parent did telephone her child's teacher to say it was entirely too much trouble to dress her son every day as if he were going to Sunday school. The teacher replied that the new dress code was concerned with neatness and did not require elaborate, expensive clothes.

At the end of the first year, parents and children were so completely sold that PTA groups in the city's elementary schools voted their own dress-right code into effect.

Meanwhile, educators across the country were taking note. Many agreed that there is a startling association between unkempt, bizarre school clothing and rebellious, antisocial behavior. A Chicago high school principal told the National Education Association that two-thirds of all students brought to his office as disciplinary cases were dressed as roughnecks.

A public school principal in Cleveland told us, "There's no doubt that a great many of our youngsters turn in inferior academic performances because there are not enough visible signposts to show them where fun stops and work begins."

Our current free-and-easy attitudes toward school clothing are fairly recent. In the 1920's and 30's, many of our big city public schools had quite severe standards.

WHAT A MIRROR SEES: Students preen, unaware that mirror is a two-way glass and a camera is on the other side (see diagram below) **WHAT STUDENTS SEE:** Reflections to be proud of. Answer to question posed by sign on glass is an emphatic "Yes!"

Girls were told to wear long-sleeved white blouses and dark pleated skirts. Boys were ordered to appear in an ironed shirt, tie and dark wool pants. The rule served a three-fold purpose. There was no economic competition over who owned the flashiest clothes or the biggest wardrobe. There was no distractions of the tight-sweater variety. Most important, it was clearly a no-nonsense costume.

Educators now concerned with "dress right" programs are not generally in favor of a return to this unimaginative kind of uniform. They point out, however, that the blue-jeans crowd has established its own uniform. At an age when everyone wants to be one of the crowd, it's a tough job persuading students to dare to look different.

"You can't legislate 'dress right' rules," Dr. Manch said. "The beauty of our program is that it is voluntary."

For the guidance of interested student and parent groups, here are the recommendations made by Buffalo's student council committee:

"DRESS RIGHT" CODE

Recommended for Boys: 1. Dress shirt and tie or conservative sports shirt and tie with suit jacket, sport coat or sweater **2.** Standard trousers or khakis, clean and pressed **3.** Shoes, clean and polished; white bucks acceptable (*Not recommended are dungarees or soiled, unpressed khakis; T-shirts, sweat shirts; extreme styles of shoes, including kabmail or motorcycle boots.*)

Recommended for Girls: 1. Blouses, sweaters, blouse and sweater, jacket with blouse or sweater **2.** Skirts, jumpers, suits or conservative dresses **3.** Shoes appropriate to the rest of the costume (*Not recommended are V-neck sweaters without blouses; Bermuda shorts, party-type dresses, slacks, ornate jewelry; T-shirts, sweat shirts.*)

This is not, of course, the only acceptable program. But one thing is sure. This is one needed school reform that is cheap, quick and surprisingly easy. And a willing source of information is Buffalo's Dr. Joseph Manch. And the results, as Buffalo and other American cities learned, are astonishingly good. — The End

Teen-Agers! Turn To Page 28 For "Dick Clark Speaking"

Dick Clark, TV star and newest addition to the THIS WEEK family, answers teen-agers' letters about a variety of problems, including clothes, on Page 28. Parents, too, will be interested in how "the kids' favorite adult" handles tough questions from his young audience.

THIS WEEK Magazine / November 23, 1958

Jeans, black T-shirts, leather jackets, pegged pants, bobby socks and blue suede shoes were all emblems of various teen-age groupings in the 1950s. On the theory that better dress meant better behavior, school disciplinarians hoped to get their students to "dress right." Designed by school officials and promoted by student governments, the Dress Right program gained national attention in the media, endorsement from clothing industry associations, and the enthusiastic support of school authorities across the country. The Buffalo Plan, as it became known, emerged as the model for school dress codes. William Graebner, historian of this movement, points out that dressing right also meant dressing alike. This shrank the distances that class and ethnic background opened between students. Courtesy William Graebner

---

Postwar prosperity put automobile ownership within range of many more people. In its turn the automobile for the first time put the suburbs within practical daily commuting range of the city. The suburb was an appealing place. Taxes were lower. Suburbs held out the promise of better and less crowded schools. Pleasant, spacious, quiet and safe, suburbs offered, as one historian put it, the opportunity for every kid to grow up "with grass stains on his knees."

The suburb also spoke to deeper longings for privacy and independence, scarce commodities in a crowded city. One enthusiastic proponent of suburban growth was Dr. Victor Reinstein, a Cheektowaga real estate developer. In 1951 he sketched the lure of the suburb this way: "A half century or more ago," he wrote, "most people dreamed about a place in the country for the family to live. Today, with larger incomes, and quick transportation, an ordinary man can have not only his little castle, but also a little estate around it."

All was not perfect in Camelot though. Suburbs experienced severe growing pains. Some demanded regional remedies. Managing the problems of storm sewers and sanitary waste disposal in the fifteen watersheds of Erie County, for example, was a problem that by its nature was not solvable by the individual towns. The need for expressways was another that showed the interdependence of city and suburb, but separate governments recognized no community of interest. If the city and county showed little inclination to agree, there was also division within the towns themselves. Older residents did not always welcome the influx of people who brought with them increased traffic, the possibility of industrial development and more crime, and more urgent demands for better schools and improved municipal services.

Many towns were simply unprepared for the sudden spurt of development. In the late 1950s sleepy villages like

Travelers to the United States in the nineteenth century noticed one extravagance—the yard. European cities are chockablock with dwellings. Houses share supporting walls, and are built up, not out. Though houses are most often detached in Buffalo they are set close together nevertheless. A thirty-foot front lot is not uncommon. During the period of city growth, lot size was limited by the ability to deliver municipal services, water, sewer, transportation, gas and electricity. In the suburbs, it was largely the developers who were responsible for services. Water and sewer services might have been undependable at first, but even a modest home could have a sizable yard. Henrich Collection, courtesy Buffalo and Erie County Historical Society

Newstead, Holland and North Collins had no zoning boards or plans for development. One-third of the towns in Erie County had a similar handicap. Even Cheektowaga, where some of the fastest development took place, had no public planning board at all. Suburban development, the *Courier-Express* editorialized, had become helter skelter.

The most basic problems needed solving. For example, inequities in tax rates vexed both the city and the towns. Rising property values created a need for reassessment, but suburban dwellers loudly denounced plans for reassessment as a violation of "home rule." In 1958 Cheektowaga supervisor Benedict Holtz called for a complete reorganization of the tax structure. He wasted no breath in describing the problem. "It is pretty definite that we don't know what we are doing now," he said.

In some towns police and fire protection could be woefully inadequate. Half the county population and the overwhelming portion of its area were patrolled by only one-third as many police officers as the city of Buffalo provided for the other half of the population in its greatly smaller area. Dispersion also had other effects. Houses were so widely separated in the village of Alden that it was judged impractical to install water lines and hydrants for fire protection. The same was true in the towns of Aurora, Colden and Elma. In Harris Hill, within the town of Clarence, there were fire hydrants, but they were so far apart that critics said they were useless.

Charges and counter-charges flew between city and county. Though they benefited not at all, Buffalo residents helped pay for the sheriffs and deputies which patrolled the county. County residents, in their turn, left the city, but not all of its problems. Eight of ten welfare recipients lived in the city because houses were older and cheaper. Welfare was a county responsibility and the single largest item in the budget. City residents helped maintain county highways, but city streets were a city responsibility no matter how many suburbanites made the daily commute

to jobs in Buffalo. The city was charged with protecting the cultural heritage of the county in its museums and libraries, and the health of the county in its hospitals. The Buffalo Zoo drew county visitors like a magnet. City schools had to be supported with a shrinking tax base as more affluent people moved, but at least school buildings already existed. Suburban schools had to be built from scratch.

While all large North American cities grew in the 1950s, they did not all grow the same way. They often expanded by annexation, absorbing their outlying districts. In these places, regional problems were, by and large, city problems. Toronto followed a metropolitan model of development where local governments remained autonomous, but assisted in planning and construction of regional highway and sewer projects, schools and parks, rapid transit and low-income housing. The central city preserved its place as the cultural hub of the area, supporting its theaters and museums. The Toronto area also established a metropolitan police force. Though this idea surfaced several times in Erie County, it failed to find enthusiastic supporters. Local control was valued highly and guarded jealously. Towns and villages remained committed to the proposition that smaller government was better (and cheaper) government.

There were a few successes in metropolitan thinking. One of the best attempts at cooperation was the creation of a countywide library system in 1954. It had taken seven years of difficult negotiation, but in the end the Buffalo and Erie County Public Library system was the envy of many metropolitan areas. County support of cultural institutions, like the Buffalo Museum of Science and the Albright-Knox Art Gallery, gradually increased to the point that it constituted a major source of their income. In 1960 the Buffalo Historical Society changed its name to the Buffalo and Erie County Historical Society to better reflect its mission and its funding.

In the 1950s the integration of the Buffalo and Erie County Public Library systems gained a national reputation as a model of metropolitan cooperation. In the immediate postwar period the libraries in the city were severely short of staff and money. County libraries were poorly stocked, and outside the city ninety thousand people had no library service at all. A solution was not easy to find. Bitter debates in the city and county preceded the merger, stretching negotiations over seven long years. When the systems finally linked in 1954, the substantial resources of Buffalo's libraries were finally available to the county, stimulating library construction. This branch in Amherst opened in 1969. Centralizing services dramatically reduced costs of services rendered. Photograph by Ronald M. Moscati, Courier-Express Collection, courtesy Buffalo and Erie County Historical Society

Recent supporters of mass transportation have an entirely different appreciation of this photograph from what the riders had on the day in 1950 when it was snapped. To advocates of mass transit this is a mournful scene already halfway along the slippery downward slope toward suburbanization, waste of resources, misdirection of social energy, isolation and social loneliness. But for those taking a last ride there were no tears. This was a day to celebrate. The streetcar would be gone and soon forgotten. For the postwar generation the abandonment of the streetcar in favor of the automobile represented progress, privacy, individual freedom and escape. International Railroad Company Collection, courtesy Buffalo and Erie County Historical Society

The "balloon frame" homes of the postwar suburban boom provided an affordable alternative to city living. Henrich Collection, courtesy Buffalo and Erie County Historical Society

207

Cheektowaga real estate developer Dr. Victor Reinstein was one of the most thoughtful and aggressive advocates of suburban growth. In a series of talks and published articles in the early 1950s, Dr. Reinstein disputed the diagnosis of the Buffalo Evening News *that population growth in the towns caused the disease "suburbanitis." The towns, he argued, paid more than their share of county welfare and sales tax, and they bore a disproportionate burden of road and utility costs. If the suburbs really lacked in fire and police protection, sewage disposal, schools and health facilities, the suburbs, he pointed out, would be "the ones clamoring for annexation to Buffalo. Just the opposite is the admitted fact."*

One of Reinstein's arguments for the suburbs brings to bear the international concerns of the time. Reinstein was deeply interested in civil defense. Because suburban growth spread people over a wider area, moving from a "vulnerable" city made good sense in the atomic age, he said. Recent thinking has stressed that nuclear war would make for a global catastrophe, but in 1951 nuclear bombs were smaller and there were far, far fewer of them. An atomic attack would have been more localized. For a brief time the idea of suburb as shelter was plausible. From the Collections, courtesy Buffalo and Erie County Historical Society

Dr. Victor Reinstein
Courtesy of Julia Reinstein (Mrs. Victor Reinstein)

Fake Newspaper threatening Atomic War.

From the Collections, courtesy Buffalo and Erie County Historical Society

In the 1950s rock 'n roll for the first time brought black music to white teenagers. From a powerful clear-channel radio station in Niagara Falls, and at local dances, George "Hound Dog" Lorenz delighted interracial audiences. Though it was a powerful force for racial harmony, music could not fully obscure racial tensions. On Memorial Day in 1956 fights at the Crystal Beach amusement park swelled into a minor riot on the deck of the returning Canadiana, a popular ferryboat. All aboard thought the brawl had the flavor of a race riot. An FBI investigation later concurred. Courtesy Buffalo and Erie County Historical Society

Since World War II the cultural distance between city and suburb has widened. While an economic boom of unprecedented length encouraged growth, opportunity was not spread evenly. Movement within the county tended to create economic and ethnic enclaves. A segmented society was nothing new, of course; ethnic neighborhoods had existed from the beginning of the city's history, and affluent areas of the city were easily identifiable. The positive side of this trend is embodied in a

to the industrial North. Black history, retaining some elements of an African past, shaped over hundreds of years by slavery, and molded by creative responses to post-Civil War discrimination, resulted in a distinctive culture. The experience of blacks in Northern cities recalls the European immigration of the nineteenth century in so many ways that blacks too might be thought of as immigrants. But the experience is not altogether typical. It was so hard for this group to become part of the mainstream,

After World War II, expressways could whisk commuters into the cities, and away from many of its problems. Courtesy University Archives, State University of New York at Buffalo

cherished generalization: Buffalo has always been known as the "city of good neighbors." What seems to be different about the last four decades is that the suburbs offered escape and insulation on a scale not possible before. In the older city upper-class neighborhoods were close to middle-class neighborhoods. Working-class families often nestled in the interstices. After World War II, expressways could whisk commuters into the cities, and away from many of its problems. Investment followed the escape route.

• • •

The suburbs tended to homogenize their residents. Schools strove for uniformity. Housing developments attracted people within a narrow income range. Ethnic differences lessened. If these new communities more nearly approximated the long-held democratic symbol of the melting pot, the old ethnic ties and a sense of belonging weakened. One historian of local Jewish history, for example, described suburbia as "lethal" to the group's identity. Even in the city, identification with an ethnic group became less, with one notable exception. Of the many changes which took place in the postwar generation, the rise of the black community is the most striking.

This history is complex. A combination of factors pushed and pulled American blacks from the rural South

and so much would be given up if they did, that American blacks, as one sociologist put it, were "in" but not "of" American society.

Blacks were lured North by the promise of jobs in two world wars. In the 1950s and 1960s mechanization of agriculture forced out countless small family farms. As tenant farmers, sharecroppers who bartered for seed, many blacks paid their rent in kind, and owned no land at all. They were least able to weather the competition from machines. Those who did own land found it difficult to obtain the credit they needed from white-controlled banks. Between 1960 and 1965 two million blacks moved North. By the 1960s nearly half the blacks in America were living outside the South.

In Buffalo the black community was historically small. But in the twentieth century it experienced a phenomenal growth related to the economic disruptions in the South. A few over thirteen thousand lived in the city in 1930, but by the later 1940s there were thirty thousand blacks, and by the 1960s, eighty-five thousand. The newcomers were as unprepared as any other immigrant group to cope with the demands of urban and industrial life.

As a rule, northern cities were also unprepared to bear the increased burden of these new millions. Educational systems creaked and groaned. Housing, increasingly restricted, became impossibly difficult to obtain. Buffalo was no exception. In 1947 one observer said "we have now reached rock bottom on the houses available [to blacks] for purchase." While the black experience was an immigrant experience in many ways, it differed in one crucial way. Time would shrink cultural differences between European immigrants, but race would continue to create distance between blacks and whites.

In the 1940s reports that pointed with pride to the progress in lowering racial discrimination now seem most to show the limitations of the understanding of the problem at the time. A field representative for the State Commission Against Discrimination noted that the Buffalo area had made the best effort in the state. "Even in the Tonawandas, where it had been rumored that negroes could not be seen on the streets after dark," he said, "negroes can now be found working in industrial plants."

Courier-Express/Ric Delaney

Razing may be delayed, but demolition of the historic Michigan Ave. YMCA appears inevitable
... offer still open to responsible party to take over building

'Y' Demolition Delayed Again

By CAMILLE CURRO

The wrecking ball threatening to demolish the nearly-half-century-old Michigan Ave. YMCA may have to wait another ten days or so.

According to John P. Juhfahl, general executive of the Metropolitan YMCA, the building won its second reprieve on Monday, with a final decision on its future postponed "on a day-to-day basis" until Jan. 7.

"We'll have our annual meeting then, and will have to make a decision by that time. We have to stop worrying about it," Kuhfahl said.

Offered Free

Last month, the YMCA offered the branch at 585 Michigan Ave. free to any responsible party who could raise at least $30,000 a year for utilities and maintenance.

"While several interested groups have come in to see it or talk about it, none have the money to operate it," he said.

Various Plans

"We're 'gun-shy.' We don't want to give the building to anyone who can't pay to keep it going," he added.

A Dec. 6 date to demolish the four-story structure was bypassed, as was another deadline on Monday — the last postponement hinging on efforts of a city agency which is trying to secure federal money to run a program in the structure, said Kuhfahl.

Earlier efforts to make the "Y" a drug rehabilitation center, a haven for homeless men, or a clinic for alcoholics were scrapped when community opposition developed.

Another proposal to expand BUILD's half-way house program into the "Y" was turned down by the black civic action group earlier this month.

Despite highly successful membership drives in the late 1950s, the branch suffered from declining attendance and increasing costs in the late 1960s.

Costs Increase

From 1965 to 1970, membership dropped from 2,165 to 907, and the number of groups using the building dropped from 185 to 47. But annual operational costs rose from $98,000 to $103,000.

In 1974, the branch closed its doors, though some $35,000 was

still spent annually for security, heating and water bills to keep the building in shape.

It opened 47 years earlier, one of four new branches built in a "Jubilee Campaign" undertaken by the Metropolitan YMCA.

$1 Million Raised

"Nearly $1 million was raised, and the South Buffalo, Delaware, Humboldt and Michigan Branches were built," said Kuhfahl.

Large contributions for the Michigan Branch came from Mr. and Mrs. George Matthews, Sears, Roebuck & Co., and from a Chicago, Ill. man named Julius Rosenwald.

Rosenwald was making offers all over the country to donate $25,000 to any city which would build a YMCA specifically for blacks," said Kuhfahl.

"While the branch was built primarily by whites, it was built for blacks. It was built at a time when the conscience of the country was leaning toward a concept of 'separate but equal' facilities," he said.

As such, the facility included residence halls, and food

services comparable to the Downtown YMCA, which was used by whites.

Railroad Men

Some early members of the branch recalled how it became a favorite "home" for black war veterans and for southerners who moved here to work.

In Buffalo's railroad heyday, black porters and stewards stayed at the Michigan "Y," along with young black professionals, said Kuhfahl.

It became a center for community meetings as well as for youth activities ranging from athletics to craft work. Several churches were founded at the "Y," holding services there until they built their own facilities.

And, during the 1940s and 1950s, eighth graders from all the schools in the neighborhood gathered there each year for graduation parties, compliments of the Buffalo Urban League.

It remains to be seen — by Jan. 7 — if any other groups will be gathering in the old landmark, or if the wrecking ball will be called to do its work.

Established in 1923 with the financial backing of Courier-Express *owner George B. Mathews and Sears Roebuck philanthropist Julius Rosenwald, the Michigan Avenue YMCA became a focus of black self-help. This was a segregated facility of course. It was not until 1954 that the Supreme Court found that separate was inherently unequal. Like other ethnic groups parceled off by prejudice, the black community did not permit the separation to disable or demoralize them; it was too strong and resilient for that to happen. Lillian Williams, a historian of Buffalo's black community, described the Y as an important source of racial pride. It was founded by a number of individuals associated with conservative black leader Booker T. Washington. One of them, Dr. Ivorite Scruggs, argued that disadvantage could become the basis of cutural unity and strength. "We must choose between fear of segregation on the one hand and on the other racial progress; we must choose between developing the best within us in our own institutions, built along the lines of other groups and a means of self-expression for us, or merely content ourselves with becoming a minor part of institutions fostered by other groups." Designed by black architect John Brent, the building opened in 1928. Photograph by Ric Delaney,* Courier-Express *Collection, courtesy Buffalo and Erie County Historical Society*

211

Dr. Jesse E. Nash, shown here (standing second from right) at a ground-breaking ceremony, served as pastor of the Michigan Avenue Baptist Chruch from 1892 to 1953. That church had a long history of activism, serving before the Civil War as a stop on the Underground Railroad. Nash also broke ground in the field of civil rights. The Buffalo Baptist Association cited his remarkable record for a lifetime of aggressive service in community affairs. In addition to the respect he gained from other denominations during his tenure as pastor, Nash was influential in founding the local chapter of the NAACP, and he helped organize the Buffalo Urban Leargue. Mary B. Talbert Collection, courtesy Buffalo and Erie County Historical Society

Between 1970 and 1980 the city continued to leak its population. Nearly one Buffalonian in four moved from the city. To ascribe the move to the suburbs to "white flight" alone would be a serious distortion. There were other powerful inducements to move. The postwar economic boom cooperated with a baby boom to create an appetite for new and modern houses, good schools, spacious yards, better roads, more attentive snow removal, and elbow room away from the demands of the extended family. "White flight" did play a part in depopulating city neighborhoods. More usefully the process can be considered as the flight of the affluent. Blacks, as a rule, did not share in the affluence, but moved into houses they could afford. Sometimes whole neighborhoods became available through the real estate scare tactic of block busting.

As whites moved to the suburbs, blacks moved north and east, leaving the Ellicott and Cold Spring districts with only half the people that formerly lived there. The oldest neighborhoods close in to the city were virtually abandoned, and by 1980 there were twenty-five hundred vacant lots in the city. While most whites did not move to the suburbs to escape blacks, it is also true that few blacks moved to the suburbs. The effect was an increasingly segmented population, divided into enclaves of income level, and

race. In 1973 the student body of Sweet Home High School was 3 percent black. Of fifteen hundred students at Williamsville South, seven were black. In Buffalo's public schools nearly half the students were black

in 1973. Photograph by Frank J. Schifferle, Courier-Express Collection, courtesy Buffalo and Erie County Historical Society

Streetcars may have made suburban sprawl in Erie County a possibility even if the automobile had never been invented. Without the automobile though, there would never have been suburban shopping malls. Buyers could stroll in the malls as they once did down Main Street. And they could do it inside, away from the weather. Downtown department stores, such as Sattler's, Hens and Kelly, Sibley's, Flint and Kent were once the anchor of the business district. They fell into eclipse as the popularity of malls rose. Photograph by Ron Schifferle, Courier-Express Collection, courtesy Buffalo and Erie County Historical Society

During the late 1950s to the mid-1960s the University of Buffalo broke into the major leagues. Student population grew by half. Research funds increased seven times. In 1962 the school became a member of the State University system. Governor Nelson Rockefeller's grand vision called for a campus of eighty thousand students, a megaversity on the order of Ohio State or the University of Wisconsin. The decision to locate the new campus of the University of Buffalo in Amherst remains controversial. A downtown location would have been a squeeze, and there was concern that urban problems would become university problems. Chester Kowal, Buffalo's mayor, was preoccupied with a criminal indictment for corruption in a garbage collection scandal. Frank Sedita, the skilled politician who replaced Kowal, became a vocal advocate of a waterfront campus, but momentum had already shifted, and powerful financial interests opposed a downtown location. The university faculty failed to endorse the move. Proponents of downtown revitalization consider it the single largest mistake in Buffalo's history. Had the campus been

built there, it is likely that the city would have rivaled Toronto as a cultural center. Instead growth dispersed into Amherst,

mostly undeveloped at the time. Courtesy University Archives, State University of New York at Buffalo

Problems

A swarm of problems plagued Buffalo and Erie County in the 1960s and 1970s. Political turmoil in the city made it impossible to attract the new campus of the University of Buffalo downtown. Feuding between county and city interests frustrated cooperative efforts at development. Racial tensions mounted as chronic underemployment continued in black neighborhoods. Cultural and generational tensions related to the Vietnam War alienated "town" from "gown." The "oil shocks" depressed local industries. Schools reeled from a desegregation order. Roads, bridges, water mains and sewers came dangerously close to the end of their useful life span. The city and county lost population.

Possibly the most symptomatic of all the recent troubles of the area was the process that has been termed "deindustrialization."

Industry and commerce had made the Buffalo area great. But recently the long-term energy crisis, the aging of industrial plants, the introduction of labor-saving technology, foreign competition, loss of local control, and the need for greater profits all contributed to the deindustrialization of Erie County. In the 1970s the whole of the industrial Northeast experienced lean years. This area was hit particularly hard. One Buffalo banker went so far as to liken the problems that beset the local economy to the problems of the third world.

In Buffalo's heyday, wealth tended to stay in the local

community; the Niagara region was once rich in local ownership. The mansions on Delaware Avenue recall this fantastic prosperity. In the brewing and milling industries, shipping, manufacturing and rail interests, locals controlled their own businesses. They profited as the area profited. Lately, often with government help, a few firms have been bought by local investors—American Brass, Dunlop Tire, Barrister Information Systems. More often the opposite has occurred: outside investors acquired local companies.

In the twentieth century larger parent corporations acquired, reorganized, and then orphaned local firms. There was little that regional interests could do to save an industry reacting to worldwide forces. Business and commerce moved farther toward a dependent position on the fringe of the world economy. As with so many other industrial concerns, the fate of Bethlehem Steel, which closed in 1983, was not decided in Erie County. Management and ownership were elsewhere, removed from the human repercussions of the plant closing. The corporation's strategy for profit was not local; instead, it was, increasingly, international. In its traditional niche of strength, heavy industry, the Niagara region found it hard to compete. What happened to Bethlehem Steel is a case study of the problems of deindustrialization in Erie County.

Because it encouraged world trade to bypass this area the opening of the St. Lawrence Seaway was one of the most fateful events in the economic history of Erie County. In the first year of the Seaway's operation Buffalo's transshipment of grain fell by nearly half. It continued falling to about a fifth of its peak. This result should have been expected, but the belief in progress was so deep and abiding that contemporaries had no sense of foreboding. The postmaster of Buffalo, Dr. Joseph R. Hawn, was one who was obliged to plan for the future and manage the expected expansion. In 1958 Dr. Hawn said, "Buffalo can't help but become one of the greatest metropolitan areas in the country when the St. Lawrence Seaway is completed." "In a few years," he continued, "there will be solid residential neighborhoods all the way from East Aurora, Orchard Park and Clarence." County population leveled off, in fact, and shortly thereafter began its decline.
Courier-Express Collection, courtesy Buffalo and Erie County Historical Society

For a century or more, the billowing smoke in Erie County's skies signaled prosperity. The failure of the smokestack industries is a recent and wrenching phenomenon. Big Steel began its decline in Erie County even before the energy crisis curtailed the national appetite for the metal. Many trends conspired to bring the mighty factory down. The aging Bethlehem plant delivered only modest profits in the 1970s, idling along at a little over 3 percent returns when even bank certificates of deposit available to private individuals yielded well into the double digits. Sometimes, as in 1977, the plant posted dramatic losses. Decisions that deeply affected the fate of the plant were not made in Erie County; it was part of a giant corporation. Modernization of Bethlehem plants elsewhere drained resources that might have improved the Lackawanna facility. American technology enabled foreign steelmakers to build more efficient and less polluting new plants. Even the strength of the dollar hurt by making Lackawanna's product dearer on the world market. New sources of ore in North America and abroad made the lakeside location less attractive than it once was. Requirements to retrofit furnaces to make them cleaner added to costs. The company accumulated a huge debt. On the eve of tremendous losses, Bethlehem closed down its operations in Lackawanna in 1983. The downward slide had taken thirteen years.
Courier-Express Collection, courtesy Buffalo and Erie County Historical Society

215

Buffeted by a bad national image that followed the blizzard in 1977, and long accustomed to bad news, Buffalonians "had been down so long it looked like up to them." Uncertain about recovery, local boosters engineered the "Mouth Off, Buffalo!" campaign to combat the jokes told at the city's expense. A later version built around the "Talking Proud" slogan hoped to raise spirits and educate Western New Yorkers about the many advantages of the Niagara region. Taken up as a football cheer, and punctuated with the thousands of wagging foam-rubber charging-buffalo hand-taunters, the campaign succeeded in receiving national attention when the networks carried local sports events. Critics noticed how the belligerent and ungrammatical tone of the campaign overshadowed the attempt to show why so many Western New Yorkers love their home. This reflected uncertainty too. Courier-Express Collection, courtesy Buffalo and Erie County Historical Society

Well liked, but plagued with the city's problems, Buffalo Mayor Stanley Makowski wryly posed with this life jacket. A deputy mayor under popular three-term mayor Frank Sedita, Makowski assumed the post in 1974 when the mayor resigned because of ill health. The new mayor was obliged to preside over some of the bleakest days in the city's history. He faced large budget deficits, a 15 percent unemployment rate, and the layoff of eight hundred city workers. Even the weather proved troublesome. Makowski's tenure in office was a casualty of the furious winter of 1976-1977. After the strain of coping with the blizzard, he declined to run for a second term in 1977. Courier-Express Collection, courtesy Buffalo and Erie County Historical Society

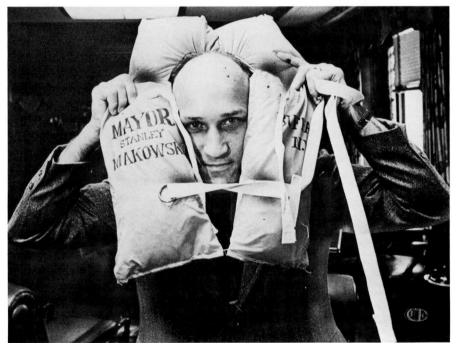

In the 1970s O.J. Simpson thrilled fans of the Buffalo Bills with his speed, great hands, and intelligent play. The first to break two thousand yards rushing in a season, "the Juice" was one reason that Rich Stadium in Orchard Park (with one of the largest seating capacities in the league) hosted sellout games for a decade. The deeper reasons for the game's popularity are worth pondering. After all, nothing real hinges on the outcome of a football game. Daniel Boorstin, the conservative critic of American culture, denounced sports as "pseudoevents." But Boorstin underestimated the role that sports play in providing societies with a secular meeting ground, a community of interest that transcends race and class, and—especially for difficult economic times—the occasional excuse to celebrate. Photograph by Robert S. Bukaty, Courier-Express *Collection, courtesy Buffalo and Erie County Historical Society*

Whites left the city in far greater numbers than blacks. City public schools, as a result, developed a higher proportion of minority students. In 1976 Federal Judge John Curtin ruled that the board of education and other agencies were responsible for a program of systematic segregation that reinforced a trend already under way. Efforts to voluntarily bus twenty-five hundred students came too late to solve a problem that was decades in the making. A small white backlash followed. It was trifling compared to the big trouble in Boston, Philadelphia and elsewhere. And Buffalonians determined that those problems would not be repeated here. Creative solutions to school segregation followed. Photograph by Ron Schifferle, Courier-Express *Collection, courtesy Buffalo and Erie County Historical Society*

This "head shop" closed for business as the bright lure of the Age of Aquarius dulled in the reality of drug abuse. Courier-Express *Collection, courtesy Buffalo and Erie County Historical Society*

217

Cheap fossil fuels powered the postwar economic boom. By the 1970s, however, the economy of Western New York was running on empty. Disruption in the oil markets of the Middle East had far-ranging effects locally. Gasoline was once so cheap that the only thing that seemed to limit the size of American cars was their ability to fit in standard garages. After the Arab oil embargo in 1973 the cost of all fuels followed the dizzying upward curve of imported oil. Once the advantage of cheap fuel evaporated, industry declined. Like the rest of the country, the Niagara region endured inflation and recession at the same time. There were special disadvantages here. Steel-making and automotive industries, so important locally, suffered as Americans bought more foreign autos. Substitution of plastic and aluminum for steel in smaller, lighter cars further hobbled Erie County's economy. Photograph by Paul Pasquerello, Courier-Express Collection, courtesy Buffalo and Erie County Historical Society

City schools inherited and demonstrated all the region's problems. Like local industry, the schools were aging by the 1950s. Half were built at the turn of the century or before. Through the Depression and war years no new elementary schools were built at all. The population of school children fell from a high of ninety thousand in 1930 to sixty thousand in 1960. Then the numbers leveled off. Roy W. Nagle Collection, courtesy Buffalo and Erie County Historical Society

Downtown urban renewal projects undertaken with federal subsidies met with mixed success in the 1970s. The St. Paul Mall was still mostly vacant six months after its opening. Photograph by Schapter, Courier-Express Collection, courtesy Buffalo and Erie County Historical Society

In the 1950s Buffalo's streets had become hopelessly clogged. At the outset of construction of the Youngman Highway in 1961, one Buffalo Chamber of Commerce official described the venture as "fundamental to the city's redevelopment program." Convenient toll-free expressways now ring the city. They efficiently carry traffic to the suburbs, to the airport, and to the Thruway. Solutions are always provisional though, and carry their own new problems.

Completed in 1967, the Kensington Expressway truncated city neighborhoods, reinforcing racial separation on the east side. The Scajaquada Expressway plunges through Delaware Park, which was described as vacant land in the original plans. Construction required another esthetic sacrifice in the loss of the fine old boulevards and traffic roundabouts like Lincoln and Humbolt Parkways and Agassiz Circle. Historian Mark Goldman

excoriated this process as "absurd and destructive," and the expressways themselves as a "monstrous gridiron." We know now that mass transit could have solved Buffalo's traffic problem. But the perception of the time, wedded as it was to the idea of progress embodied in the automobile, could not see that anything of much value was being lost. Courtesy Buffalo and Erie County Historical Society

A century of frustration welled up in the decaying neighborhoods of American inner cities in the 1960s. The year 1967 witnessed the worst of the long hot summers of urban rioting. Though Buffalo did not escape these troubles entirely, damage was minor compared to the destruction in such cities as Detroit, Los Angeles and Cleveland. One reporter recorded these impressions on June 28, 1967, the day following a night of rioting. "There were no overturned cars. No lines of burned out buildings. No brick-strewn streets. Smoke from the smouldering fires did not hang heavy in the air. This was not Watts, this was not Hough. You had to look—not too hard—but you had to look to find the damage. It did not rise up and assault your sight of itself. Here and there, a pile of glass on a sidewalk and a jagged black hole in the window above. On the next block, a smashed neon sign. Somewhere a burglar alarm clanged." Courier-Express Collection, courtesy Buffalo and Erie County Historical Society

One of the reasons that Buffalo did not erupt into sustained urban violence was the stability and organization of the black community. BUILD (build unity, independence, liberty, dignity), newly formed with the help of a scholarly and shrewd veteran activist from Chicago named Saul Alinsky, quickly capitalized on violence in the streets. Alinsky believed that federal antipoverty programs had sapped the strength of local leadership and protest. The remedy was direct engagement of local authorities. BUILD went directly to Mayor Frank Sedita with a list of demands that included withdrawal of police from riot areas, improved playground facilities, and two thousand jobs for inner-city youth. Sedita pledged to "attack the causes of our common problem and not merely treat its symptoms." Courtesy Buffalo and Erie County Historical Society

BUILD

UNITY

INDEPENDENCE

LIBERTY

DIGNITY

Students at the University of Buffalo hoaxed the local media in 1964. A group of conspirators chose one of their number to impersonate a potentate from an imaginary kingdom. When the turbaned "Thallus of Marchantia" landed at the Buffalo Airport, he was greeted by the jeer, "Thallus, go back to your palace!" Banners protested the treatment of Jews in his country. Counter demonstrators shouted "No malice to Thallus!" Police extended protective custody. Newsmen had not bothered to consult an atlas for information about Marchantia, and film of the confrontation appeared on television. Meanwhile the "ruler" explained to police that a thallus *of* marchantia *was the stem of a liverwort plant, and that he was a biology major from Brooklyn. College disciplinarians were not amused, and threatened suspension. The Thallus was eventually fined fifty dollars for disturbing the peace. This episode has a prankish, harmless, "happy days" feel to it. In a few short years though, the issues that divided students from authorities would be serious and dangerous. Courtesy University Archives, State University of New York at Buffalo*

All the "town-gown" tensions between university students and city authorities during the Vietnam War years were played out on a stage that the pugnacious sheriff Michael A. Amico helped to set. A courageous cop honored with the Buffalo Evening News "Man of the Year" award in 1963 for his testimony in the Senate Valachi hearings on organized crime, Amico was later to be much less popular with university students. As chief of the Buffalo Narcotics Bureau in the late sixties, Amico conducted a series of highly visible raids to seize marijuana and make arrests. Use of the illegal drug among some had assumed the air of civil disobedience in protest of the nation's longest and least popular war. Amico parlayed his pledge to "get the goods on dope pushers" into a winning election campaign for sheriff. He declared "This is war!" on the day of his election. The sheriff arrested hundreds of students, and even faculty, but complained that very few went to jail. Critics charged that Amico was grandstanding for political gain. Courtesy University Archives, State University of Buffalo

Tensions between the police and the university did not begin with Vietnam War protests. Local police felt hamstrung when a series of Supreme Court decisions required them to abide by national rules. Since the "revolution" of the sixties was intellectual as well as social and legal, the university became the focus of conservative criticism. In 1965 one tough cop who dealt with youth crime identified the biggest problem in controlling youth as "the do-gooders at the University of Buffalo who study sociology, waltz before the legislators and tell them 'You are going to hurt these children.'" The political protest of the Civil Rights movement, and the groundswell of feeling against U.S. involvement in Vietnam spilled over into a cultural clash between the generations. The so-called sexual revolution and the use of mind altering drugs grated on an older generation steeled in the total patriotic involvement of World War II. This war was different, the aims less clear, the tactics confusing, the enemy hard to identify. The more one knew about the war in Vietnam, the more likely one was to oppose it. After a time it appeared that the only reason for continuing the war was that it had already lasted so long. Universities led the way in questioning the propriety of the war, and the University of Buffalo became a leading center of protest. Vice President Spiro Agnew, who later had

his own problems with the law, dismissed student protesters as "elite snobs" and "nattering nabobs of negativity." But the war dragged on and the protests grew. In the spring of 1970 when police fired tear gas that permeated the Main Street campus

of the University of Buffalo to disperse crowds, student newspapers denounced the "invasion." The climate of confrontation had been long in the making. Courtesy University Archives, State University of New York at Buffalo

Though Buffalo reported half the crime of similar-sized cities like Denver and Mineapolis during the early 1970s crime rates did rise. By the late 1970s the city ranked fifth of thirteen major American cities surveyed in reported crime. Rising crime rates provoked the Buffalo Division of Youth to encourage residents to volunteer as "Block Parents." After 1975 the blue signs that hung in windows notified lost or endangered children that a friendly adult was inside. Was this a measure of a society growing more lonely and alienated? Or had the community become more caring? By the 1980s the postwar baby boom, which strained the system (as one demographer put it) "like a pig through a python," had passed. With fewer men in their teens and twenties, crime began dropping substantially and consistently. From the Collections, courtesy Buffalo and Erie County Historical Society

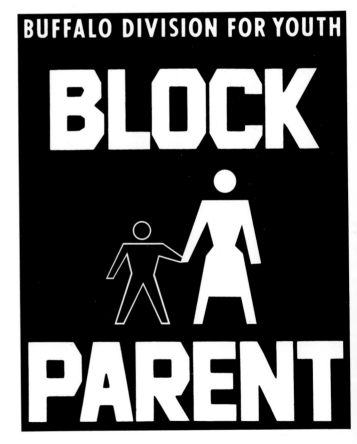

Music was often the vehicle of protest in the 1960s. If still not quite respectable, rock music had become big business by the mid 1970s. American culture is so flexible that even thoroughgoing challenges to the system can be absorbed into the mainstream. In less secure political systems a gathering such as this 1975 Rolling Stones concert in Rich Stadium might be the occasion of fear and trembling by the authorities. In fact, such may have been the case in America just a few years before when rock concerts were obliged to find rural venues like Woodstock and Altamont. Once involvement in Vietnam ended there was only the music: politics had, for the most part, disappeared. This throng signaled that an accommodation had been reached. Photograph by Ric Delaney, Courier-Express Collection, *courtesy Buffalo and Erie County Historical Society*

Joseph F. Crangle, whom Buffalo mayor Frank Sedita called "second to none in political savvy and moxie," became chairman of Erie County's Democratic party in 1965, at the age of thirty three. Crangle successfully navigated Erie County's stormy political waters for the next twenty-three years. He began as a protege of the wily Peter J. Crotty, who controlled the party before him. Crangle's power grew statewide and extended nationally. Crangle played a role in the political successes of Robert Kennedy and Daniel Patrick Moynihan. He became a member of the Democratic National Committee. Crangle's long-standing estrangement from the city's Democratic mayor was complicated enough. The end came for him as a consequence of backing a losing candidate in the race for county executive. After Vincent J. Sorrentino replaced him in 1988, Crangle exchanged power for influence, and remained active as a television commentator and political mentor. Crangle's extraordinary tenure will be remembered alongside the powerful Democratic machine polls of the nineteenth century. Courier-Express Collection, courtesy Buffalo and Erie County Historical Society

There were hopes that a high-technology corridor (like Boston's Route 128 or California's Silicon Valley) would spontaneously generate along a light rail line from Buffalo to Amherst. But the expectations went awry when delays in construction of the six-mile underground section forced costs up astronomically. Many businesses along the above-ground section on Main Street could not survive the disruption. The extension to Amherst, to be built with federal money, never materialized, as economic conservatives shifted planning away from emphasis on mass transit. Instead this development has been piecemeal. A group of high-technology firms did group close to downtown in an area that wags have dubbed "silicon alley." North and east of Buffalo, Amherst has enjoyed the greatest growth. Courier-Express Collection, courtesy Buffalo and Erie County Historical Society

Even the weather seemed to be against Buffalo in the late 1970s. Plummeting temperatures accompanied the blizzard winds of seventy miles an hour that smashed into Western New York on January 28, 1977. Transportation came to a halt as thousands found themselves stranded on area roads. President Jimmy Carter declared the region a disaster, and the army was pressed into service to clear the streets. More cars were stranded when beleaguered city authorities prematurely decided to allow travel again. Nearly two dozen deaths were determined to be storm-related, and the national news media carried all the grim details. Newsweek concluded "no American city was hurt as much as Buffalo by the winter weather." Pundits drew parallels to a gloomy economic forecast. Interestingly, people who braved the blizzard do not usually recall the difficulties. More often, resilient Buffalonians mention how helpful their neighbors were. They remember who was assigned to pull the sled to the market, who had the best party, who shoveled which driveway. Not a few fondly remember being stranded in area restaurants and bars. Tee-shirts shout, "I survived the Blizzard of '77." A black-tie "blizzard ball" marks it annually. The area also supports a counter-cultural spoof, the "lizzard ball." Photograph by Ron Moscati, Courier Express Collection, courtesy Buffalo and Erie County Historical Society

View down Main Street. Photograph by
Marc Murphy, © *1987 all rights reserved*

The past is a difficult enough terrain, obscured and clouded by time, carved by present-day beliefs, distorted by nostalgia. When the historian becomes a futurist, it is a more perilous venture. In that errand, all is speculation and expectation. There is the daunting example of the apocalyptic visions and happy endings that have gone so wildly askew. Whether the news is good or bad, the futurist must remember that forecasts are arguments built in shifting sands. Sometimes the present yields strong clues. Occasionally we know enough of a mystery to predict an ending. There are several trends in the recent history of the Niagara Frontier that will stretch into the near future: continued suburban development, deindustrialization, the infusion of high technology, county population loss, racial desegregation, recolonization of the city by the young and professional. Taken together, these trends permit a cautious optimism.

The decision to build a university center of the state system in Amherst has had far reaching effects. While the city of Buffalo lost another 5 percent of its population in the 1980s, Amherst continued its phenomenal growth. Called a "boom town in the rust belt," upscale Amherst is, without question, Erie County's recent success story.

Suburbs have had to defend themselves against the charge that they were bedroom communities, and that they were boring. New York City's mayor asserted that the suburbs (surely he meant the rest of the state) were "sterile." The charge could not be more misplaced with Amherst. Though the town is barely 3 percent black and hispanic, the tendency toward ethnic homogenizing is somewhat lessened by the university. Especially in the technical and scientific fields, the school has attracted significant numbers of Asians. In addition, development has not been unplanned. Town authorities responded to the charges that they would allow wall-to-wall asphalt by scaling back their projections of growth. Current hope is that Amherst will expand to 175,000 over the next half

century. They may not be able to hold this line; the population already stands at about 115,000. Shopping centers, commercial office complexes, restaurants, and movie houses have multiplied at a surprising rate. People once needed to travel downtown for these amenities.

Some futurists predict Buffalo's eclipse by this vigorous suburb. But it is too soon to count the city out. The belief seems founded in the assumption that growth elsewhere must continue to come at the expense of the city. This is a latter-day version of the short-sighted fear that the development of Black Rock would proceed only at the cost of Buffalo's forward movement. There is no escaping that the metropolitan area depends on the city's cultural, human and natural resources. The term "civilization" was originally a description of the growth of cities. Becoming "civil" meant partaking of the cultural advantages of the city, of its diversity, of its zing and juice. Art and historical museums, a fine orchestra, inexpensive and interesting ethnic restaurants, good schools, national sports teams, a thriving art and theater community, libraries, attractive parks and a surprising number of universities and small colleges all serve to make the city one of the most livable in North America.

Two other trends also bode well for the city. The first has to do with the kind of lives we are more likely to lead. As more women enter the workplace, families have gotten smaller. The lure of a large lawn is somewhat diminished when there are not several children available to manage it. In any case, two-career households leave less time. Older housing stock, still affordable, has begun to be valued for its beauty, authenticity and sturdiness. Neighborhoods like Parkside and Linwood-Oxford have reclaimed the city for the upwardly mobile and professional middle-class.

The second trend is economic and technological. A telecommunications revolution has made it possible to de-centralize activities like banking, insurance, and money

227

brokerage. The ability to exchange information instan-
taneously means that one need no longer be in Manhattan,
or Chicago, or the San Francisco Bay area to be in contact
with business. The gleaming new buildings downtown
reflect the impact of the new technology. Servicing these
concerns benefits firms involved in advertising, law,
software marketing, communications, furnishing, and
office maintenance. Sometimes this growth, as in the
business of advertising, has been extraordinaily volatile.

The availability of reasonably priced houses close to
downtown is one of the city's greatest attractions for the
middle management which make up the bulk of the work
force for these companies. One would have to draw the
salary of a sultan to live so comfortably so close in to the
financial centers of New York City. Other factors conspire
to make the city more desirable. Cheap gasoline once made
a long commute affordable. As a result of the oil shocks of
the 1970s some families in the outlying districts found
themselves "fossil fuel poor." Although prices have fallen
since (and risen again), and people have adjusted with
smaller and more efficient cars, the memory of long lines at
the pumps has convinced many that living closer to work
is desirable.

This area of the country is often called the "rust belt."
Aging smokestack industries came to symbolize the decline
of the Northeast. Unfortunately, Buffalo and Erie County
has been one of the best examples of the process. The "sun
belt" was usually seen as the beneficiary of local decline.
Real and threatened moves to the Tex-Mex border, and the
export of jobs to Europe and the Far East, made for an
uncertain or declining prognosis for local labor.

Metaphors can be coercive though. Rust is irrever-
sible. Few trends in American economic history have
lasted for long; none have lasted forever. Technological
innovation has most often been disruptive in the short run,
beneficial in the longer term.

It should be remembered that the South and the
Southwest have risen again on the strength of two factors,
air-conditioning and available water. The rescued bayous,
reclaimed deserts and dry pueblos of the Southern Rim are
perilously dependent on scarce resources. Geography has
provided the steady lake breezes which are Erie County's
air conditioning. The greatest store of fresh water in the
world is at Buffalo's front door.

For much of our history the city turned its back on the
lake, thinking of it only instrumentally—at best regarding
it as a highway; at worst, as a sewer. Twenty years ago
scientists who gauged the effect of pollution predicted the
rapid aging and the imminent death of Lake Erie. It now
constitutes one of the area's best hopes. For example, it
takes a hundred thousand gallons of water to make an
automobile. The demand for water in the year 2000 is
projected to be ten times greater than it was at
mid-century. The resurgence of Lake Erie, the return of
fish in the Niagara River, the hope for an accessible
waterfront look forward to a time when water resources
will be among this nation's most precious reserves.

One thing is certain. The painful dislocations of
the past fifteen years will not last very far into the
twentieth century, at least not in the form that has been
witnessed. There are, of course, many reasons to worry,
some of them new.

Erie County played a vital role in creating the nation's
prosperity. It now suffers consequences in the deterioration of the human and natural environment. The residues
of past chemical pollution lie at the bottom of the water-
ways, or in inadequately protected dumps that occasionally leach toxics to groundwater. The "infrastructure"—
that is, the water mains, sewers, bridges and roads—
sometimes dates back a century or more. So far the need to
retrain older factory workers has not successfully been
met. The creation of new jobs in lower-paid service
industries will not replace the wages of experienced steel
and automobile workers. American civilization has solved
the problem of production, but the problem of distributing
the surplus (while still maintaining our drive) remains
acute. Most ominous for dwellers of city and county, there
is the possibility for the development of a permanently
dependent inner-city underclass.

The results of national history, these are deep and
thoroughgoing problems that, if they are to be solved,
require national attention.

But there are also good reasons to be optimistic.

The financial resurgence of downtown has demanded
a new, educated work force. Though some firms have
trouble recruiting to the area, they have less difficulty
maintaining their personnel once they see what is
available here. Townhouse development is attracting
young middle income professionals to the city. They bring
with them demands for a greater responsiveness of the
political system, of improvement in schools, better
maintenance of the parks, more opportunity for recreation,
more varied entertainment, and increased support of
cultural institutions.

By the turn of the next century there will be ninety
thousand people living in the area who have a direct
connection to the University of Buffalo, as alumnae,
faculty, employees and independent contractors. Add these
to the graduates of fifteen other local colleges and Erie
County may boast of a substantial educational resource.
There is also a more direct role for the university as the
flagship of graduate education for the state system. A
nationally ranked law school is an asset to local business.
Dentistry, nursing, and medical research provide a
technical pool which holds local health care standards
high. Programs that incubate innovation, like the New
York Technology Development Center in Amherst, and the
cooperative UB-Calspan venture point the way. The University of Buffalo's most futuristic engineering (the new
ventures in earthquake research and superconductivity)
are already boosting the reputation of the region as a good
prospect. When these technologies transfer and spinoff to
private industry, there is every indication that the area
will benefit.

228

University-sponsored research and development facilities in Amherst have already assisted private firms. The blurry image is a machine at the Amherst campus Earthquake Center that tests the effect of vibration on structures. Although Erie County geology is friendlier than California's, the need to know about how materials behave under stress is as great here as elsewhere. The ability to simulate these conditions means that researchers need not experience an earthquake to prepare for one. The center has already assisted utility, welding, heavy equipment and construction companies, manufacturers associations, subway engineers, and even an agency of the Chinese government. Other centers do research in subjects as varied as toxicology and electrooptics. Their facilities and faculties make state-of-the-art research available for cooperative ventures with industry. A final verdict on the value of these initiatives to Erie County's economy will await the decision by outside firms to locate here. Photograph by David S. Ottavio, courtesy State University of New York at Buffalo

Whether in high technology or low, the backbone of the recovery will likely be small business, because, proportionally, it creates more jobs. Office space is readily available. The bargains are as good as can be found in medium-size cities, and costs are far less than in the largest cities. This helps to encourage small business. In addition, a trained and disciplined industrial work force already exists for small manufacturing and industry to capitalize. The resilience of Erie County's people (who have weathered booms, busts, and blizzards) is one of its greatest assets.

The dizzying journey from frontier village to boom town, then decline, and now to recovering metropolitan area has taken a scant century and a half. A national image to the contrary, the quality of life in Buffalo and Erie County remains high. The city is a gem in the rough, set among the more polished suburbs. The climb back from population loss and industrial failure will not be easy; it would be misleading to say otherwise. Enthusiasm for the role of free enterprise notwithstanding, redevelopment here will not be accomplished without massive federal transfusions and special state tax incentives. Nor will it be possible without a cooperative local spirit, and careful planning. Area fortunes will rise as the fortune of the city rises. That renaissance will ultimately turn on a commitment to the belief that cities are permanent features of the American landscape. And that they, and the exurbs that they nourish, are worth preserving.

The Prudential, or Guarantee Building, is one of Buffalo's architectural treasures. Begun in 1894 and completed in 1896, this building was the masterpiece of architect Louis Sullivan. Sullivan, brilliant, arrogant, and sour, was the inventor of the skyscraper. "Form follows function" was his famous dictum that imitators so often abused. In the heart of the city a great deal of use had to be gotten out of a limited space. Like the Buffalo economy, this skyscraper was built on a superstructure of steel. The walls, covered in elaborate terra cotta designs, bore only their own weight. By the 1970s the Guarantee Building had badly deteriorated. There had been a fire, and it became a candidate for demolition. In the 1970s dedicated preservationists found a way to link federal and state money with private developers. It has been restored to its former beauty. Courtesy Buffalo and Erie County Historical Society

Changes in women's roles have been profound. Most now expect to have a work career before and after the years of child-rearing. The revolt against sex stereotyping stemmed partly from the women's movement, partly from legislative initiative and court mandate, and partly from economic necessity. While women still experience significant salary differences from their male counterparts, they have begun to move into better paying non-traditional occupations. Pioneer gender benders like this member of the construction team for the rapid transit line have become an increasingly common sight in the 1980s. Photograph by Mike Osterreicher, Courier-Express Collection, courtesy Buffalo and Erie County Historical Society

The successful and innovative BUILD Academy on Fougeron Street became one of the magnet schools in 1977. Experimental in its form, the BUILD Academy placed its emphasis on black history and black culture. Closely connected to the activist organization, the school also sought to link parents to the educational process. BUILD Academy did not avoid controversy, with the most interesting clash being philosophical. Democratic thinking reinforced by recent court decision has stressed equality of opportunity. By degrees American schools have become more pluralist and "color blind." BUILD was an outgrowth of the civil rights movement, and sought to raise black consciousness. Some school board members were concerned that by serving special interests the BUILD academy violated democratic tenets, and the spirit of the desegregation decision. Courtesy Buffalo and Erie County Historical Society

The Parkside neighborhood in North Buffalo has often been sighted as an example of the city's resurgence, and a pattern that other urban areas might follow. In Europe and Britain houses acquire prestige with age. In the United States the opposite has most often been the case. The high demand for houses in this neighborhood defies the American rule. Designated in 1987 as an area of national historic preservation, the streets adjcent Delaware Park bear the mark of Frederick Law Olmsted's imagination. Not quite "gentrified," the neighborhood is stable, racially and economically integrated, and improving. Older long-time residents stayed through a period of uncertainty when nearby neighborhoods were the victims of block busting in the 1960s. Parkside has also attracted many young professional people. Convinced of the utility of small voluntary groups, a strong neighborhood association has been watchful for pockets of contageous urban blight. The group secured federal money for several upgrading projects, and local support for day-care programs. The supervised "tot lot" pictured here is one of Parkside's attractions. Courtesy Martha Hipkens

The Allentown Art Festival held each June along Delaware Avenue and adjacent streets routinely attracts three hundred thousand. Visitors share an occasion to buy artwork and see each other. The vibrant throng drawn to the festival demonstrates the will and wherewithal of the Buffalo area to bounce back. After all, Athens in its Golden Age had fewer people than Buffalo does now—fewer, in fact, than visit the Allentown Festival each year. The festival also presents an opportunity to chart the more outré in local fashion. In 1986 one young woman appeared with her hair spiked, and dyed white to match the stoat that she kept on a leash. Photograph by Joe Traver, Courier-Express Collection, courtesy Buffalo and Erie County Historical Society

When Dr. Roswell Park arrived in Buffalo in 1883 he was already a renowned surgeon. Park was among the first to understand that the free market would be less important in pioneering medical research than government funding would

Charles Burchfield began as a designer for the famous Buffalo-based Birge and Sons Wallpaper Company. He resigned in 1929 to devote full time to painting in his Gardenville studio. Over the next forty years his reputation grew as an observer of the poignant and quirky in the natural and social world of this region. A museum which bears his name, the Burchfield Art Center on the Buffalo State College campus, is one of many institutions friendly to developing the fine arts in this region. Courtesy Burchfield Art Center

be. The three-room research laboratory he founded at the University of Buffalo in 1898 has grown to occupy eight city blocks. The first such facility of its kind, Roswell Park Memorial Institute gained a world-wide reputation for its work in the field of cancer research. Roswell Park acts as a magnet to draw international talent and federal grant money to Buffalo. The institute carries 375 scientists and physicians on staff. Dr. Herbert Hauptman, research director at the affiliated Medical Research Foundation of Buffalo, became the institute's first Nobel Laureate in 1985, winning the prize for chemistry. Government investment has begun to pay a dividend as Roswell Park attracts private biotechnology and pharmaceutical firms to the area. Courtesy Medical Research Foundation of Buffalo

Since 1976 Buffalo has energetically pursued creative solutions to the problem of segregation in its schools. Where other cities have resorted to coerced busing, here "magnet schools" attract white students to integrated classrooms by offering fine teaching in innovative programs. Special curricula for early childhood, science education, an honors program, a "futures academy," and a school that specializes in the visual and performing arts have enjoyed national recognition. These integrated schools are so popular that admission must now be determined by lot. Courtesy Buffalo Board of Education

When the pollster George Gallup surveyed cultural changes since World War II the most profound shift was not the change in religious values, the attitude toward civil rights, or the perception of the military; it was in how people perceived their own bodies. In the nineteenth century, the body was viewed as an unrechargeable storage battery. Draw it down too quickly and you would have no energy left. In the last fifteen years we have come to believe the opposite. Exercise energizes. The change from observer to participant has come on so fast that city authorities have not been able to

keep pace. Delaware Park, formerly given over to the leisurely game of golf, became the focus of more intense athletic training, running, soccer, basketball, bicycling. In the early 1980s a concession was made to bicyclists in carving out a lane from Delaware Park's ring road. Later, bicyclists were obliged to share the lane with the others enjoying the park—runners, the parked cars of softballers, walkers, roller-skaters, and the occasional horse. Runners then complained that there were too many bike riders in the jogging lane, and bicyclists must again find their way

between traffic and joggers. Looking for an answer community groups called for closing the ring road to automobiles. New York City and Boulder, Colorado found a solution to this problem in a few gallons of paint. Bike lanes and jogging lanes were separated there. Authorities will face more of these cultural controversies as new groups with greater (and sometimes conflicting) demands move into the city. Courier-Express Collection, courtesy Buffalo and Erie County Historical Society

Pilot Field, in the heart of downtown Buffalo's Joseph Ellicott Preservation District, represents a bold attempt at downtown revitalization. The stadium opened in the spring of 1988, and the Triple-A Buffalo Bisons have attracted a million or more fans to their new home each year since. Attendance has given a substantial boost to the downtown economy, and the stadium has become a source of regional pride.

Recognized nationally as one of the finest new ball parks in the country, Pilot Field is also one of downtown's newest architectural gems. Designed by HOK Sports Facilities, it incorporates elements and materials that complement its historic neighbors, the Ellicott Square Building, and the Old Post Office Building, now the City Campus of Erie County Community College. As one of the new wave of baseball stadia, Pilot Field captures some of the best features of earlier ball parks like Ebbetts Field and Wrigley Stadium,

including natural grass, clear sight lines and an intimate scale. It combines these with the most up-to-date facilities for team comfort, training, and safety, as well as fan comfort. Courtesy Bison Baseball, Inc., photograph by Ron Moscati

The Erie Community College city campus has set an example in its creative reuse of the old post office. Before it was turned over to the college in 1979, the gothic structure was a horror show relic, dingy with a century of accumulated soot. Cleaning the outside has provided the downtown skyline with a building that fully lives up to its inclusion on the National Register of Historic Places. Students now enjoy a redesigned interior space that takes advantage of the atrium once used to light the mail sorting floor. Photograph by Marc Murphy, © 1987 all rights reserved

Photograph by Marc Murphy, © 1987 all rights reserved

234

Bibliography

Adler, Selig, and Connolly, Thomas E. *From Ararat to Suburbia: The History of the Jewish Community of Buffalo.* Philadelphia: Jewish Publication Society of America, 1960.

Advasio, J. M., and Carlisle, Ronald C. "The First Americans: Pennsylvania Pioneers." *Natural History,* December 1986, pp. 20-33.

Barnett, Richard J. *The Lean Years: Politics in the Age of Scarcity.* New York: Simon and Schuster, 1980.

Berkhofer, Robert F., Jr. *The White Man's Indian: Images of the American Indian From Columbus to the Present.* New York: Vintage Books, 1978.

Bilotta, James D. "Western New York and the Sectional Controversy: 1840-1860." Master's thesis, State University of New York at Buffalo, 1972.

Bingham, Robert W. *Cradle of the Queen City: A History of Buffalo to the Incorporation as a City.* Buffalo: Buffalo Historical Society, 1931.

Brown, Richard C., ed. *Niagara Land: The First 200 Years.* Buffalo: *Courier-Express.* 1976.

____, and Watson, Bob. *Buffalo: Lake City in the Niagara Land, An Illustrated History.* Woodland Hills, Cal.: Windsor Publications, 1981.

Buffalo. Buffalo and Erie County Historical Society Archives. "The Polish Immigrant, Buffalo, and the Church" (by Carl L. Bucki).

Buffalo. Rosary Hill College. History Proseminar Papers, 1959. "Buffalo in World War II."

Buffalo. State University of New York at Buffalo Archives. "The Buffalo, New York Negro, 1855-1875: A Study of the Family Structure of Free Negroes and Some of Its Implications" (by Herbert G. Gutman and Laurence A. Glasco, 1968).

Buffalo. Buffalo and Erie County Historical Society Archives. "Stephen Humphreys Gurteen and the American Origins of Charity Organization" (by Verl S. Lewis).

Buffalo Architecture, A Guide. Cambridge, Mass.: *Courier-Express,* 1976.

"Buffalo's Little Italy: Un-American Codes and Modes." *Buffalo Express,* 27 May 1891, p. 1.

Buffalo Yacht Club. *The First 125 Years of the Buffalo Yacht Club.* Buffalo: Buffalo Yacht Club, 1985.

Carpenter, Niles. "Nationality, Color, and Economic Opportunity in the City of Buffalo." *University of Buffalo Studies* 5 (June 1927):95-194.

Ciliberti, Nancy. "Irish Domestic Servants in Buffalo, New York, During the Nineteenth Century." Master's thesis, State University of New York at Buffalo, 1981.

Dunn, Walter S., ed. *History of Erie County, 1870-1970.* Buffalo: Buffalo and Erie County Historical Society, 1972.

Eberle, Scott G. *Re: Collections, Artifacts and Manuscripts at the Buffalo and Erie County Historical Society.* Buffalo: Buffalo and Erie County Historical Society, 1986.

Ellison, Ismar. "The Germans of Buffalo." *Publications of the Buffalo Historical Society* 2 (1880):117-144.

Fleishman, Richard K., Jr. "Violence in Buffalo: The 1913 Streetcar Strike." *Niagara Frontier* 30 (1983):3-20.

Fosdick, Myrtilla C. *When Buffalo Was Young.* Buffalo: Otto Ulbricht and Co., 1925.

Fox, Austin. *Designated Landmarks of the Niagara Frontier Including Buffalo, Niagara Falls, and Nearby Canada.* Buffalo: Meyers Enterprises, 1986.

____, ed. *Erie County's Architectural Legacy.* Buffalo: Erie County Preservation Board, 1983.

Friedman, Beverlee. "The Development of the Black Community in Buffalo in the 1920s." Student paper, State University of New York at Buffalo, 1968.

Gerber, David. "Modernity in the Service of Tradition: Catholic Lay Trustees at Buffalo's St. Louis Church and the Transformation of European Communal Traditions." *Journal of Social History* 15 (Spring 1982):655-683.

Geschichte der Deutschen in Buffalo und Erie County. Buffalo: Reinecke & Zesch, 1898.

Glasco, Laurence A. *Ethnicity and Social Structure: Irish, Germans, and Native-Born of Buffalo, N.Y., 1850-1860.* New York: Arno Press, 1980.

____. "The Life Cycles and Household Structure of American Ethnic Groups: Irish, Germans, and Native-Born Whites in Buffalo, New York, 1855." In *Family and Kin in Urban Communities 1700-1930,* edited by Tamara Hareven, pp. 121-143. New York: New Viewpoints, 1977.

Goldman, Mark. *High Hopes: The Rise and Decline of Buffalo, New York.* Albany: State University Press, 1983.

Goodyear, George F. *Goodyear Family History, Part III.* Buffalo: Privately printed, 1976.

Graebner, William. *Coming of Age in Buffalo: Teenage Culture in the Postwar Era.* Buffalo: Buffalo and Erie County Historical Society, 1986.

Graf, Hildegarde. "Abolition and Anti-Slavery in Buffalo and Erie County." Master's thesis, University of Buffalo, 1939.

____. "The Underground Railroad in Erie County." *Niagara Fronter* 1 (Winter 1953):69-71.

Grande, Joseph A. *Peter B. Porter and the Buffalo Black Rock Rivalry.* Buffalo: Buffalo and Erie County Historical Society, 1982.

Graymont, Barbara. *The Iroquois in the American Revolution.* Syracuse, N.Y.: Syracuse University Press, 1972.

Gredel, Stephen. "Early Polish Pioneers in Buffalo." *Niagara Frontier* 10 (Summer 1963):37-56.

Gurteen, S. Humphreys. *A Handbook of Charity Organization.* Buffalo: The Courier Co., 1882.

Heubusch, Carol A. "How the Great Glaciers Changed the Niagara Frontier." *Hobbies* 38 (1958):55-64.

Hewett, Marie. "'Elephant Joe' Josephs, A Folk-Hero From Buffalo's Past." *New York Folklore* 10 (Summer-Fall 1984):35-45.

Hill, Henry Wayland. *Municipality of Buffalo, New York: A History, 1720-1923.* 4 vols. New York: Lewis Historical Publishing Company, 1923.

History of the City of Buffalo: Its Men and Institutions. Buffalo: *Buffalo Evening News,* 1908.

Horton, John T. Williams, Edward T., and Douglass, Harry S. *Northwestern New York: Erie, Niagara, Wyoming, Genesee, and Orleans Counties.* 3 vols. New York: Lewis Historical Publishing Company, 1947.

Irwin, Dudley M., Jr. *The Buffalo War Council: How One*

City Met the Challenge of Total War. Buffalo: Saxer and Pfeiffer Printing Co., n.d.

"The Italian Colony in Buffalo." *Buffalo Courier,* 8 May 1898, p. 8.

Johnson, Chrisfield. *Centennial History of Erie County, New York.* Buffalo: Matthews and Warren Printers, 1876.

King, Cy, ed. *Erie County Time for Action.* Buffalo: *Buffalo Courier News,* n.d.

Koperski, Katherine. "The Message of an Angel: Children's Guardian Angel Stories and Buffalo's Polonia." *New York Folklore* 10 (Summer–Fall 1984): 135-144.

Kusmer, Kenneth L. "The Social History of Cultural Institutions: The Upper Class Connection," *Journal of Interdisciplinary History* 10 (Summer 1979):137-146.

Lankes, Frank J. *The Ebenezer Society.* West Seneca, N.Y.: West Seneca Historical Society, 1963.

Mogavero, I. Frank. *A Brief History of the Diocese of Buffalo.* Rev. ed. Buffalo: Diocese of Buffalo, 1956.

Palmer, A. D., Jr., ed. and comp. *Buffalo Airport 1926-1976.* Buffalo: Niagara Frontier Transportation Authority, 1976.

Percy, John W. *Pioneer Suburb: A Comprehensive History of Kenmore, New York.* Kenmore, N.Y.: Partners' Press, 1974.

————. *Tonawanda, The Way It Was: A History of the Town of Tonawanda From 1805-1903.* Kenmore, N.Y.: Partners' Press, 1979.

Perry, David C. "The Politics of Dependency in Deindustrializing America: The Case of Buffalo, New York." In *The Capitalist City,* edited by Joe R. Feagin and Michael Peter Smith, pp. 113-137. Oxford: Basil Blackwell Publishers, 1987.

Reinstein, Victor. *The Practical Side of Suburbanitis.* Speech before Chamber of Commerce and Young Republicans Club, 13 February 1951 at Hamburg, New York. Mimeographed.

————. "Towns' Answer to Suburbanitis." *Cheektowaga News,* 7 December 1950.

Richman, David. "The University Relocation Controversy," Student paper, State University of New York at Buffalo, 1975.

Roth, Roberta. "The Amherst Campus." Student paper, State University of New York at Buffalo, 1972.

Seller, Maxine S. "Ethnic Communities and Education in Buffalo, New York: Politics, Power, and Group Identity, 1838-1979." Buffalo Community Studies Graduate Group Occasional Paper No. 1, State University of New York at Buffalo, 1979.

Severance, Frank H. *Studies of the Niagara Frontier.* Publications of the Buffalo Historical Society, vol. 15. Buffalo: Buffalo and Erie County Historical Society, 1911.

————. "Underground Trails." In *Old Trails on the Niagara Frontier,* edited by Frank H. Severance. Buffalo: Matthews Northrup Co., 1899.

Shaw, Ronald. *Erie Water West: A History of the Erie Canal, 1792-1854.* Lexington, Ky.: University of Kentucky Press, 1966.

Shelton, Brenda K. "Social Reform and Social Control in Buffalo, 1890-1900." Ph.D. Dissertation, State University of New York at Buffalo, 1970.

Sholes, Elizabeth C., and Leary, Thomas E. *From Fire to Rust: Business, Technology and Work at the Lackawanna Steel Plant 1899-1983.* Buffalo: Buffalo and Erie County Historical Society, 1987.

Skulicz, Ann T. "Rise of the Buffalo Polonia, 1887-1900." B.A. thesis, University of Buffalo, 1951.

Smith, H. Perry, ed. *History of the City of Buffalo and Erie County.* 2 vols. Syracuse, N.Y.: D. Mason & Company, 1884.

Spears, A. W. *The Peace Bridge, 1927-1977, and Reflections on the Past.* Buffalo: The Buffalo and Fort Erie Public Bridge Authority, 1977.

Sweeney, Daniel J., ed. *History of Buffalo and Erie County, 1914-1919.* Buffalo: Committee of One Hundred, 1920.

Tesmer, Irving H., ed. *Colossal Cataract: The Geologic History of Niagara Falls.* Albany: State University Press, 1981.

Totten, Christine M. *Roots in the Rhineland: America's German Heritage in Three Hundred Years of Immigration, 1683-1983.* New York: German Information Center, 1983.

Weisman, Marilyn. "Buffalo Women's Wheel and Athletic Club." Women's History seminar paper, State University of New York at Buffalo, 1972.

Williams, Lillian Serece. "The Development of Black Community: Buffalo, New York, 1900-1940." Ph.D. Dissertation, State University of New York at Buffalo, 1979.

Wolck, Wolfgang. "Sounds of a City: Types and Characteristics of the Speech of Buffalo and Its Ethnic Groups." *New York Folklore* 10 (Summer-Fall 1984):7-22.

Woodward, Jane S. Men of Medicine in Erie County, 1821-1971. Buffalo: Medical Society, County of Erie, 1971.

Young, James Harvey. *The Toadstool Millionaires: A Social History of Patent Medicines in America Before Federal Regulation.* Princeton: Princeton University Press, 1961.

Yox, Andrew P. "The Myth of Persistence of Families in the Orchard, an East Buffalo Neighborhood." *New York Folklore* 10 (Summer-Fall 1984):89-103.

Zenkert, Charles A. "The Flora of the Niagara Frontier; Ferns and Flowering Plants of Buffalo, N.Y., and Vicinity." *Bulletin of the Buffalo Society of Natural Sciences* 16 (August 1934).

Index

A

abolition, 66, 84, 105, 107, 166
Adam, James Noble, 169
Adam, J. N. and Company, 169
Adam, Meldrum and Anderson, 142
Adam, Robert Borthwick, 142, 169
Adams, John Quincy, 32, 37
Addington, Samuel, 66
Adler, Selig, 85, 236
Advoasio, J. M., 23
African Repository, 105
Afro-Americans. See Black Americans
Agassiz Circle, 219
Agnew, Spiro, 222
Agrarian Movement, 30, 64
Agriculturists, 20
Akron, 10, 51, 57, 141
Albright, John T., 152
Albright-Knox Art Gallery, 136, 152, 206
Albro, John, 26
Alden Township, 57, 66, 105, 130, 146, 196, 198
Alden Bath House and Sanitarium, 146
Alinski, Saul, 220
Allen, Lewis, F., 30, 32, 47, 48, 49, 168
Allen, William Ethan, 26
Allentown Art Festival, 232
Almshouse (Buffalo), 126
Alsatians, 72, 74
Altamont, 223
American Brass, 214
American Colonization Society, 105, 109
American Express Company, 58, 59
American Federation of Labor, 160
American Red Cross, 176
Americanization, 83
Amherst, 16, 46, 48, 202, 207, 214, 224, 226, 228
Amherst Library, 207
Amico, Michael, 221
Angola, 122
Anguish, Henry, 25
Anti-Masonic Party, 31, 64
Anti-Saloon League, 191
anti-Semitism, 85
antislavery, 104, 105
architectural style, 33, 51, 62, 151, 193
Armistice Day (Nov. 11, 1918), 178
Association for the Encouragement of Manufactories, 55
Aurora Township, 26, 47, 48, 57, 60, 66
atomic war, 208
Aurora, 105
Aurora Academy, 132
Austria, 91
automobile, 155, 201, 202, 203, 204, 207, 219

B

Baker, Benjamin, 66
Baker, Nelson H., 114, 148
Baldwin, Stanley, 189
banks, 55, 56, 179
Barnett, Richard J., 235
Barrister Information Systems, 214
Battle of Ridgeway, 70, 71

Batavia, 10
Bavaria, 78
Becker, Philip, 78
Bell Aircraft, 202
Belt Line Railroad, 145, 158
Berkhofer, Robert F., 235
Bethlehem Steel, 90, 152, 214, 215
Bidwell and Banta Shipyard, 57
Bidwell, Major Daniel, 68
Bilotta, James D., 235
bicycling, 233
Bingham, Robert W., 235
Bird, William A., 32, 52
Birge Wallpaper Company, 58
Birney, James, 105
black Americans, 73, 98, 99, 104, 105, 109, 176, 179, 210, 211, 212, 217
Black Rock, 16, 20, 21, 22, 26, 27, 28, 32, 36, 37, 42, 47, 49, 57, 87, 103, 168, 226
Blasdell, 48, 49, 154, 155
Blasdell, Herman, 154
Blasdell Park Store, 48
Bliss, Franklin, 178
blizzards, 225, 230
block busting, 212
Block Parents, 222
bloodletting, 117
Board of Trade, 55
Bohemians, 123
Boone, Pat, 204
Boorstin, Daniel, 217
Boston, 217
Boston Township, 26, 47, 48
Botanical Gardens, 148
Breckenridge Street Presbyterian Church, 41
Brent, John, 211
Breslin, Jimmy, 75
Broadway Auditorium, 173
Broadway-Fillmore, 87
Broadway Market, 87
Brown, Richard C., 235
Brown, William Wells, 107
Buck, George, 178
Buffalo Airport, 181, 192, 201
Buffalo Automobile Club, 184
Buffalo and Erie County Historical Society, 206
Buffalo and Erie County Public Library, 206
Buffalo and Fort Erie Public Bridge Company, 188
Buffalo and Susquehanna Iron Company, 165
Buffalo and Williamsville Electric Trolley, 155
Buffalo Athletic Field, 144
Buffalo Baptist Association, 212
Buffalo Bills, 201
Buffalo Bisons, 234
Buffalo Board of Health, 116, 119
Buffalo Chamber of Commerce, 170, 219
Buffalo City Commission Government, 191
Buffalo City Hall, 36, 193
Buffalo Club, 65
Buffalo Common Council, 78, 135
Buffalo Council of Churches, 191
Buffalo Creek, 10, 25, 28, 52, 103, 104, 117

Buffalo Division of Youth, 222
Buffalo East Side Railway, 153
Buffalo Emporium, 108
Buffalo Evening News, 140, 187
Buffalo Express, 167
Buffalo Female Academy, 134
Buffalo Fine Arts Academy, 60, 63, 65
Buffalo Gaslight Company, 58, 59
Buffalo General Electric Company, 181
Buffalo General Hospital, 60, 65
Buffalo Harbor, 28, 30, 36, 51, 52, 55, 69
Buffalo high schools, 193
Buffalo Historical Society. See Buffalo and Erie County Historical Society, 60, 65
Buffalo Industrial Area, 201
Buffalo Insane Asylum, 212
Buffalo Lithia Water, 120
Buffalo Medical Association, 60
Buffalo Medical and Surgical Journal, 120, 121
Buffalo Medical Journal, 117, 118, 126
Buffalo Medical Society, 117
Buffalo Museum of Science, 192, 194, 206
Buffalo Narcotics Bureau, 221
Buffalo Normal School, 134, 135
Buffalo Opera House, 62
Buffalo Parks Commission, 56
Buffalo Pitts, 167
Buffalo Psychiatric Center, 60
Buffalo Public Library, 194
Buffalo Savings Bank, 55, 179
Buffalo Seminary, 38
Buffalo service clubs, 187
Buffalo Socialist Newspaper, 161
Buffalo Society of Natural Sciences, 194
Buffalo State College (State University College of New York at Buffalo), 232
Buffalo State Hospital, 144, 149
Buffalo State Teachers College, 187
Buffalo theaters, 62, 63, 187
Buffalo Urban League, 212
Buffalo War Council, 202
Buffalo Yacht Club, 23
Buffalo Zoo, 206
BUILD, 220, 231
Burchfield, Charles, 232
Burchfield Center (Suny College at Buffalo), 232
Burwell, Dr. Bryant, 73
bus transportation, 203
Bushe, Myron, 57
Busti, Paul, 14, 17, 25, 27, 29

C

Calhoun, John C., 15
Canada, 75, 106
Canadiana, 145, 209
Canal Street, 30, 55, 74, 94
Canisius College, 82, 135, 229
Canisius High School, 134, 135
Capen, Samuel P., 152
Caroline, 31, 44, 45
Carlisle, Ronald C., 235
Carpenter, Niles, 176, 235

Carter, Jimmy, 225
Catholics, Roman, 74, 78, 80, 87, 90, 91, 110, 113, 114, 134, 154
Cayugas, 10
Centennial Park, 196
Cazenovia Park, 148
Central Park, 145
Central Intelligence Agency, 191
Central Presbyterian Church, 107
Chamber of Commerce, 173
Champlain, Samuel de, 13
Chapin, Cyrenius, 25, 193
Charity Organization Society, 112, 113, 115
Charlevoix, Fr. F. X., 8
Cheektowaga, 26, 73, 87, 92, 201, 202, 205, 206, 208
Cherry, Hamilton, 48
Chicago, 140, 228
Children's Friend, The, 122
"Chinaman's" lighthouse, 39
Chippewa Market, 88
cholera, 117, 118, 19, 120
Christi, Ned, 30
Ciliberti, Nancy, 235
Citizens Association, 123
City Charter, 124
City-County Hall (1876), 193
Civil Rights Movement, 222
Civil Service Reform Association, 123
Civil War, 59, 67, 68, 69, 75, 99, 109, 138, 140, 167, 168, 212
Clarence Hollow, 10
Clarence Township, 10, 21, 22, 26, 46, 57, 60, 66, 105, 206, 215
Clay, Henry, 15, 32, 105
Clemens, Samuel, 167
Cleveland, 220
Cleveland *Herald,* 167
Cleveland, Steven Grover, 32, 49, 168, 193
Clinton, DeWitt, 18, 28, 32, 36
Clinton, George, 26
Clinton, George W., 60
Cocco, Dominic, 94
Colby, Ezekiel & Nathan, 26
Colden, 206
Cold Spring Schoolhouse, 65
Collins Township, 47, 66, 105
Colton, Bishop Charles, 134
Commercial Advertiser, 30, 66, 108
Committee of Public Defense, 69
Compromise of 1850, 66
conscription, 69, 176
Community of True Inspiration, 79
Como, Perry, 204
Concord Township, 26, 47, 66, 69
Confederacy, 109
Congressional Medal of Honor, 202
Connolly, Thomas E., 235
Consolidated Aircraft, 181
Corning, Erastus, 53
Cornplanter, Jesse, 100
"Cosmopolitan, The," 80
Courier, 140
Courier Express, 187, 194, 204, 211
Courthouse Park, 33, 66
Cradle Beach, 122
Crangle, Joseph, 224
Crotty, Peter J., 224
Crystal Beach, 145, 209
Cummings, John, 26

Curtiss Field, 176, 171
Curtiss, Glenn, 181
Curtin, John, 217
Czernina, 87

D

Daily Courier, 66
Dart, Joseph, 50, 51, 52, 73
Daughters of the American
  Revolution, 111
Dawes, Charles, 189
Day, David, 28
deindustrialization, 214, 226
Delaware Lake, 151, 203, 219, 231
Delaware Park, 135, 144, 145, 147,
  149, 176, 223
Dellwood Ballroom, 204
Democratic party, 75, 80, 89, 140,
  168, 224
Demokrat, 80
Denver, 222
Depression, 218
Der Weltberger, 77, 80
Detroit, 204, 220
Dickens, Charles, 126
divorce, 94
doctors, 117, 118, 144
Dodge, Mabel, 111
Donovan, William "Wild Bill," 191
Dorsheimer, William, 144, 147
Douglas, Fredrick, 99
Dress Right, 205
Du Bois, W. E. B., 98, 99
Dun Building, 166
Dun, R. G. and Company, 166
Dunlop Rubber and Tire Company,
  181, 184, 202, 214
Dunn, Walter S., 235
Dupont de Nemours and Co., E. I.,
  181
dyemaking, 129
D'Youville College, 134, 137,
  138, 184
Dwight, Theodore, 66

E

Eagle Street Theater, 107
East Aurora, 30, 58, 64, 65, 163, 215
East Boston Lumber Company, 49,
  50
East Hamburg Friends Institute,
  132
Ebenezer Society, 62, 79, 80
Eberhardt community, 158
Eberhardt, Louis, 156, 157, 159
Eberle, Scott, 235, 240
Eden Township, 26, 47, 48, 66, 92,
  105
Eden Center, 93
Eggleston, Alanson, 26
Eggertsville, 77
"Elephant Joe" Josephs, 80
Eliot, Charles W., 152
Ellicott, Benjamin, 26
Ellicott, Joseph, 13, 14, 18, 20, 24,
  26, 27, 28, 29, 31, 193
Ellison, Ismar, 235
Elma, 206
Elmlawn Cemetery, 154
Elmwood-Franklin, 134
Elmwood Music Hall, 174, 196
Emerson, Henry P., 132, 133
epidemics, 115
Erie Canal, 18, 30, 34, 36, 47, 50, 51,
  53, 57, 59, 64, 85, 130, 162, 202
Erie Community College, 234
Erie County Agricultural Society,
  48
Erie County Medical Society, 60

Erie County parks, 180
Erie County Parks Commission,
  180
Erie County Savings Bank, 55
European revolutions of 1848, 84,
  118
Evans Township, 47, 57, 66, 105
Evans, Oliver, 51

F

factories, 57, 58, 59, 176, 181, 184,
  196, 198
Fargo, William F., 58, 59, 66, 69, 138
farming in Erie County, 18, 19, 25,
  26, 30, 47, 48, 49, 180, 195
Favorite Prescription, 138
Fenians (Irish), 69, 70, 71, 75
Federal Bureau of Investigation,
  209
Felician nuns, 89
Fillmore, Abigail Powers, 64, 65
Fillmore, Caroline McIntosch, 65
Fillmore, Millard, 30, 31, 60, 62,
  63, 64, 65, 66, 67, 69, 107, 109,
  168, 193
Finney, Charles Grandison, 60, 105
First Presbyterian Church, 41
Fitch, Benjamin, 127
Fitch Institute, 127
Flint, Austin, 60, 117, 118, 119
Flint and Kent Department Store,
  142, 213
Fleishman, Richard K., Jr., 235
Follett, Ella, 131
Follette, William, 130
Folsom, Frances, 168
Foslom, Oscar, 168
Ford Motor Company, 184, 196
Fort Erie, 16, 38, 42, 188
Fort George, 16, 21
Fort Niagara, 13, 16, 20, 21
Fort Porter, 69, 176, 188
Forward, Oliver, 28, 37
Fosdick, Myrtilla C., 235
Fosdick, J. S., 134
fossil fuel, 228
Foster, Orin, 136
Fox, Austin, 235
Franklin Square, 193
Fredonia, 93
Free Soil Party, 33, 66
Fresh Air Mission, 122
Friedman, Bervelee, 235
Fronczak, Dr. Francis, 90
Front Park, 148
Fugitive Slave Law, 109
Fuhrmann, Louis, 31, 60, 77, 173,
  176, 178

G

Gallup, George, 233
Guarantee Building, 230
Garfield, James, 80
Garrison, William Lloyd, 105
Gerber, David, 85, 235
germ theory of disease, 120
General Motors Corporation, 184,
  198
German American Bank, 82
Germans, 72, 74, 77, 78, 79, 80, 82,
  83, 84, 89, 110, 118, 133, 135, 229
Germany, 78
Getzville, 92
Gilded Age, 140
glaciation, 10
Glasco, Laurence A., 235
Golden Medical Cure, 140
Golden Medical Discovery, 140
Goldman, Mark, 219, 235

Goodyear, George F., 235
Gorham, Nathaniel, 13
Graebner, William, 205, 235
Graf, Hildegarde, 105
Grand Island, 10, 44, 47, 48, 49, 50,
  85, 145, 194
Grande, Joseph A., 235, 240
Granger, Erastus, 15, 25, 28
Graves, John, 125
Graymont, Barbara, 235
Great Depression, 194, 195, 196, 197
Great Upheaval of 1877, 112, 140
Gredel, Stephen, 235
Green, E. B., 152
Grey Nuns of the Cross, 134
Griffin, James, 76
Griffon, 15
Grover Cleveland High School, 135
Grundy, Felix, 15
Gurteen, S. Humphreys, 112, 113,
  115, 235

H

Hall, Nathan, 60, 64
Halpin, Maria, 168
Hamburg Driving Park
  Association, 48
Hamburg Township, 26, 48, 49, 57,
  77, 148, 154, 156, 196
Hamilton, Frank Hastings, 60
Hamlin, Cicero Jabez, 58
Hammond, Jabez, 26
Harding, Warren G., 178
Harris Hill, 206
Hauptman, Herbert, 232
Haven, Solomon, 64
Hawn, Joseph R., 215
Hershey, John, 25
head shop, 217
Hengerer, William, 130
Hengerer's Department Store, 142
Hennessey, Louise Huber, 131
Hens and Kelly, 213
Heubusch, Carol A., 235
Hewett, Marie, 235
Higgins, James W., 191
Hill, Henry Wayland, 235
Hines, Rev. Thomas, 114
Hipkens, Martha, 231
Hitchcock, Appololos, 26
Hi-Teen Club, 204
Hodge, Joseph, 25
Holland, 26, 48, 66, 105, 128, 129,
  155, 206
Holland Land Company, 13, 14, 17,
  18, 19, 20, 25, 26, 27, 30, 47, 64
Holland Land Purchase, 13, 14,
  18, 31
Holmes, Oliver Wendell, 138
Holy Angels School, 134
Holz, Benedict, 206
Homeopathic College, 119
homeopaths, 118, 119
Hoover, Herbert, 196
Hopkins, Timothy, 26
Horton, John T., 235
hotels, 33, 35, 62, 66, 69, 139
Houdaille Corporation, 202
Howard, George, 57
Hubbard, Elbert, 163, 173
Huber, Ida Stukie, 131
Hughes, Charles Evans, 134
Humbolt Park, 148, 149, 192
Humbolt Parkway, 219
Humphrey, Arthur, 226
hurdy-gurdy, 94
Hydraulics, the, 118
hydropower generation, 77, 129

I

Il Coriere, 95
infrastructure, 228
Innocents Abroad, 167
International Peace Bridge, 188,
  189, 192, 227
International Railway Company,
  160, 200, 201
Ireland, 73, 74
Irish Americans, 73, 74, 75, 76, 95,
  110, 113, 123, 166
iron, 129
Iroquois Confederation, 13
Irvin, Leslie L., 181
Irwin, Dudley M., 235
Italian Americans, 73, 76, 92, 93, 94,
  95, 113, 123
Italy, 93, 94

J

Japanese management, 163
Jefferson, Thomas, 15
Jewett, Sherman S., 144, 147
Jewish immigration, 85, 86, 87,
  166, 210
Jesuits (Society of Jesus), 10, 229
Johnson, Charles and Oliver, 26
Johnson, Ebenezer, 38, 117
Johnson, William, 20, 25
Josephs, Joseph, 80
Johnson, Crisfield, 235
Jubilee Water Works, 42

K

Keeler, Jane, 187
Kellogg, Frank, 189
Kellogg, Spencer, 162
Kelsey, Samuel, 26
Kenefick, Daniel J., 193
Kenmore, 132, 156, 158, 159, 184,
  194, 198
Kensington Expressway, 219
Ketchum, Jesse, 134, 135
King, Cy, 235
King, John, 25
King, W. L. MacKenzie, 189
Kinney, Didymus, 26
Kleinhans Music Hall, 196
Knoche, Philip, 61
Knox, Seymour, 134, 136, 152
Koperski, Joseph E., 91, 92
Koperski, Katherine, 91
Kowal, Chester, 214
Kuechener, "Water John," 42
Kuhn family, 61
Ku Klux Klan, 191
Kusmer, Kenneth L., 235

L

Lackawanna, 90, 114, 174, 180, 215
Lackawanna Iron and Steel
  Company, 152
Ladies General Aid Society, 69
Lafayette, Marquis de, 28, 32, 33,
  34, 37
Lafayette Square, 29, 48, 66, 173,
  175, 178, 179
Lake Erie, 9, 25, 148, 149, 228
Lake Ontario, 9, 20
Lake View Brewing Company, 82
Lancaster Township, 26, 48, 57, 66,
  105, 131
Lancaster Academy, 132
Lancaster Opera House, 131
Lane, Ezekiel, 20
Langdon, Jervis, 167
Langdon, Olivia, 167
Lankes, Frank J., 235
Larkin Girls, 163

Larkin, John D., 163
LaSalle, Robert, 9, 14
La Voce Della Verta, 95
La Vendetta, 95
Leary, Thomas E., 235
LeCouteulx, Louis, 24, 25
Letchworth, William Pryor, 57, 127
Lewis, William, 26
Lewiston, 20, 21, 27
Liberal Club, 123, 124
Liberia, 105
Liberty Bank, 82
Liberty Loans, 176
Liberty party, 66, 105
libraries, 207
Liedertafel, 77, 80, 83
L'Imparzial, 95
Lincoln, Abraham, 63, 66, 67, 69, 80
Lincoln Parkway, 219
Linwood-Oxford, 226
Livingston, William, 58
Logan, Alexander, 25
Loomis, Frank, 123
Lord, Mary E. (Mrs. J. C.), 125, 126
Lord, Rev. John C., 107, 125
Lorenz, George "Hound Dog," 209
Los Angeles, 220
Love, John, 29
Love, Maria, 111
lumbering, 129
Lusitania, 173
Lutherans, 78

M
MacKenzie, William L., 31, 44
McClure, George, 16, 21
McKinley, William, 151, 152, 170
machine manufacturing, 129
Madison, James, 15, 28, 105
magnet schools, 233
"maid of the mist," 11
Makowski, Stanley, 216
Maltby, William, 26
Manhattan, 228
Manufacturers and Traders Bank, 55, 56
Manufacturer's Club, 170
Marine Bank of Buffalo, 55, 56
Marsh, John, 105
Martin, Darwin, 164
Martin Luther King Park, 148
mass transportation, 207
Mather, Alonzo, 188
Matthews, George B., 211
Mechanics Association, 55
Medaille College, 229
Medical Research Foundation of Buffalo, 232
Memorial Auditorium, 196, 197
Message to Garcia, A, 163
metalworking, 129
Mexican Expedition, 172, 173
Michigan, 69, 70
Michigan Avenue Baptist Church, 106
Michigan Avenue YMCA, 211
Middaugh, Martin, 20, 25
Milburn, John, 125, 152
milling, 129
Minneapolis, 222
Mogavero, I. Frank, 235
Monroe, James, 32
Montreal, 134
Mook, Anna, 131
Morgan, William, 31
Morris, Robert, 13
Mt. Olivet Cemetery, 15
Mt. St. Joseph School, 134
"Mouth Off, Buffalo" campaign,

216
Municipal Ownership League, 123

N
Nardin Academy, 134
Nash, Jesse E., 212
National Association for the Advancement of Colored People (NAACP), 99, 212
National Association of Colored Women's Clubs, 98
National Guard, 172, 173, 174, 175, 176, 201
National Linseed Oil Trust, 162
Native Americans, 10, 11, 13, 85, 100, 103, 104
Navy Island, 31, 44
Neumann, John, 30, 43
Newark. *See* Niagara-on-the-Lake
New Deal, 201
Newstead Township, 51, 57, 66, 206
Newsweek, 225
New York Central Belt Line Railroad, 156
New York City, 228
New York Grange, 180
New York State Legislature, 134, 135
New York State Building (Buffalo Historical Society), 151
New York Technology Development Center, 228
New York Tribune, 167
Niagara, 23
Niagara Falls, 9, 15, 32, 44, 57, 77, 126, 150
Niagara-on-the-Lake, 16, 21
Niagara Mohawk Power Corporation, 57, 181
Niagara Movement, 99
Niagara River, 9, 10, 106, 148, 228
Niagara Square, 29, 36, 174, 180, 187, 193
Nice, John, 148
Nicholas I, Czar, 87
Nichols School, 134
Noah, Mordecai Manuel, 50, 75
Norris, Major James, 11
North Collins Township, 6, 154, 206

O
Ogden Land Company, 103
Ohio State University, 214
oil, 214, 218
Oishei, John R., 184
Olmsted, Fredrick Law, 144, 145, 148, 231
Orchard Park Township, 26, 62, 105, 156, 201, 215, 217
Osborn, Maurice, 49
Our Lady of Victory Association, 114
Our Lady of Victory Home, 114
outdoor relief, 114

P
padrone, 93, 123
Palace Hotel, 139
Palace Park, 154
Palmer, A. D., Jr., 235
Palmer, George, 56
Pan-American Exposition, 129, 150, 151, 152, 156
Park, Julian, 127
Park, Roswell, 232
Park School, 134
parks, 150, 202
Parker, James F., 152
Parkside, 144, 145, 148, 156,

226, 231
Pearl Harbor, 201
Peoples Common Sense Medical Adviser, 139
Perry, David C. 235
Perry, Oliver Hazard, 23
Phelps, Oliver, 13
Philadelphia, 160, 217
physicians, 115
Pierce-Arrow Company, 155, 176, 184
Pierce, Ray Vaughn, 138, 139, 140
Pilot Field, 234
Pitt, John A., 58
Pitass, John, 87, 89
Pitts, H. A., 167
Pitts, J. A., 167
Pointsett Barracks, 31, 45, 48
Poland, 85, 87, 89
Poles, 73, 85, 87, 90, 91, 92, 93, 113, 123
police, 123
Polish National Catholic Church, 90
Polonia, 89
Pomeroy and Company, 59
poor relief, 127
Pius IX, Pope, 62, 69, 72
Porter, Barton and Company, 26
Porter, Cyrus, 156
Porter, Laetitia Breckenridge Grayson, 32
Porter, Moses, 20
Porter, Peter A., 68
Porter, Peter B., 15, 22, 26, 28, 32, 36, 45, 52, 103
Potter, Allen, 148
Pratt, Hiram, 30, 52
Pratt, Pascal, 55, 56, 57, 58, 144
Pratt, Samuel, 59
Pratt and Letchworth, 176
Preparedness Day Parade, 173, 175
preservationists, 230
Presley, Elvis, 204
Progressive Movement, 169
Prohibition, 188, 190, 191
Protestants, 80, 110, 111, 113, 123
Prudential Building, 230
Prussia, 89
Public Works, Department of, 123, 197
Putnam, James, 125

Q
Quakers, 62, 103, 104, 105

R
railroads, 52, 53, 56, 129, 180
rail strike, 140
Ransom, Asa, 26
Rathbun, Benjamin, 31, 35, 45
Red Jacket, 17, 100, 103, 104, 109
reformers, 123
Reinstein, Victor, 235
religious holidays, 87
Republican party, 66, 80, 89, 140, 168, 224
revivalism, 104, 141
Rich, Charles, 51
Richman, David, 235
Rich Stadium, 217
Rich-Twinn House, 51
Richardson Building, 121
Richardson, Henry Hobson, 144, 148
Richmond, George, 26
Riverside Park, 148
Rockefeller, Nelson, 214
rock 'n roll, 209

Roesch, Charles, 193, 194, 196
Rolling Stones, 223
Roos, Jacob, 82
Roosevelt, Franklin D., 195, 197
Roosevelt, Theodore, 45, 123, 152, 170
Roosevelt, Theodore, Inaugural Site, 170
Roswell Park Memorial Institute, 232
Roth, Roberta, 235
Roughing It, 167
Rumsey, Aaron, 57
Rumsey, Bronson, 55
Rumsey, Dexter, 144, 147
running, 233
Russia, 89
Russian Jews, 86

S
Sacred Heart Academy, 134
St. John, Gamaliel, 21
St. John, Margaret (Mrs. Gamaliel), 16, 21, 22
St. Joseph's Cathedral, 62
St. Joseph's Collegiate Institute, 134
St. Lawrence Seaway, 215
St. Louis Church, 24, 41, 72, 74
St. Margaret's School, 134
St. Mary's Benevolent Society for the Deaf and Dumb, 134
St. Michael's Church, 135
St. Patrick's Day Parade, 76
St. Paul's Episcopal Church, 41, 113
St. Paul Mall, 219
St. Peters German Evangelical and Reformed Church, 61
St. Stanislaus Church, 87, 89
St. Stanislaus School, 88, 89
Salisbury, Charles, 48
Salisbury, Smith, 48
Sardinia Township, 26, 30, 66, 105
San Francisco, 228
Sattler's Department Store, 213
Scajaquada Expressway, 219
Schaefer, Philip G., 80
Scheu, Solomon, 78
Schoellkopf, Jacob, 57, 77
Schwab, Frank X. 190, 191, 192, 193, 194, 195
Scott, Winfield, 20, 31, 38, 45
Scranton, 52
Sedita, Frank, 214, 216, 220, 224
Seedorf, Henry, 155
Selkirk, John, 59
Seller, Maxine S., 235
Senecas, 103, 104
Seneca Chief, 29, 36
Senza Paura, 95
Shea, Michael, 187
Sheehan, William, 75, 224
Shelton Square, 195
Severance, Frank H., 235
Shaw, Ronald, 235
Shelton, Brenda, 123, 235
Sholes, Elizabeth C., 235
shipbuilding, 129
Sibley's Department Store, 213
Simpson, O. J., 217
Sisters of Charity Hospital, 60, 62
slavery, 98, 104, 105, 106, 107, 109
Skulicz, Ann T., 235
Smallwood, 125
Smart-Weed, 138
Smith, Alfred E., 189
Smith, H. Perry, 235
Snyder, 77
Social Gospel, 111, 113

Social Service Building, 115
South Buffalo, 76
South Park, 148
Southern Rim, 228
Spaulding, Elbridge G., 58, 59
Spanish-American War, 151
Springville, 57, 60, 104, 105, 141
Springville Academy, 132
Spears, A. W., 235
Stapleton, Jim, 100, 141
State Commission Against
    Discrimination, 211
State University College at Buffalo,
    135
streetcar, 207, 213
Steele, Oliver, 60
steel making, 129, 215, 218
Stone, Christopher, 26
Sturges, 191
sugar making, 129
Sullivan Expedition, 11
Sullivan, Louis, 164, 230
Supreme Court, 211, 222
Sweeney Company, 142
Sweeney, Daniel J., 235
Sweet Home High School, 212

T
Taft, William Howard, 170
Talbert, Mary, 99
Talbert, William H., 98
"Talking Proud" slogan, 216
Tappan, Lewis, 166
Taylor, Jacob, 26
Taylor, Zachary, 30, 64, 66
temperance, 105, 107, 110, 115, 141
Temple of Music, 152
Tesmer, Irving J., 235
Thallus of Marchantia, 221
Thayer brothers, 29, 34, 193
Thompson, John, 26
Timon, John, 60, 62, 72, 74
Toledo, 140
Toledo Blade, 167
Tompkins, Daniel D., 16
Tom Sawyer, 167
Tonawanda Township, 25, 30, 43,
    51, 61, 69, 73, 85, 103, 130, 132,
    147, 148, 154, 156, 176, 180, 181,
    184, 194, 198, 202
Tonti, Enrico, 15
Toronto, 206
Totten, Christine M., 235
Townsend, Harriet, 110
Townsend, Jonathan, 26
Tracy, Albert H., 28
Treaty of Ghent, 16
Trico Products Corporation,
    184, 202
trolleys, 154, 155, 156, 158, 160, 178
Trowbridge, Josiah, 60, 117
"true women," 143
Tubbs, Samuel, 26
Turnverein, 84
Twain, Mark, 167

U
Underground Railroad, 38, 66, 105,
    106, 212
Union Continentals, 66, 67
Unitarian Church of Our Father,
    63, 66
University of Buffalo, 60, 90, 118,
    126, 127, 136, 137, 152, 201, 214,
    221, 222, 228, 232
University of Wisconsin, 214
Upper Canada, 14, 15, 16, 31, 44
U.S. Coast Guard, 188, 190, 196

V
Van Buren, Martin, 33, 45, 66
Van Wey, Jonas, 26

Vanderbilt, Cornelius, 53
Vietnam War, 214, 221, 222, 223
Villa, Pancho, 172

W
Wadsworth, James, 56
Wales Township, 26, 66
Ward Pumping Station, 42, 171
Ward, Samuel Ringwold, 66, 105
War Hawks, 15
War of 1812, 16, 17, 20, 21, 22, 23,
    26, 28, 36, 38
Warsaw, 66
Washington, Booker T., 99, 211
Washington, George, 11, 37, 104
weather, 8, 9, 225
Webster, Daniel, 105, 109
Weisman, Marylyn, 235
Weld, Theodore Dwight, 105
welfare capitalism, 163
Wells, Bob, 204
Wells Fargo and Company, 59
Wells, Henry, 58, 59
West Seneca Township, 47, 62, 66,
    79, 80, 154, 202
West Side (Buffalo), 76, 94
West Virginia, 140
Western New York Antislavery
    Society, 107
White, Andrew D., 123
White, James, 144
White, Seneca, 103
Whitheaven settlement, 50
Whitman, Charles S., 173
Wilcox, Ansley, 45, 124, 170
Wilkeson, Samuel, 28, 36, 59,
    105, 193
Williams, Jonas, 26, 27
Williams, Lillian Serece, 211, 235
Williamsville, 10, 20, 21, 26, 27, 38,
    43, 47, 50, 60, 61, 66, 105, 148,
    153, 156
Williamsville Classical Institute,
    61, 132
Williamsville South, 212
Wilson, Peter, 10
Wilson, Woodrow, 172, 173,
    174, 175
Winney, Cornelius, 25
Wolck, Wolfgang, 235
Woodward, Jane S., 235
Women's Christian Temperance
    Union, 190
Women's Educational and
    Industrial Union, 110
women's suffrage, 174
Woodstock, 223
World's Dispensary, 138
World War I, 82, 84, 98, 129, 172,
    173, 175, 176, 178
World War II, 83, 84, 201, 202,
    204, 222
Works Progress Administration,
    197
Wright, Frank Lloyd, 164
Wright, Asher, 104

Y
York, Duke of, 189
Youngman Highway, 219
Young, James Harvey, 235
YMCA, 56
Youngmen's Association, 60
Youngs, Jasper, 198
Yox, Andrew, 83, 235

Z
Zenkert, Charles A., 235
Zimmerman, Adam, 25
Zimmerman, Ida, 132
Zimmerman, William A., 25

About the Authors

Scott G. Eberle

Dr. Scott G. Eberle, research historian at the Buffalo and Erie County Historical Society, is also the author of *Re:Collections,* the Society's award-winning collections catalogue. He writes a column by that same name for the Society's quarterly newsletter. He is curator of *Yesterday's Tomorrow: Buffalo's Pan-American Exposition*, on exhibition in the Historical Society's Museum. Eberle received a Ph.D. in American Social and Intellectual History from the State University of New York at Buffalo. He is currently working on another book, *The Human Factor,* which examines the influence of psychiatry in early twentieth-century business.

Joseph A. Grande

Dr. Joseph A. Grande, professor of history at D'Youville College, has authored *Peter B. Porter and the Buffalo-Black Rock Rivalry* in the "Adventures in Western New York History" series published by the Historical Society. Among his other publication credits are four articles included in *Niagara Land, the First 200 Years,* a national bicentennial series published by the *Courier-Express.* Born in Malden, Massachusetts, he received a B.S. summa cum laude from Buffalo State Teachers' College, an M.A. in history from the State University of New York at Buffalo and a Ph.D. in American History from Notre Dame. Grande is active in community historical activities, having served as president of the Tonawanda-Kenmore Historical Society, historian for the village of Kenmore and president of the Erie County Preservation Board. He is currently president of the Historical Society's Members Advisory Committee.